Jesus the Christ

Jesus the Christ

The Historical Origins of
Christological Doctrine

NILS ALSTRUP DAHL

Edited by Donald H. Juel

FORTRESS PRESS ▪ MINNEAPOLIS

Library of Congress Cataloging-in-Publication Data

Dahl, Nils Alstrup.
  Jesus the Christ : the historical origins of christological
  doctrine / Nils Alstrup Dahl ; edited by Donald H. Juel.
      p.   cm.
  Includes bibliographical references and index.
  ISBN 0-8006-2458-0 (alk. paper)
  1. Jesus Christ—History of doctrines—Early church, ca. 30-600.
  2. Bible. N.T.—Theology. I. Juel, Donald. II. Title.
BT198.D25 1991
232'.09'015—dc20   90-44551
                                                                  CIP

The paper used in this publication meets the minimum requirements of American National Standard for Information Sciences—Permanence of Paper for Printed Library Materials, ANSI Z329.48-1984.   (∞)™

Manufactured in the U.S.A.   AF 1-2458

95   94   93   92   91   1   2   3   4   5   6   7   8   9   10

Contents

Foreword

THE PUBLICATION of an essay collection is seldom heralded as a singular event. Most journals give such collections only cursory reviews. The publication of these essays by Nils Alstrup Dahl is an exception. It should be marked as a significant occasion.

One can learn a great deal about a scholar by observing the nature of his or her publications. Dahl has written few books; the essay is his preferred genre. He sketches an idea or a new direction and packs it into a few pages, then leaves to students and colleagues the task of tracing the implications, while he moves on to something new. His work has ranged over a broad spectrum of New Testament issues covering the Gospels and Paul, moving restlessly from text criticism to Christology to epistolography to historical matters. His doctoral dissertation, *Das Volk Gottes*, defended during the German occupation of Norway in 1941, sounded a theme that appears throughout his work: the Jewish roots of the early Christian movement and the continuing significance of the Jewish people for Christian identity.

Dahl's essays, numbering well over a hundred, have appeared in scores of Festschriften and in virtually every scholarly publication in Europe and the United States, but few have read more than a small portion of his work. Few, therefore, have recognized that the essays arise from a coherent view of early Christianity against its historical background; not many realize that Dahl has sketched out a comprehensive picture of the development of Christian tradition. Reading through this collection of Dahl's essays affords scholars a glimpse of something not available elsewhere in his work.

The essays in this volume deal with New Testament Christology, with an eye to theological and trinitarian matters as well. The few Yale students privileged to hear Dahl's lectures on New Testament Christology have some sense of the depth and breadth of his thinking. Those who know his work only through publications may know only an essay or two, like "The Crucified Messiah" or "The Problem of the Historical Jesus." His historical arguments arise from painstaking attention to exegetical matters, as becomes apparent in chapter 1, "The Messiahship of Jesus in Paul." They also depend upon careful attention to literature from the first-century environment, as in "Eschatology and History in Light of the Qumran Texts." "Sources of Christological Language" affords a glimpse of a whole program for New Testament Christology, while "Trinitarian Baptismal Creeds" begins to construct a bridge between the New Testament and later creedal formulations, showing how language used to speak of Jesus necessarily involved language used to speak of God (the theme of "The Neglected Factor in New Testament Theology"). In "The Crucified Messiah and the Endangered Promises," Dahl offers an approach to a biblical theology, tracing implications of his historical and exegetical work. Only when the essays are seen together does one get the sense of a coherent proposal.

What also becomes apparent is that the approach sketched in these essays cannot easily be categorized. Dahl's work does not fit into any particular school. He acknowledges his indebtedness to the giants of the past. Included as appendices are his review of Bultmann's *Theology of the New Testament* and an appreciative retrospective of Julius Wellhausen's contribution to New Testament studies. What he appreciates about such towering figures is not so much their great syntheses as their exegetical and historical rigor—and their ability to pose significant questions. Dahl's "The Crucified Messiah" develops an offhand suggestion made by Wellhausen in his *Einleitung*.

An awareness of and appreciation for Bultmann's work is apparent throughout Dahl's essays on the historical Jesus and New Testament Christology. Yet, disagreements are also apparent. Dahl is dissatisfied with the idealistic heritage of the history-of-religions school; he wants to protect the particularity of the early Christian movement from absorption into a history of ideas.

Dahl is also far more aware than most of his German contemporaries of the Jewish setting from which early Christianity arose. And, while appreciative of Albert Schweitzer's work, which had a dominant influence on Bultmann and the whole of twentieth-century biblical scholarship, Dahl has demonstrated that "consistent eschatology" cannot serve as a unifying theme for writing an early Christian history, any more than it can for a history of dogma.

The appendixes are included, therefore, both to highlight the debt Dahl believes scholarship owes to such figures as Wellhausen and Bultmann and to offer insight into his own view of the art and craft of biblical studies. That his work does not fit within any acknowledged school is an important sign that he is an original thinker, rare in any generation.

The collection and publication of these essays makes available to the scholarly community a body of work that has been insufficiently appreciated. Those familiar with the three volumes of collected essays published by Augsburg (*The Crucified Messiah, Jesus in the Memory of the Early Church*, and *Studies in Paul*—now all out of print) will recognize that all of the essays in the first of the three have been included in this volume. In addition, there are five new essays: "The Neglected Factor in New Testament Theology," *Reflections* 75 (1975) 5–8; "Julius Wellhausen on the New Testament," *Semeia* 25 (1982) 89–110; "The Crucified Messiah and the Endangered Promises," *Word and World* 3 (1983) 251–62; "Trinitarian Baptismal Creeds and New Testament Christology," previously unpublished (a related essay, "Trinitariske dåps-bekjennelser og nytestamentlig teologi," was published in *Svensk exegetisk årsbok* 48 [1983] 119–43); and "Sources of Christological Language," previously unpublished.

Now available as part of a collection, the essays may help to shape an agenda within biblical studies that offers considerable promise, both intellectually and theologically. Dahl's work deserves a hearing it has yet to receive. We are grateful to Fortress Press for providing so important a resource to those who may otherwise never have been exposed to some of the most stimulating work of this century.

DONALD H. JUEL

9

Abbreviations

AGWG	Abhandlungen der (k.) Gesellschaft der Wissenschaften zu Göttingen (new ed.)
AnBib	Analecta biblica
BZ	*Biblische Zeitschrift*
BZAW	Beihefte zur *Zeitschrift für die alttestamentliche Wissenschaft*
BZNW	Beihefte zur *Zeitschrift für die neutestamentliche Wissenschaft*
DTT	*Dansk teologisk tidsskrift*
GGA	*Göttingische gelehrte Auzeigen*
HNT	Handbuch zum Neuen Testament
IEJ	*Israel Exploration Journal*
JBL	*Journal of Biblical Literature*
JSJ	*Journal for the Study of Judaism*
JTS	*Journal of Theological Studies*
MeyerK	Meyer, Kritisch-exegetischer Kommentar über das Neue Testament
MPG	Migne, *Patrologia Graeca*
MPL	Migne, *Patrologia Latina*
NGWG	*Nachrichten der Gesellschaft der Wissenschaften in Göttingen*
NovTSup	*Novum Testamentum,* Supplements
NTS	*New Testament Studies*
REJ	*Revue des études juives*

RGG	*Religion in Geschichte und Gegenwart*
RHPR	*Revue d'histoire et de philosophie religieuses*
RQ	*Revue de Qumran*
RSR	*Recherches de science religieuse*
SBT	Studies in Biblical Theology
SEÅ	*Svensk exegetisk årsbok*
ST	*Studia theologica*
Str-B	Strack and Billerbeck, *Kommentar zum Neuen Testament*
SUNT	Studien zur Umwelt des Neuen Testaments
TDNT	*Theological Dictionary of the New Testament*
TLZ	*Theologische Literaturzeitung*
VC	*Vigiliae christianae*
ZNW	*Zeitschrift für die neutestamentliche Wissenschaft*
ZTK	*Zeitschrift für Theologie und Kirche*

Jesus the Christ

1

The Messiahship
of Jesus
in Paul

PAUL'S CHRISTOLOGY can be stated almost without referring to the messiahship of Jesus. Nevertheless, one will scarcely deny that the question whether Jesus was the Messiah or not was crucial in the life of the onetime persecutor and later apostle. The problem of this apparent contradiction is often too quickly bypassed. I hope that a few observations and reflections of a philological, historical, and theological nature will contribute to the clarification of the problem.

PHILOLOGICAL OBSERVATIONS

The philological question concerns the meaning of the word *Christos*. Is the name still employed by Paul as a title, or is it only a proper name?[1] Preliminary study leads to the following negative conclusions:

1. In the Pauline letters *Christos* is never a general term but always a designation for the one Christ, Jesus (on the contrary, see Acts 17:3; 26:23).
2. *Christos* is never used as a predicate; Paul never says, "Jesus is the Christ," or the like (otherwise Acts 18:5, 28).
3. A genitive is never added; Paul does not say, "the Christ of God."

4. The form *Iēsous ho Christos* is not to be found in the earliest text of the epistles. (It does occur in the Textus Receptus in 1 Cor. 3:11.)

In order to understand the sense of the apostle's statements, it is not necessary for Paul's readers to know that *Christos* is a term pregnant with meaning. Even if one understands "Christ" only to be a surname of Jesus, all the statements of the epistles make good sense. This does not exclude the possibility that the name "Christ" bears a fullness of meaning. However, the messiahship of Jesus is not stressed.

Nonetheless, the name "Christ" is not completely fixed as a proper name. The interchangeability of the forms *Christos Iēsous* and *Iēsous Christos* is already an indication of this.[2] Furthermore, it is clear that *Iēsous* has remained Jesus' proper name. The confession reads: "Jesus is Lord" (Rom. 10:9; 1 Cor. 12:3) or "Jesus Christ is Lord" (Phil. 2:11), but not "Christ is Lord." Elsewhere Paul speaks of the Lord Jesus or the Lord Jesus Christ, but not of the Lord Christ. Romans 16:18 and Colossians 3:24 constitute only apparent exceptions, since both contrast serving the Lord who is Christ to serving other lords.

Paul says "Christ" and "the Christ," as well as "Jesus Christ" and "Christ Jesus." The varying forms are fixed by grammatical and stylistic considerations as well as by habits of speech. As a rule a simple form, either "Christ," "the Christ," or "the Lord," stands as the subject of a sentence.[3] Complete liturgical-sounding forms, such as "[our] Lord Jesus Christ" are used primarily in the genitive and in prepositional phrases and occur frequently at the end of a sentence.[4] Moreover, Paul always writes *(ho) kyrios (hēmōn) Iēsous Christos*, but if the name "Lord" follows, he alternates between "Jesus Christ" and "Christ Jesus." Furthermore, Paul obviously avoids the dative form, *Iēsou*, which is identical with the genitive; for that reason "Christ" is placed before "Jesus" in dative constructions. Paul says *en Christō Iēsou*, but on the contrary *dia Iēsou Christou*.[5]

In the use of the article we can observe that the genitive *tou Christou* is placed after an articular noun, whereas only *Christou* is used after an anarthrous noun.[6] The article is used with the dative when it is not governed by a preposition.[7] Otherwise, *Christos* is used most frequently without an article; where the article is used, it is to be explained as an anaphora. In an analogous fashion the forms *Iēsous* and *ho Iēsous* likewise alternate.[8] However, the article with *Christos* may, in a few cases, show that the content of the noun has not been fully lost.

Formal considerations by themselves hardly account for the variations in the mode of expression. One can also observe that Paul preferred one or another expression for specific contexts.[9] However, one should not overemphasize the significance of the particular forms of a name that are chosen at different times. This is confirmed by the frequent textual variants; only rarely do they transgress the bounds of customary Pauline usage or alter interpretation.

At this point, as at many others, the terminology of the Pastorals differs from that of the genuine letters. In the Pastorals, the form "Christ Jesus" completely dominates. From one Pauline epistle to another the different forms appear with varying frequency, but no single letter exceeds the bounds established by the others. It has been assumed that *ho Christos* is used in the sense of "the Messiah" in Ephesians (and Colossians), thus differing from the other Pauline epistles.[10] I have not been able to find this view confirmed by clear evidence, however. Even in these epistles it is never *necessary* to understand *Christos* as a messianic title.

Only contextual exegesis can decide to what degree the notion of the messiahship of Jesus is found in a particular passage. Generally this does not yield, I admit, an unequivocal result. But there is at least one passage, Romans 9:5, where the result is unambiguous. Anyone who knows the original meaning of the name understands that the Christ belongs to Israel precisely as Messiah. There are other places as well where the careful reader would detect messianic connotations. In most of these cases,[11] though not in all,[12] the definite article is used with *Christos*. Paul speaks most clearly of the messiahship of Jesus in Romans 1:2-4, but it is still questionable whether *Christos* is to be especially stressed in the expression "Jesus Christ our Lord."

The result appears to be slight but does signify something. The name "Christ" does not receive its content through a previously fixed conception of messiahship but rather from the person and work of Jesus Christ. An *interpretatio christiana* is carried out completely. Nevertheless, the name "Christ" retains a certain peculiar connotation in contrast to the true proper name "Jesus." The name "Christ" has content: it connotes more of the nature and significance of Jesus. This is not, however, to distinguish between the person and the office. Everything that Jesus is and does, he is and does as the Christ. In Paul the name "Christ" is not a title to be detached from the person and work of Jesus Christ. As matters stand, it is only natural that in individual cases one cannot clearly distinguish

17

between statements where the name "Christ" is used only as a proper name and others where the appellative force is still felt. The only relevant question is how far and in what manner the messiahship of Jesus is expressed in all that Paul says.

HISTORICAL SETTING

The historical question primarily concerns the place of Pauline usage within the framework of general early Christian usage. Within the non-Pauline works of the New Testament, *Christos* is used as an actual title in Matthew, Mark, Luke, Acts, John, 1 John, and Revelation.[13] As a part of Jesus' name, *Christos* is used chiefly in the form *Iēsous Christos*.[14] On the other hand, only infrequently is the simple *(ho) Christos* used as a designation of the person (thus 1 Peter and Hebrews).[15] In the New Testament the sequence *Christos Iēsous* is found almost exclusively in Paul.[16]

From this evidence several historically informative inferences can be made: Paul's letters represent a strikingly advanced stage in the evolution that transformed *Christos* from a messianic designation to Jesus' second proper name. Certainly this historical development has not moved in a single straight line; the theological content of the name could always be reactualized.[17] It is quite probable that from the very earliest period many Gentile Christians understood "Christ" as a proper name (cf. Acts 11:26) and only later were taught its significance. One must be aware that the epistles may provide a somewhat one-sided view of the apostle's usage. To Jews he may have spoken in another manner (cf. Acts 17:3; 18:5; 26:23). To them the messiahship of Jesus must have been set forth more thematically. This means we must also reckon with the probability that the messiahship of Jesus had for Paul himself a greater significance than emerges directly from the usage of the name "Christ" in his epistles.

The usage in the other New Testament writings cannot be understood as a further development of Pauline but only of pre-Pauline usage. This terminological independence probably reflects christological tradition independent of Paul. This is especially important for evaluation of the Johannine writings. The first clear case of Pauline influence upon usage may be seen in Clement and Ignatius, especially in the formula *en Christō Iēsou*. Paul's unemphatic use of *Christos* presupposes that it is part of the standard Christian vocabulary. His usage can be explained only by assuming that the confessions and proclamation of the Aramaic-speaking church were summarized in the affirmation: "Jesus is the Messiah." One must also presuppose that there was a pre-Pauline, Greek-speaking church in which "Christ" was used as a name for Jesus. His dignity was expressed through other titles, especially *kyrios*.[18] Paul already assumes the *interpretatio christiana* of the messianic title *Christos*.

This forces us to face the question of the origin of Pauline Christology, a topic we can treat only briefly here. Some have asserted that Paul applied to Jesus his Jewish messianic conceptions, setting within this framework Jesus' earthly life as a proleptic manifestation of the transcendent Messiah (W. Wrede, M. Brückner).[19] Studies in the history of religions have proved that the situation is more complicated. The terminology of Pauline Christology and its content stem from many sources, and even terms with Old Testament and Jewish roots cannot all be derived from messianic ideology. Above all, it can hardly be doubted today that the basic elements of Paul's Christology were already present in pre-Pauline Hellenistic Christianity.[20] The christological differences between Palestinian and Hellenistic communities were hardly as great as Wilhelm Bousset, for example, assumed. What provides the content of the word "Christ" in Paul is less Paul's pre-Christian messianic concept than the pre-Pauline Christology of the church.

Perhaps at this point we may go one step further along the uncertain path of historical conjecture. On the road to Damascus, Paul was convinced that the crucified Jesus was really the Messiah. The important point is not that he applied his conception of the Messiah to Jesus, but rather that he was now called to proclaim the faith in Jesus the Messiah that he had sought to destroy earlier. Peter and his fellow disciples probably recognized that Jesus was the Messiah before they understood what his messiahship involved. Paul, on the other hand, always understood the terms "Messiah" and "Christ" applied to Jesus as they were interpreted by Christians.

Nevertheless, or perhaps precisely for that reason, Paul's proclamation of Christ has a unique character. The revelation of the Son of God signified for him an abrupt break with the past. There is a correlation between this experience and his emphasis that through the cross and resurrection of Christ the old had actually passed away. Even to know Christ "according to the flesh" is to remain in the past. To be sure, for Paul the earthly Jesus is the Christ, the Son of God, born of the seed of David; but Jesus' Davidic birth and life meant not kingly, messianic grandeur but rather humiliation, obedience, and suffering.

The résumé of the gospel in Romans 1:2-4 conforms to a traditional christological pattern (cf. 2 Tim. 2:8 and further Acts 2:30-35; 13:23-37 and Mark 12:35-37). What is peculiarly Pauline is the emphatic contrast between "according to the flesh" and "according to the Spirit of holiness," whereby Davidic birth and resurrection are related antithetically. The summary of the gospel in Romans 1:2-4 foreshadows the two great antitheses of Romans: flesh and spirit, law and Christ. The early Christian interpretation of Jesus' messiahship, which Paul took over, receives a specifically Pauline sharpening.

THEOLOGICAL SIGNIFICANCE

The theological question is complicated because Jesus' messiahship is not a dogmatic element that can be isolated from Paul's total Christology. To say that Christ is "God's Son" is to say much more than "Jesus is the Messiah." Nevertheless, Jesus' divine sonship includes his messianic office.[21] In Paul one should not even try to distinguish between a theocratic and a metaphysical understanding of "Son of God."

The lordship of Jesus expressed by the title *kyrios* transcends all Jewish concepts of messiahship. The preeminence of this title was favored both by the antithetical analogy to the many divine "lords" of the Oriental–Hellenistic–Roman world and by the use of *kyrios* by Greek-speaking Jews to render the Tetragrammaton. The disciples may have addressed their earthly master as "our Lord"; this same address was later used to invoke the risen Christ. Yet the significance of Psalm 110 ought not to be overlooked; to say "Jesus is Lord" implies that he is the messianic sovereign at God's right hand.[22] *Kyrios* is to some extent an appropriate rendering of "Messiah" because it has royal connotations that *christos* would not have communicated to a Greek. At this point the *interpretatio graeco* and the *interpretatio christiana* coincide.

The content of the messianic idea has been changed in many respects by the Greco–Christian interpretation, but much has been preserved. One basic aspect of Jesus' messiahship is that he is the fulfiller of the Old Testament promises. Christ died for our sins and rose on the third day "according to the scriptures" (cf. Rom. 1:2f.; 1 Cor. 15:3f.). Paul took up the scriptural proof for Jesus' messiahship and developed it further. In the extant epistles, to be sure, we find only traces of such scriptural proof.[23] Later the messianic idea was preserved chiefly in the context of Christian interpretation of the Old Testament; often the proof of Jesus' messiahship from Scripture was no longer an integral part of the dogmatic structure. In Paul, however, this is not the case; for him the messiahship of Jesus is essential for the inner coherence of his Christology.

Because Jesus is the Messiah, the Christ-event is understood as an eschatological event. The parousia of Jesus is described with features taken from early Christian eschatology.[24] However, Paul understands the coming of Jesus, his death, and his resurrection as eschatological events. "When the time had fully come, God sent forth his Son";[25] as the "first-born from the dead" Jesus was raised.[26] Christ is the "last Adam," the "second man."[27] (Is this to be seen as a Greco–Christian interpretation of "Son of Man"?) Christ died "to deliver us from the present evil age" (Gal. 1:4). In Colossians 1:15-20 reconciliation is the eschatological counterpart to creation. The exaltation of Jesus is proclaimed as a heavenly, eschatological enthronement.[28]

In addition to the christological interpretation of the Old Testament and the eschatological interpretation of the Christ-event, the ecclesiology of Paul is an indirect witness to the significance of the messiahship of Jesus. Because Jesus is the Messiah, the ones who believe in him are the "saints" of the end of time, the *ekklēsia* of God, the true children of Abraham, and part of the "Israel of God."[29]

Even Paul's doctrine of salvation must be considered in this context. The coming, the death, the resurrection, and the exaltation of Christ are events that signal the end of time and mark the end of the old aeon and the inauguration of the new. The doctrine of the justification of the sinner, the concept of dying and rising "with Christ," and the idea of the new being "in Christ" must be understood within this eschatological framework.[30] Jesus' messiahship is the latent presupposition for all of this.

The same applies to the Pauline doctrine that Christ is the end of the law. Faith in Christ implies for Paul that God bestowed eschatological justification and salvation through him, apart from the law. The believer is therefore justified while a sinner and not as one who is just through the law. Whoever insists on the validity of the law for the believer does not simply err, but denies the grace of God and the efficacy of Christ's death (cf. especially Gal. 2:15-20). Only because he has freed sinners from the law can Christ grant them the gift of eschatological righteousness—and only in this way can he be the Christ. That the messiahship of Jesus stands in contradiction to the law as the final codification of the God-man relationship is the basic assumption common to Paul the persecutor and Paul the apostle.

For the apostle the law is undeniably the law of God. Only those who are redeemed by Christ and who die with him to the law are freed from the law. Freedom from the law has as its presupposition that Christ himself was under the law, became the "curse," and died to the law.[31] Thus it was essential for the Pauline–Christian interpretation of Jesus' messiahship that Christ belonged, according to the flesh, to Israel. This is necessary not only for liberation from the law but also for fulfillment of the promises (Rom. 15:8; cf. Gal. 3:16). For Paul the incarnation of the Son of God is not an abstract assumption of humanity but rather a coming "from the seed of David," under the law (Rom. 1:3; Gal. 4:4).

Because the inseparability of Christ and Israel is grounded in the promise of God, it is not invalidated by Israel's lack of faith. Therefore Paul says in Romans: "to the Jew first." Paul's collection for and overall relation to the early apostles and the Jerusalem church confirm that for him Israel retained a special role. Paul apparently attached little importance to teaching pagans the meaning of the name "Christ." But his entire work as an apostle is conditioned by the messiahship of Jesus. Paul could become the apostle to the Gentiles because the crucified and risen Jesus was the Messiah of Israel; his work as the apostle to the Gentiles aimed, in turn, at the salvation of Israel (Rom. 11:11ff.).

In the end "all Israel will be saved," for Jesus continues to be Israel's Messiah. For Paul the parousia is somehow tied to Jerusalem: "The Deliverer will come from Zion, he will banish ungodliness from Jacob" (Rom. 11:26; cf. also 2 Thess. 2:4, 8). This nonspiritualized, Old Testament messianic expectation cannot be regarded as an isolated and inconsequential rudiment in the Son of God and kyrios Christology. On the contrary, this confirms that Jesus' messiahship actually had a fundamental significance for the total structure of Paul's Christology. If Paul reckoned with a double resurrection and a messianic interregnum (cf. 1 Cor. 15:23-28), this would be another testimony to the importance of the messianic idea.[32]

According to Paul, Christ is the Lord of the church, and the church is his body. It is noteworthy that the unity of Christ and the church has been emphasized in our time. This unity, however, is fatally misunderstood, if by it the church is glorified and the sovereignty of Christ is in any way impugned. Against an eccle-siastical arrogance the apostle himself has already raised a protest in Romans 11:17-24. That the Christ is and continues to be the Messiah of Israel preserves the lordship of Christ over the church and serves as a constant reminder that the church of the Gentiles exists only out of the free grace of God.

Notes

[1]As a rule, this question is treated briefly in expositions of Pauline theology and in commentaries, e.g., E. von Dobschütz on 1 Thess. 1:1 (*Die Thessalonicher-Briefe* [MeyerK. Göttingen: Vandenhoeck & Ruprecht, 1909]) and H. Lietzmann on Rom. 1:1 (*An die Römer* [HNT 8; Tübingen: Mohr, 1928]). The most detailed treatments in recent years are L. Cerfaux, *Christ in the Theology of St. Paul* (trans. G. Webb and A. Walker; New York: Herder & Herder, 1959) 480–505, and W. Kramer, *Christ, Lord, Son of God* (trans. Brian Hardy; Naperville, Ill.: Allenson, 1966).

[2]*Christos Iēsous* is quite well attested in manuscripts (Gal. 5:24; 6:12; Eph. 3:1, 11; Col. 2:6); in comparison, *Iēsous Christos* occurs infrequently (1 Cor. 3:11; Gal. 3:1).

[3]Only rarely "Jesus" (1 Thess. 4:14); "Jesus Christ" or "Christ Jesus" (Rom. 8:34; 2 Cor. 13:5; Gal. 3:1); "the Lord Jesus" (1 Cor. 11:23; 2 Thess. 2:8 v.l.; cf. 1 Thess. 3:11). The usage in 2 Thess. 2:16 is unique.

[4]In the introductory greetings, *apo . . . kyriou Iēsou Christou* is a standard formula; cf. also Eph. 6:23; Phil. 3:20; 1 Thess. 1:1; 2 Thess. 1:1, 12. The genitive *tou kyriou* is usually found with *charis; tou kyriou hēmōn Iēsou Christou* also occurs with *onoma, patēr, parousia, hēmera*, etc. Finally, *dia Iēsou Christou tou kyriou hēmōn* and *en Christō Iēsous tō kyriō hēmōn* are frequently used formulas.

[5]*En Iēsous Christō* only in Gal. 3:14 (cod. ℵ and B); *dia Christou Iēsou* in Rom. 2:16 (cod. ℵ and B). *En tō Iēsou* in Eph. 4:21 is striking.

[6]In 1 Cor. 11:3 and Col. 1:7 the nouns are only formally anarthrous.

[7]2 Cor. 11:2; Eph. 2:5; 5:24; 6:5; Col. 3:1. Without the article only in Gal. 2:19: *Christō synestaurōmai.*

[8]Cf. Blass–Debrunner, *A Greek Grammar of the New Testament* (trans. and ed. R. Funk; Chicago: University of Chicago Press, 1961), particularly ¶ 260, 1. The articular form is found regularly in comparisons; *kathōs kai ho Christos* (Rom. 15:7; Eph. 5:2, 23, 25, 29; cf. 1 Cor. 12:12). Ephesians deviates from the pattern of the other epistles mainly in the frequency of formulas like *en tō Christō* (1:10, 12, 20; cf. 3:11).

[9]Cf. on this Cerfaux, *Christ in the Theology of St. Paul,* 481–84; the overly ingenious work of W. Schmauch, *In Christus* (Gütersloh: Bertelsmann, 1935); and Kramer, *Christ, Lord, Son of God* 19–64.

[10]Thus von Dobschütz, *Die Thessalonicher-Briefe,* 61. Similarly, but more cautiously, R. Bultmann, *Theology of the New Testament* I (trans. K. Grobel; New York: Scribner's, 1951) 80. Cf. also nn. 6 and 7 above.

[11]1 Cor. 10:4; 15:22; 2 Cor. 5:10; 11:2f.; Eph. 1:10, 12, 20; 5:14; Phil. 1:15, 17; 3:7. But in no case in Paul can *Christos* be translated "Messiah."

[12]Cf. 1 Cor. 1:23; Rom. 15:8; Gal. 3:16. In 1 Cor. 1:23 we certainly do not find any antithesis to a Messiah who is not crucified.

[13]On the other hand, in 1 and 2 Peter, James, Jude, and Hebrews, as in Paul, it is never necessary to understand the term as a title.

[14]This is true above all in Acts in the expression "the name of Jesus Christ" (2:38; 3:6; 4:10), which perhaps sheds light on the origin of the usage.

[15]Cf. also 2 John 9; Matt. 1:17; 11:2; Acts 2:31; 8:5; 26:23; Rev. 20:4, 6; etc. Here the appellative significance is still clear to some degree, whereas it is not in the Apostolic Fathers (1 Clement, 2 Clement, Ignatius, Polycarp).

[16]*Christos* is to be understood as a title in Matt. 1:18 (cod. B only) and in Acts 3:20 and 5:42, but as a proper name in Acts 24:24; the textual history is ambiguous. Later the sequence *Christos Iēsous* is found in Ignatius (*Magn.* 8:2; 10:3 v.l.; *Rom.* 6:1 v.l.; etc.) and in Polycarp (*Phil.* 8:1), as well as in the Old Roman Symbol. On the other hand, it occurs in 1 Clement only in the Pauline expression *en Christō Iēsou* (32:3; 38:1); the expression occurs frequently in Ignatius, even alongside the non-Pauline *en Iēsou Christō* (Ign. *Eph.* 8:2; 10:3, etc.).

[17]Cf. the secondary insertion of the article in 1 Cor. 3:11 and Acts 5:42; 9:34. *Iēsous ho Christos* occurs also in 1 Clem. 42:1 and Ign. *Eph.* 18:2. It is strange that later Christ's priestly dignity in particular has been bound up with the name "Christ"; cf., e.g., Tert. *Adv. Marc.* 3.7; Cyr. *Kat.* 10.4, 11, 14 (already in Just. *Dial.* 86:3; 141:3?). The concept of the threefold office is likewise combined with the name "Christ" (Eus. *Hist. Eccl.* 1.3; Dem. *Ev.* 4.15; 8; preface; similarly Calvin *Inst.* 2.15 and many after him).

[18]W. Bousset's perception here must not be obscured by all the criticism of his *Kyrios Christos* (trans. J. Steely; Nashville: Abingdon, 1971). Yet we must also reckon with the possibility that already in Judaism "Messiah" was on the way to becoming a proper name (cf. the *malka mešiḥa* of the Targums and *Christos Kyrios* in Lam. 4:20 and Ps. Sol. 17:32—unless the text has undergone Christian alteration).

[19]W. Wrede, *Paul* (trans. E. Lummis; London: P. Green, 1907); M. Brückner, *Die Entstehung der paulinischen Christologie* (Strasbourg: J. H. E. Heitz, 1903).

[20]Cf. Bultmann, *Theology* I, 123ff.

[21]This is clearly the case, e.g., in Rom. 1:3-4; Gal. 4:4; Col. 1:13; 1 Thess. 1:10. In the background stands the messianic-christological interpretation of Psalm 2.

[22]Cf. Acts 2:34; Rom. 8:34; 1 Cor. 15:25; Eph. 1:20; Col. 3:1.

[23]Cf. Rom. 4:25; 10:16 and 15:21; 9:33; 11:26; 15:3, 8-11; Eph. 2:13-17; 4:8; further, Galatians 3 and Romans 4. By christological interpretation of the Old Testament, Paul also arrives at a conception of the presence of Christ in Old Testament history (1 Cor. 10:1ff.). On Galatians 3, cf. below pp. 60, 155-56 with notes.

[24]Cf., e.g., 1 Thess. 4:14-17; 5:1ff.; 2 Thess. 1:7-10; 2:8; Rom. 11:26; 2 Cor. 5:10.

[25]Gal. 4:4; cf. Eph. 1:10.

[26]Col. 1:18; cf. 1 Cor. 15:20ff.

[27]1 Cor. 15:45-49, cf. v. 22; Rom. 5:12ff., cf. Eph. 2:15 and 5:31. To what extent other, perhaps gnostic, conceptions are involved does not need to be discussed here.

[28]Rom. 1:4; Phil. 2:9-11; Eph. 1:19-23; Col. 3:1f., etc.

[29]Cf. especially Romans 4; 1 Cor. 10:1ff.; Gal. 3:29; 6:16.

[30]At this point Albert Schweitzer's basic conception has essentially advanced interpretation of Paul, in spite of all the one-sidedness and poor exegesis. Concerning

the doctrine of justification, cf. H. D. Wendland, *Die Mitte der paulinischen Botschaft* (Göttingen: Vandenhoeck & Ruprecht, 1935).

[31]Gal. 4:4; 3:13; Rom. 7:4; cf. Gal. 2:19.

[32]On the problem, cf. H. Bietenhard, *Das tausendjährige Reich* (Bern: F. Graf–Lehmann, 1944).

2

The Crucified Messiah

FEW PERSONS have made greater impact upon the history of Norway than King Olav Haraldson. The anniversary of his death, July 29, is still celebrated in remembrance of the introduction of Christianity. Olav was a Viking who, after his baptism, returned to the land of his fathers and became king. With vigor and force, he pursued the work of Christianizing and unifying the land. Opposition to his brutal use of power forced him to leave the country. In the year 1030 he returned with an army but fell at Stiklestad in a battle against the peasants and local leaders who acknowledged the lordship of King Knud of Denmark, also a Christian. On both sides there were Christians as well as pagans; the war was obviously a political one. And yet, scarcely had Olav fallen when the belief arose that he had been a saint. In an amazingly short time the sentiment reversed among the people, leaders of the peasants did penance, the foreign sovereignty was thrown off, and the work of Christianizing and unifying the land was completed under the sign of the holy king and his martyr death. The figure operative in history, the originator and bearer of the ensuing development, was Saint Olav, the *rex perpetuus Norvegiae*, the Olav of saga and legend, of cultic devotion and folk traditions. The "historical" Olav Digre (i.e., Olav the Stout) is a critical-historical reconstruction of nineteenth- and twentieth-century research.

There are good reasons to question studies that fail to acknowledge some connection between the historical personality and the symbol of cult and ideology. But a gap, a contrast, does exist. The tension between historical factuality and a historically operative symbol is a generally recognized phenomenon. From the perspectives of phenomenology and history of religions, the problem of

27

"the historical Jesus and the kerygmatic Christ" will appear as a particular instance of this general phenomenon. The problem has in fact been seen in this way by the "history-of-religions school," in which the Christ of the church was understood as a "cult-hero" and a "cult-symbol." The parallel with the holy king ought to have shown that the issues thus raised are only glossed over and not really solved by Martin Kähler's formula. It is not the so-called historical Jesus but the biblical Christ who is the eminently historical and the eminently real, since his figure alone has been operative in history.

In Norway Olav and his death can be evaluated as national Christian symbols in full consciousness that the historical figure as such was quite problematic. But the situation with respect to Jesus Christ is not the same. Christian faith hangs on the fact that Jesus Christ himself, and not merely a symbolic figure, encounters us in the preaching grounded in the apostolic testimony. It revolves not around the general problem of the relationship between a historical and a symbolic figure but around the personal identity of the Christ exalted to the right hand of the Father with the Jesus of Nazareth who was crucified under Pontius Pilate.

This identity was a genuine concern also for Kähler, and his criticism of the biographies of Jesus was indeed relevant not only for dogmatics but also for historical studies. But Kähler clothed his conviction in the not entirely appropriate garb of the philosophy of history and of apologetics. Thus he failed to make sufficiently clear that the biblical picture of Jesus was historically not the only possibility, as the New Testament itself shows. Pilate, the chief priests, the Pharisees, and even the disciples prior to the passion understood Jesus differently, and none had the same picture of him as the disciples did after Easter. The possibility of offense was always present. What is necessary to faith is not a basis in scientific or philosophical interpretations of history but simply the possibility of facing all the historical facts of the case openly and without apologetic manipulations, and then not to take offense. Thus a sober historical approach is required, one that can help clarify the implications of faith without taking away the responsibility for making one's own decision.

Thus I see the primary task of research concerning the historical Jesus to be that of laying bare, as far as possible, what actually happened. The question of "how it really was" is certainly not as plain and simple as it once seemed. For what does "really" mean? Is the "real" what is in the foreground substantiated by everyone?

Or is it much more what is in the background, that which is significant in what has been and happened? So-called brute facts as such are not yet real history, for to human history there belongs always the interpretation of what happened, even when the interpretation is that of historians asking about the facts and explaining them. The proper discretion of historians emerges when they do not forcibly impose their own interpretation upon the material but rather strive to bring to expression the material at their disposal.[1] Historians must always allow their own understanding, without which they cannot work at all, to be enriched and corrected by being open to interpretations that have been given to the events by those who share in them and have been shaped by them. But the historical and real should not be identified with the historically operative, and scholarly discretion is not to be understood as anxiety in the face of radical questions.

These few remarks may be sufficient to outline my approach to the question of the history of Jesus. By means of methodological and theological considerations, and also by philosophical reflection upon the idea of history, this question could be pursued more in depth than is possible here. Nevertheless, it must be said that the really burning questions cannot be answered in principle but only through constant new encounter with the material. The clarification of conceptions and of basic questions serves a purpose for research only insofar as work with the text and with particular problems is thereby advanced. From time to time the great and fundamental questions must be asked; in this way blind alleys are exposed, false questions and alternatives are unmasked, and new ways are opened for further research. But it is seldom fruitful to dwell too long on discussion of methodology and principles. It was necessary and very useful that, in the last decade, the problem of the historical Jesus was raised anew.[2] Now we would do better to turn again to work with specific questions.

The question of the relation between the proclaimed Christ and the historical Jesus cannot be answered simply by confronting the post-Easter proclamation with the preaching and conduct of Jesus before his passion. The death of Jesus is at the center of the church's proclamation and is precisely the point at which the historical quest for the life of Jesus must start.[3] How is it possible to believe in the death of Jesus as the ground of our salvation and at the same time to make the death of Jesus the object of historical-critical research? And what is the relation between what we are able to say about it as historians and what we as members of the church confess and preach? Many questions arise, of which I select one: the question of the meaning and legitimacy of saying that Jesus was crucified as the Messiah.

CREEDAL SUMMARIES

The New Testament proclaims the death of Jesus as the death of Christ, the messianic salvation-event. Outside the Gospels, the historical particulars of the passion narrative are seldom mentioned. Allusions are found almost exclusively in the kerygmatic summaries in Acts. This fact, however, is due not only to the historicizing tendency of Luke but also to the difference between missionary preaching and hymnic-liturgical formulations (cf. also 1 Cor. 15:3ff. and 1 Thess. 2:15f.). The death of Jesus as an act of men can be contrasted with his resurrection as an act of God. When the responsibility of the Jews is stressed and the complicity of the Romans is largely ignored, it is less because Christians sought to offer a political apologetic than because in their conception of salvation history, Jewish responsibility was the significant factor, at first for preaching salvation and repentance to the Jews, and later for the church in its relation to the Old Testament and to the synagogue.

The plot against Jesus can be attributed to Satan (John 13:27; 14:30; cf. Luke 22:3, 53), and the lords of this world appear as the executors of the crucifixion (1 Cor. 2:8). In this way the cosmic, supernatural dimensions of the event are indicated. The conceptions are not really mythological, since Satan and the powers do not act directly but through human beings. Elsewhere the death of Jesus appears as an act of God, who employed the adversaries as his instruments without their knowledge or will in order to realize his secret design. Luke reconciles the different aspects by emphasizing that the Jews acted according to the design and predetermination of God (Acts 2:23; 4:28). Other writers stress only what was of theological significance: the death of Jesus is the revelation of God's saving righteousness and the act of his love (Rom. 3:25; 5:8; 2 Cor. 5:16, 21; 1 John 4:9f.). This aspect in no way denies, however, that the crucifixion was a human act and a historical fact. In John this paradox is expressed by means of the Jews being able to appear as the instigators of the "lifting up" of Jesus (John 8:28).

The relation between historical and theological aspects is more difficult to determine in those statements in which the death of Christ appears not as a passive but as an active deed. Here a whole series of images and figures is employed: Jesus has laid down his life and thereby brought about a ransom; he has on his own authority offered his life for us; through death, he has consecrated and sacrificed himself; he has overcome hostility and made peace; through his death, he has triumphed over death and the devil; through death and exaltation, he has gone to the Father; as high priest he has entered the heavenly sanctuary. Such are obviously not historical statements about phenomena that can be observed and substantiated. Furthermore, they do not claim to be. Their subject matter is rather the mystery of Jesus' death, the significance of which cannot be confirmed historically but can be preached, confessed, and praised only through faith in the Resurrected One. The death of Jesus appears as a saving event only in its unity with the resurrection, mediated through the word of reconciliation that is instituted by the Resurrected One.

Jesus' act of dying can also be conceived in ethical categories such as endurance, obedience, and love. It is rather striking in this regard that precisely the dogmatic, hymnic-doxological texts speak in this way, while the more historical reports of the Gospels maintain a modest silence about Jesus' disposition during his passion; only a glimmer of it can be seen between the lines. Where the language is direct and open about the forbearance of the suffering Christ, it is nearly always connected with Old Testament allusions (1 Pet. 2:22ff.; Rom. 15:3; indeed also Heb. 5:7f.) The obedience of Jesus appears as the eschatological counterpart to the fall of Adam (Rom. 5:19) or as an extension of the self-renunciation of the preexistent Christ, who divested himself of his equality with God (Phil. 2:6ff.). The death of Jesus is an act of his love; but the love of Christ is not to be understood psychologically, but rather the contrary: since the death of Jesus is proclaimed and believed as a saving event, it is also understood as perfect obedience and as an act of love. "Love is visible only to faith in it."[4] This applies in a special way to the love of Christ shown on the cross in its identity with the love of God.

Like the saving significance of the cross, so also the sinlessness and the forbearance, the love and obedience of the crucified are not historically verifiable phenomena. This is not first of all a given, to which modern historians must resign themselves; rather, it is already apparent from the very manner in which the New Testament authors use a language of confession and praise when they speak about the obedience and love of Christ. In the statements that are to be theologically and soteriologically understood, however, the historical is not excluded but included. This is true where the death of Jesus is spoken of as an act of God as well as where it is seen as manifesting the forbearing, obedient, and loving character of Jesus Christ. Proclamation, confession, and praise presuppose that the conduct of Jesus, visible to men and women, can be understood as an expression and an indication that here Christ, the Son of God, suffered for our sakes—not, to be sure, that it *must* be so understood: what is historical remains ambiguous, but faith cannot isolate itself from history. If the interpretation were correct that Jesus actually was a political insurgent and was rightly executed as such, and that the end of his life broke in upon him as a completely unforeseen catastrophe, that would, in fact, be fatal for faith in the Christ proclaimed in the New Testament. Thus, what is historically identifiable certainly has no constitutive significance for preaching and faith, but it is not irrelevant. This is shown also in that beside the christological hymns and formulas of the New Testament stand the passion narratives of the Gospels.

THE PASSION NARRATIVES

The passion stories are in the form of narrative accounts of what happened. This does not mean that the purely historical viewpoint was the overriding and controlling one. The evangelists and the bearers of the traditions before them participate with their whole beings in what is told here. *That* they tell, *what* they tell, and *how* they tell the story—all is determined by their faith in the Crucified One, who is the resurrected Christ. The kerygmatic-doxological statements in the rest of the New Testament presume the historical facts; a theological significance is no less implicit in the passion narratives of the Gospels. This significance is only infrequently expressed, but it determines the entire manner of the telling. In each of the four Gospels one may speak of something like a theology of the passion story.[5] The evangelists bear witness, each in his own way, that on Golgotha occurred the decisive event in the history of God's dealing with humankind.

The concern of the evangelists—kerygmatic, cultic, devotional, or whatever one wishes to call it—involves both the retention of the events in memory and a transformation of the historical picture. The passion narratives contain features that are to be characterized as legendary not only in a form-critical but also negatively in a historical sense. But they also contain historical facts. The dispute arises over the degree to which the one and the other element is present.

Various motifs within the passion narratives can be distinguished: proof from prophecy, apologetic, novelistic features, moral injunctions, dogmatic and cultic interests, and the like.[6] However, neither stylistically nor in content can one succeed in separating what is historical, legendary, or dogmatic. All such elements are intertwined; the historical is not merely historical, the theological not dogmatic and rational. As a whole and in its parts, the passion story is condensed in content and symbolically powerful. The very manner in which it is presented expresses the inner participation of the narrator and the hidden dimension of what happened.

With reference to the creedlike statements about the death of Christ, the expression "pathos-formula" has been employed.[7] The designation is not entirely fitting. Form-critically it is imprecise, and with respect to content it is not wholly appropriate. But it does render one service: it exposes the inadequacy of precise categories of style, content, and function. As in the "liturgical" formulas so also in the passion narratives, we must be aware of the "pathos" in order to discover what is at stake. Pathos is missing in none of the evangelists, but it is strongest in Mark, no doubt because he depicts the passion story with blunt realism without alluding to the latent authority of the Son of God in the direct dogmatic manner of Matthew and John and also without highlighting the nobility in the suffering of the perfect martyr as in Luke.

None of the evangelists has recounted the passion story without pathos, disinterestedly, like a neutral reporter. Historical interest is present, even if it at no time becomes an end in itself. Mark cites authorities (14:51; 15:21); he gives information about what motivated the opponents of Jesus (15:10; cf. 12:12-13), how it happened that Jesus was arrested alone and without greater sensation (14:1-4, 10f., 43ff.), and upon what juridical basis he was condemned (14:55ff.; 15:2). Whether or not he has given the historically correct answers, he is moved by the question of what happened and how it came about. In Matthew it is not very different. In the passion narrative as elsewhere, Luke emerges as the "historian" among the evangelists; he makes it clear that Jesus must be accused before Pilate as a political insurgent (23:2, 5, 14). It is more noteworthy that even the fourth evangelist—and he in particular—strives to set forth clearly the causal connections that led to Jesus' death. Perhaps even more than in Luke, he gives the political aspects of the trial special prominence (John 11:45ff., 57; 12:10f., 17ff.; 18:13f., 19f., 29ff.; 19:6ff.). It is questionable to what extent Luke and John have at their disposal historical reports that go beyond Mark. If they do not, these two evangelists exhibit an all the more notable sense of history.

From a literary point of view, the passion narratives are characterized by the tension between events in the foreground that can be observed by all and their mysterious background, that which happened within what happened.[8] Concealed within the earthly event is the mystery of God, which first became manifest to the disciples through the appearances of the resurrected Christ in order that it might be revealed through their preaching. In John the distinction between outward happenings and their deeper significance is explicitly stressed. The high priest's comment that it would be better that one man die for the people than that the whole nation perish is political. Without knowing it, however, he speaks as a prophet of the vicarious suffering of Christ (John 11:49ff.). Pilate formulates the title on the cross in order to annoy the Jews, but the inscription in three languages proclaims for all the world that the one crucified is the "King of the Jews," the promised Messiah (John 19:19ff.). The inscription is understood in the same way in the Synoptics, even if it is not as clearly expressed. In the passion narratives, the accusation against Jesus is an indirect testimony that the crucified is the Christ, while in the passion formulas he is directly proclaimed and praised as such.

The engagement of faith and the pathos of the account thus do not exclude a historical interest on the part of the evangelists, but rather include it. This interest is interwoven with the concern of faith, but it is not completely one with it. The mystery, the death of Jesus as a saving event, is only to be grasped in faith, which is simultaneously faith in the resurrected Christ. A fact that can be historically confirmed can belong only to the foreground of the event. Christians may legitimately ask about historical fact, however. What was first held together in the pathos of the passion narratives becomes separated for us who belong to a later, sophisticated generation: here confession, preaching, and faith; there historical research. Moreover, to pursue the historical interest we must work critically and avail ourselves of all means and methods of historical study at our disposal.

AN UNSETTLED QUESTION OF ALBERT SCHWEITZER

It cannot be said in advance how far it will be possible to obtain a certain, unambiguous answer to our historical questions. What really happened in the death of Jesus? How did the course of events lead to his condemnation? What circumstances, motives, and contributing causes were of significance? What light does the death of Jesus shed upon his previous life and his preaching? We can expect, in any case, to make some advances, for in reality little has been done with these questions in the last decades. This is a result of misgivings about the nineteenth-century biographies of Jesus but is not a legitimate consequence of the reaction against them. For the historical question about the death of Jesus in its relation to his previous life was not settled by the demise of psychologizing biographies; rather, it became acute. Albert Schweitzer had asked this question in his "Sketch of the Life of Jesus," which originated in connection with a work on the Lord's Supper.[9] Later he formulated it clearly and powerfully in his debate with Wrede, even if his own answer was no more than an arbitrary conjecture.[10]

A new quest for the historical Jesus cannot simply and unreflectively continue or resume the line of the old biographical research without an awareness of the insights for which we are indebted to M. Kähler, among others, and form critics. We should not be induced, however (perhaps by a new conception of history), to neglect our obligations to take up anew genuine, unsolved problems of older research. Recent research has unjustly taken from Schweitzer's work only the problem of eschatology and the "delay of the parousia" and has ignored the chief problem with regard to Jesus' life, namely, the problem of the nonmessianic character of Jesus' public ministry in relation to his messiahship affirmed by the sources. Schweitzer's main asset as a New Testament critic lay in his ability, trained through the history of research, to see essential problems and to ask sharp questions. Nineteenth-century German research into the life of Jesus had a double outcome: Wrede and Schweitzer. The correspondence and the difference between the two types of solutions led Schweitzer to formulate the alternatives: "The inconsistency between the public life of Jesus and his Messianic claim lies either in the nature of the Jewish Messianic conception, or in the representation of the Evangelist. . . . *Tertium non datur*."[11]

Contemporary research has scarcely gone beyond these alternatives, although the literary analysis and tradition-criticism following Wrede have become keener and more penetrating (Bultmann and others), while the interpretation of the self-consciousness of Jesus in light of Jewish messianic ideas has been carried on with more learning and greater circumspection than in Schweitzer (e.g., by Joachim Jeremias and Erik Sjöberg). The advocates of the two typical solutions have appealed to solid arguments and have pointed out the difficulties in the opposing attempts at solutions. But at the same time, both sides have a common difficulty. In the early Christian confession and kerygma, Jesus was proclaimed as the Anointed One (Messiah, *Christos*). This fact cannot be easily accounted for either by supposing that Jesus in no sense intended to be the Messiah or by assuming that he combined in his own person the role of heavenly Son of man with that of Suffering Servant. Does there exist a third possibility beyond the alternative explanations in terms of community dogmatic or Jewish messianism?

THE INSCRIPTION OF THE CHARGE

If we are to proceed beyond the impasse, we must achieve clarity about one matter: was Jesus actually crucified as a messianic pretender, as the evangelists say? This is contested by Bultmann, for example, who asserts that Jesus was condemned and executed not as Messiah but as a messianic prophet; the view that Jesus should die as Messiah belongs to the dogmatic motifs of the passion story.[12] The motif is undoubtedly dogmatic, but must it therefore be unhistorical? This question cannot be answered by a priori considerations. Historically both alternatives are conceivable: Jesus could have been crucified either as a messianic pretender or as a false prophet and agitator. The motif is firmly anchored in the sources. To be sure, one cannot argue on the basis of the proceedings before the Sanhedrin (Mark 14:55ff. par.), for its historicity is indeed questionable. Moreover, Bultmann may be right that the accusation in Mark 15:2 is a secondary expansion parallel to 15:3-5. But this does not prove that the inscription of the charge in 15:26 is also secondary.[13] More probably, the question of 15:2 was formulated in view of the inscription "King of the Jews," which is firmly fixed in the tradition. Furthermore, this title occurs in the Barabbas episode and in the scene where the soldiers do mock homage to Jesus; it is presupposed in the reviling of the crucified (Mark 15:9, 12, 16ff., 32). This is not easy to explain if the motif is really secondary.

Mark's presentation is confirmed by the fact that the crucifixion of Jesus as "King of the Jews" is also a chief motif of the Johannine passion narrative, which on the whole, is not dependent upon the Synoptics (cf. John 18:33ff.; 19:1-3, 12-15, 19-22).[14] Thus in any case the motif must be very old. John gives it a spiritualized meaning; in Matthew and Luke it is less prominent than in Mark.[15] The formulation "King of the Jews" stems neither from proof from prophecy nor from the Christology of the community. In general, early Christians hesitated to use the title "king" for Jesus. Could the formulation really represent the historicization of a dogmatic motif? This is highly implausible. It is difficult to imagine a form of the passion story that was merely a historical report and equally difficult to imagine any stage in the passion tradition that did not presuppose the messiahship of the crucified. The crucified-Messiah motif belongs to the substance of the passion story, though its historicity is still not proved.

THE CHRISTIANIZING OF THE TITLE "MESSIAH"

Another consideration is decisive: That the title "Messiah" was inextricably bound up with the name of Jesus can be explained only by presupposing that Jesus was actually crucified as the Messiah. Otherwise one falls into great difficulties and cannot make historically understandable the title's Christian meaning and its wide use as another name of Jesus.[16] At this point I can only sketch the results of more extensive work. In all the writings in the New Testament Jesus is proclaimed as the Christ. But the name "Christ" is not the expression of any particular christological conception but is rather a common denominator for the various conceptions that are found in the New Testament. In the oldest sources, the Pauline epistles, *Christos* always denotes the one Christ, Jesus. It is not a colorless proper name, however, but an honorific designation, whose content is supplied by the person and work of Jesus Christ. Where *Christos* appears as a more general term for the Messiah announced in the Old Testament, there are often signs of later theologizing, which is also to be seen in patristic literature. For example, in Luke, as in Justin, the primitive kerygma "Christ died . . . according to the scriptures" has developed into two statements: "the Anointed One must suffer," and "Jesus is the Anointed One." Actually, what these writers and many after them present as the Old Testament doctrine of the Messiah has been conformed to their image of Jesus the Christ.

Thus from the beginnings of Greek-speaking Christianity (within a few years of the crucifixion), the name "Christ" as applied to Jesus must have been firmly established. This presupposes that

Jesus was already designated "the Messiah" and "Jesus the Messiah" in Aramaic-speaking regions. To this extent the Christology of the primitive community from the very first must have been a Messiah Christology. To be sure, Jesus was also spoken of as "Son of man" and "Servant of God," but these designations never appear as predicates. In the kerygma and confession it is not "Jesus is the Son of man" or "Jesus is the Servant of God," but always "Jesus is the Messiah" and, further, "Jesus is the Son of God" or "Jesus is Kyrios." The content of the predicate "Messiah" was determined essentially by the crucifixion and resurrection of Jesus and only to a limited extent by a previous conception of the Messiah.

From the very first, faith in Jesus as the Resurrected One was faith in him as the Messiah. This is not to be explained by the Easter event alone. To a Jew of Jesus' time it was not a completely foreign idea for someone to be raised from the dead or to be exalted to heaven; likewise, a person of the past could return at the end time. Such statements might apply to Enoch and Elijah, perhaps also to Moses, Melchizedek, and others (cf. also Mark 6:14ff.; 8:28). However, none of this in itself has anything to do with the Messiah or messiahship. From the discovery of the empty tomb (if it is historical) and from the appearance of the Resurrected One, it could be inferred that Jesus lives and is exalted to heaven. But his resurrection would not necessarily mean that he is the Messiah. In the resurrection stories in the Gospels, the messiahship of Jesus is not especially stressed apart from specifically Lucan formulations (Luke 24:26, 46).[17] The resurrection does mean, however, that Jesus was vindicated by God vis-à-vis his adversaries. If he was crucified as an alleged Messiah, then—but only then—does faith in his resurrection necessarily become faith in the resurrection of the crucified Messiah. In this way the distinctiveness of the Christian idea of the Messiah, in contrast to the Jewish, was given from the outset. Whether it is said that God will send the foreordained Messiah, Jesus (Acts 3:20f.), or that Jesus is enthroned as Messiah (Acts 2:36), or that Christ died for our sins (1 Cor. 15:3) is a matter of minor importance in this context.

Jewish messianic expectations do not explain the meaning of the name "Messiah" assigned to Jesus. Neither can it be said that the title "Messiah" is the necessary contemporary expression for the conviction that Jesus is the eschatological bringer of salvation. This is no more valid than the older assertion that messiahship was the necessary garb for the archetypical religious self-consciousness of Jesus. Jewish eschatology did not know just one salvation figure; in addition to the royal Messiah there was the eschatological high priest, the prophet like Moses, Elijah redivivus, the warrior from Ephraim; and there were still other figures. Expectation, as we now see clearly, was not systematized so that the other figures were taken as forerunners of the true Messiah; instead they were parallel figures. What remained constant were the eschatologically interpreted statements of the Scriptures; on particular questions exegesis had its freedom. Scriptural passages could be connected in various ways, and certain figures are combined and even identified with each other; they could also go unnoticed.

Rarely has it been made clear how strange it is that precisely the title "Messiah" was applied to Jesus and became his name. The title stems from the figure in Jewish eschatology that has almost nothing at all in common with the New Testament picture of Christ. "The Messiah," used absolutely as an eschatological term, designates the political Messiah, the king of the house of David. Accordingly, in the New Testament *Christos* is in more than one place a synonym for "King of Israel" (or "King of the Jews"), while nowhere is it necessary to presuppose another significance. And since it is not necessary, it should not be done. We may assume that in popular piety, as in the synagogue prayers, the Messiah-King was the dominant figure; this is also the figure for which the broadest basis is to be found in Holy Scripture. The first Christians, however, found prophecy of the Christ neither exclusively nor even principally in the parts of the Old Testament that were interpreted messianically in the narrow sense in Judaism.[18] Not only were the prophecies about the Son of David referred to the Messiah Jesus; testimonies to him were also found in the texts about the prophet like Moses, the eschatological high priest, the Son of man, the Servant of the Lord, the messenger of salvation (Isa. 52:7), the pierced one (Zechariah 12), and in many passages that in Judaism were not at all interpreted as referring to an eschatological figure. If the prophecies in Malachi 3 were not often referred to Jesus, it is only because John the Baptist had already been identified—by Jesus himself (?)—with the coming Elijah.[19]

Jesus' name, Messiah, surely implies that in him and through him the promises of God were fulfilled; but remarkably little attention was devoted to the specifically messianic prophecies of the Old Testament. But this means that the application of the title "Messiah" to Jesus cannot have had its origin in the study of Scripture and in the discussion of the first Christians with Jews. Both are only secondary factors. The messiahship of the crucified Jesus is rather the presupposition that lies at the root of all the scriptural evidence *de Christo*. Since the central place of the name "Messiah" cannot be explained from the preaching of Jesus, there remains only one possibility: the title "Messiah" was inseparably connected with the name of Jesus because Jesus was condemned and crucified as a messianic pretender.

We may now draw two important conclusions. First, that Jesus was crucified as King of the Jews is not a dogmatic motif that has become historicized in the passion narratives; precisely to the contrary, it is a historical fact that became centrally important for the formulation of the first Christian dogma: Jesus is the Messiah. Second, the confession of Jesus as the Messiah is not to be understood as a "re-Judaizing" of the preaching and person of Jesus but, on the contrary, as a thorough, radical Christianizing of the Jewish title of Messiah.

THE GOSPELS AND THE MESSIAHSHIP OF JESUS

From what precedes, the data given by the evangelists can be evaluated. They too presuppose the concept *Christos* as reinterpreted in Christian terms. Only in a few places is the name put into the mouth of Jesus (Matt. 23:10; Mark 9:41; John 17:3). Matthew makes rather extensive use of the Christian concept of Messiah in the gospel story. Luke characteristically uses Old Testament language, speaking of Jesus as the anointed of God. Knowledge of the contrast between Jewish messianic doctrine and New Testament faith in Christ is most clearly expressed in John.[20] As a general conception not directly applied to Jesus, *Christos* appears in the question about the Messiah as son and as Lord of David (Mark 12:35-37 par.) as well as in the prophecy about false christs arising (Mark 13:21 par.). It seems certain that before the passion Jesus did not openly claim to be the Messiah.

Matthew understands Peter's confession at Caesarea Philippi as a prototype of the Christian confession of Christ. But this is a secondary interpretation.[21] Mark's version is different but in no way disinterested. Peter's confession must be read in light of the themes of the messianic secret and of the disciples' misunderstanding. Peter speaks the truth; Jesus is indeed the Christ. But Peter does not yet understand the implications of this truth. He cannot accept the idea of the passion because he sees in Jesus the Messiah (contrast in Matthew). This means that, according to Mark, Peter still understands the name "Messiah" in a Jewish sense. A beatitude addressed to Peter would be impossible in Mark; the true messiahship of Jesus remains a secret even to the disciples until the passion and resurrection. Furthermore, the Marcan form of the pericope takes up a motif that appears in another context (Mark 8:28; cf. 6:14f.). But it may be a historical recollection that even in his lifetime Jesus was "one who was hoped to be the Messiah, but who not only at the moment of failure, but in his entire message and ministry, disappointed the hopes that were placed in him."[22]

May we suppose that Jesus himself gave a new interpretation to the concept of Messiah? For this assumption there is only one piece of real evidence, the question about the son of David (Mark 12:35-37). In it is contained an indirect messianic claim. The answer to the problem of the seemingly self-contradictory statements of Scripture lies in the concrete messiahship of Jesus, who, as a man, is son of David but, as the Exalted One, is his Lord. Here the Christian concept of Messiah is indeed presupposed. And for precisely this reason the pericope is probably a product of Christian scriptural interpretation. It belongs to those elements of the tradition whose historicity cannot be demonstrated because of their close conformity to the kerygma of the church.[23]

The designation "Son of man" in Jesus' words in the Gospels is and remains enigmatic, no less so because the pre-Christian origin of the Similitudes of Enoch (37–71) has now once again become doubtful. If I am right that the name "Messiah" must have stood at the center of the early community's confession and preaching, it becomes impossible to consider all the traditional Son of man sayings as constructions of the community. A kernel of traditional, genuine Son of man sayings must have existed as a point of departure for the Gospels' widespread use of "Son of man" as Jesus' self-designation.[24] But this does not prove that Jesus, drawing upon peculiar apocalyptic traditions, understood himself as the hidden Son of man. In the words of Jesus most widely accepted as authentic, either the Son of man is an eschatological figure not clearly identified with Jesus (Mark 8:38 par.), or Jesus speaks of himself noneschatologically as Son of man (i.e., as an individual man). Thus in the latter case it is not clear that he claims to be the Son of man of Daniel 7 (Matt. 8:20 Q; 11:19 Q). Those passion predictions that might most plausibly be considered authentic are not joined to any titles.[25]

Did Jesus think that he was the eschatological Son of man? Criticism and exegesis of the words of Jesus transmitted by tradition cannot answer this or the more general question of messianic self-consciousness with certainty. The Gospels were written by men who believed that Jesus was the Christ, the Messiah, as Christians understood that term. The preserved Son of man sayings have been interpreted from this perspective. But in themselves they are remarkably ambiguous. Negatively it can be maintained that Jesus before his passion made no express and unequivocal claim to messiahship (cf. John 10:24f.). But does this exclude the possibility that in some sense he thought himself the Messiah? Positively it might be said that if Jesus regarded himself as Messiah, "he thought of his messiahship essentially in the categories of an apocalyptic conception of the Son of Man," though admittedly he transformed the apocalyptic image he appropriated.[26] But is this presupposition correct? Can any advance toward the solution of this problem, so vexing for contemporary research, be made if we begin with the idea that the crucifixion of Jesus as messianic pretender must be taken to be a historical fact? It is along this course that we must proceed.

Of course, caution is needed. I agree with Käsemann that we cannot reconstruct a life of Jesus, since we do not have the requisite knowledge of his external and psychological development.[27] But from this it does not follow that historical questions about causal relationships neither can nor ought be asked at all. There is certainly some purpose in asking about the causes and effects of Jesus' death; moreover, questions must be asked, whether we find the task pleasant or not. Answers can be given only incompletely and approximately; the best claim can only be to a high degree of probability. But this is not only because of the nature of the sources but just as much because of the general problems that are bound up with the use of causal explanations in historical research. Nevertheless the historian cannot work without the concept of causality, even if it must be used with caution.[28]

We know little with certainty about the motives that led the authorities to take legal steps against Jesus, but we can conjecture some things with good reason. Jesus' sovereign attitude to the prescriptions of the law, his relation to the poor and to many suspect individuals, and especially his public appearance in the temple— all this, in conjunction with his eschatological preaching, could appear to be a revolt against the established religio-political order. The messianic hopes of Jesus' followers may have been sufficient to occasion the charges raised against him. With Bornkamm we have to speak "not of Jesus' non-messianic history before his passion, but indeed of a movement of broken messianic hopes."[29]

The fact that Jesus was arrested alone is one indication, among others, that there can be no serious questions of a messianic-political movement under Jesus' leadership (in spite of Robert Eisler, among others). Jesus was crucified as a messianic pretender, but he did not himself claim to be the Messiah, at least not publicly. A. Schweitzer wanted to explain this apparent contradiction by assuming that Judas betrayed the messianic secret. This theory was a necessity for Schweitzer's whole construction, but it belongs in the realm of historical fiction. From Jesus' crucifixion as "King of the Jews," no direct conclusions can be drawn about Jesus' messianic self-consciousness before the passion. To be sure, Jesus' activities are likely to have given rise to the question, among both followers and opponents, whether or not he thought himself to be the Messiah. The authority with which he invested his actions makes this understandable. But it must have been his opponents who put messiahship in the foreground and made it the decisive question of life and death. It is very doubtful that a precise historical report lies behind the synoptic account of the proceedings before the Sanhedrin. The essential point, however, would seem to be historically accurate. The inscription of charge presupposes that Jesus was accused before Pilate on the ground that he made a royal-messianic claim. If so, one may further infer that Jesus, confronted with that charge that he thought himself to be the Messiah, accepted the accuracy of the charge by his silence, if not in any other way.[30]

The claim to be the Messiah was thus extorted from Jesus. He did not raise it on his own initiative—at least not expressly and directly. However, before the accusation made in the face of impending death, he did not deny he was the Messiah. From this, one might try to argue back to a previous messianic consciousness and perhaps find a point of contact in possible Jewish ideas about a suffering Messiah. But the line of argument is uncertain. We may say with greater confidence that Jesus could not deny the charge that he was the Messiah without thereby putting in question the final, eschatological validity of his whole message and ministry. Furthermore, it may be said that willingness to suffer is implicit in Jesus' behavior and attitude throughout his preaching.[31] This was verified by his willingness to die a rejected and ridiculed Messiah. We are able to say almost nothing at all from a psychological viewpoint about Jesus' attitude during the passion. But we may take it as a historical fact that Jesus did nothing to avoid his condemnation and crucifixion as "King of the Jews." Only in the form of this "good confession" before Pontius Pilate does a "messianic claim" of Jesus become historically accessible. But this is precisely the one thing that is a necessary presupposition for the New Testament gospel of the crucified Messiah.

CONCLUDING REMARKS

The contradiction between Jesus' nonmessianic public appearances and his messiahship is to be explained neither from the nature of Jewish messianic ideas nor by the tension between historical facts and the conceptions of the evangelists. There is a third possibility. Indeed many things can and must be explained by analysis of sources and traditions, and it is conceivable that Jesus appropriated certain ideas on Jewish messianism. The real explanation, however, is to be sought in the historical event itself; the inconsistency stems from Jesus' crucifixion as the Messiah, although he never made an express messianic claim. He did not deny the accusation that he acted the role of Messiah when it was raised against him. This fact had a determinative significance for the Christian kerygma and thus for the ideas of the evangelists. The end of Jesus' life stands at the heart of the gospel; the historical Jesus, like the kerygmatic Christ, is the crucified Messiah.

There is no gap between the historical Jesus and the preaching of the church; rather, there exists a close and inseparable connection. We have not achieved this result by abstracting from historical matters of fact in order to ask only about the "continuity of the gospel in the discontinuity of the times" (Käsemann). Nor is this to say that we have reckoned with a conception of Heilsgeschichte with its own laws and its own continuity, detached from general history. Rather, the question has been simply historical, and the continuity I see is first of all a historical, causal continuity. This continuity is not purely theological or ideological; the church's preaching of Christ is not to be traced back to the self-consciousness of Jesus or to his preaching. What we have found, rather, is a complex series of actions and reactions of various people who were involved in the events. Not only the conduct of Jesus and his disciples but also that of Caiaphas and Pilate was of decisive significance. What applies to the external course of the events is also true for the theological interpretation. The formulation of the confession "Jesus is Messiah" presupposes the formulation of the charge and was occasioned by it. It is quite probable that the title "Messiah" was first brought forth as an expression of false expectation, as an accusation and as a mockery of Jesus. Only later, after the appearance of the risen Lord, was it taken up as a unifying expression of confession and preaching. With this, the ambiguity of the historical continuity becomes quite clear. Only by faith in the resurrection has the scandal of the crucified Messiah been overcome.

The preaching of the resurrected Christ still makes the death of Jesus a saving event for us. The truth of the gospel does not permit validation through historical investigation. However, it seems arbitrary to isolate the message and the life of Jesus from his death as the crucified Messiah in order to seek the essence of Christianity in the "so-called historical Jesus" isolated in such a way. I find it equally impossible to see historical research as something standing beside the kerygma with parallel access to the significance of Jesus, unless the crucifixion should finally become a dispensable symbol for the proper understanding of existence. Insofar as this is true, faith remains directed toward the preached, biblical Christ. This does not lead us to escape the difficulties bound up with the question of the historical Jesus, however; the kerygma is much too closely involved with the historical events for that to happen.

I am somewhat skeptical of slogans and great syntheses. If the proposal sketched here has worth, it is this: an important single question—the historical problem of the application of the title "Messiah" to Jesus—has been clearly asked and to some extent precisely answered. Some guiding principles and consequences have been laid out, but no final answers attained; old problems are cast in a new light, and broader questions raised. Thus the result is shown to be a genuinely historical one. Such a clarification—of what lends itself to historical clarification—should not be unwelcome to faith in the preached Jesus Christ.[32]

Notes

[1]M. Kähler, *The So-Called Historical Jesus and the Historic Biblical Christ* (trans. C. Braaten; Philadelphia: Fortress, 1964) 47: "For the cardinal virtue of genuine historical research is modesty." Kähler did not clearly express his opinion about the possibility of genuine historical research into the life of Jesus, but he obviously did not want to exclude this possibility.

[2]Particularly noteworthy was the article by E. Käsemann, "The Problem of the Historical Jesus," first published in 1954 and now included in his *Essays on New Testament Themes* (trans. W. G. Montague; Naperville, Ill.: Allenson, 1964) 15–47. Independently of Käsemann, however, several other scholars worked with the problem. James M. Robinson (*A New Quest of the Historical Jesus* [SBT 25; Naperville, Ill.: Allenson, 1959]) presents recent scholarship too one-sidedly as a reaction to Käsemann. My article "The Problem of the Historical Jesus" (chap. 5 in this volume) goes back to a paper read in Uppsala in 1952.

3Cf. "The Problem of the Historical Jesus," chap. 5 below.

4R. Bultmann, *Glauben und Verstehen* I (2d ed.; Tübingen: Mohr, 1954) 241.

5To clarify this point I refer to two of my essays, "Die Passionsgeschichte bei Matthäus" (*NTS* 2 [1955–56] 17–32), now "The Passion Narrative in Matthew," in *Jesus in the Memory of the Early Church* (Minneapolis: Augsburg, 1976) 37–51; and "Markusevangeliets sikte" (*SEÅ* 22–23 [1957–58] 99–112), now "The Purpose of Mark's Gospel," in *Jesus in the Memory of the Early Church* 52–65.

6Cf. R. Bultmann, *The History of the Synoptic Tradition* (trans. J. Marsh; New York: Harper, 1963) 280ff.

7J. Knoll, *Gott und Hölle: Der Mythos vom Decensuskampfe* (Berlin: Teubner, 1932) 123f., 529f., etc.

8Cf. the analysis of biblical narratives, including the exposition of the denial of Peter, in E. Auerbach, *Mimesis: The Representation of Reality in Western Literature* (trans. W. Trask; Princeton: Princeton University Press, 1953), chaps. 1 and 2, especially pp. 40–49.

9A. Schweitzer, *The Mystery of the Kingdom of God* (New York: Macmillan, 1955; German original, 1901).

10A. Schweitzer, *The Quest of the Historical Jesus* (3d ed.; London: Black, 1954) 328–49. (According to Schweitzer, Judas betrayed the messianic secret!)

11Schweitzer, *Quest* 335. Cf. against this, T. W. Manson, "The Life of Jesus: Some Tendencies in Present-day Research," in *The Background of the New Testament and Its Eschatology* (Cambridge: Cambridge University Press, 1956) 211–21.

12Bultmann, *History* 284; cf. 272–73.

13Against Bultmann, *History* 272. The historicity of the inscription of the charge has been championed recently by T. A. Burkill, "The Trial of Jesus," *VC* 12 (1958) 1–18; P. Winter, *On the Trial of Jesus* (Berlin: de Gruyter, 1961) 107–10; W. Meeks, *The Prophet-King* (Leiden: Brill, 1967) 79 n. 1.

14Cf. P. Borgen, "John and the Synoptics in the Passion Narrative," *NTS* 5 (1958) 246–59.

15Cf. John 18:36f.; 19:21f.; Matt. 27:17, 22 (Mark 15:9, 12), as well as the absence of Lucan parallels to Mark 15:9, 12, 18.

16The difficulties encountered if one seeks to understand the application of the title "Messiah" to Jesus purely from the study of the history of ideas are quite evident in the rather inadequate treatment "Jesus the Messiah" in O. Cullmann's *The Christology of the New Testament* (trans. S. Guthrie and C. Hall; Philadelphia: Westminster, 1959) 111–37. The same difficulties are present in F. Hahn, *The Titles of Jesus in Christology—Their History in Early Christianity* (trans. H. Knight and G. Ogg; London: Lutterworth, 1969) 136–239; and R. Fuller, *The Foundations of New Testament Christology* (New York: Scribner's, 1965).

17It would, of course, be otherwise if the supposition were true that the Caesarea–Philippi pericope and the transfiguration story were transposed Easter stories. But there is no basis for this assumption apart from the supposition that the disciples' faith in the Messiah was grounded in their Easter visions.

18This has been correctly seen by S. L. Edgar, "New Testament and Rabbinic Messianic Interpretation," *NTS* 5 (1958) 47–54.

19Cf. J. A. T. Robinson, "Elijah, John, and Jesus," *NTS* 4 (1958) 263–81.

20John 1:19ff.; 7:26f., 40ff.; 12:34. Cf. Bent Noack, "Johannes-evangeliets messiasbillede og dets kristologi," *DTT* 19 (1956) 129–55; M. de Jonge, "The Use of the Word 'Anointed' in the Time of Jesus," *NTS* 19 (1972–73) 246–70.

21Cf. especially A. Vögtle, "Messiasbekenntnis und Petrusverheissung," *BZ*, n.s., 1 (1957) 252–72; 2 (1958) 85–103.

[22]G. Bornkamm, *Jesus of Nazareth* (trans. Irene McLuskey et al.; New York: Harper & Row, 1960) 172.

[23]On the methodological difficulties, cf. Robinson, *A New Quest* 100ff.

[24]Cf. on this H. E. Tödt, *The Son of Man in the Synoptic Tradition* (trans. D. Barton; Philadelphia: Westminster, 1965); and E. Schweizer, "Der Menschensohn" and "The Son of Man Again," in *Neotestamentica* (Zurich: Zwingli-Verlag, 1963) 56–84 and 85–92.

[25]Mark 10:38; Luke 12:50. The word "be baptized" (or "be immersed") seems to be used here not in the Christian sacramental sense but in the more general Jewish ritual sense.

[26]Thus E. Sjöberg, *Der verborgene Menschensohn in den Evangelien* (Lund: Gleerup, 1955) 241.

[27]See my "Problem of the Historical Jesus."

[28]Cf. on this Ottar Dahl, *Om årsaksproblemer i historisk forskning* (Oslo: University Press, 1956), with an English summary: "Problems of causation in historical research."

[29]Bornkamm, *Jesus* 172.

[30]The greatest difficulty in Mark 14:55-64 is that Jesus' messianic claim is the occasion for his condemnation on the grounds of blasphemy. This is most easily explained as the viewpoint of the narrator, who knew well that the Christian confession of Jesus' messiahship was a scandal and blasphemy to Jews. It is quite probable that the high priest was concerned to find some basis for a charge before Pilate. The individual problems cannot be dealt with here. I do believe that in 14:62 the reading "you say that I am" is worthy of consideration. I regard E. Stauffer's interpretation of this verse as fantastic (*Jesus and His Story* [trans. R. Winston and C. Winston; New York: Knopf, 1960] 124, 184).

[31]E. Fuchs, "The Quest of the Historical Jesus," in *Studies of the Historical Jesus* (trans. A. Scobie; Naperville, Ill.: Allenson, 1964) 11–31.

[32]I have been unable to deal here with Christ's resurrection. But in my way of approaching historical questions, I feel a certain kinship with the work of Hans von Campenhausen, "The Events of Easter and the Empty Tomb," in *Tradition and Life in the Church* (trans. A. V. Littledale; Philadelphia: Fortress, 1968) 42–89.

3

Eschatology and History
in Light of
the Qumran Texts

TERMINOLOGY

IN THE FOLLOWING REMARKS I will use the word "eschatology" to mean doctrine of the last things, that is, statements that concern events and persons of the last days.[1] By "history" I mean socially relevant events that are the objects of reporting and research, the objects of "history" in the Greek sense.

My usage of these terms is old-fashioned. It stems from the time before Karl Barth formulated the famous sentence: "If Christianity be not altogether and unreservedly eschatology, there remains in it no relationship whatever to Christ."[2] Since that time several theologians have tended to designate as eschatological anything that has anything at all to do with Christ. The meaning of the word "eschatology" has thus become so ambiguous that anyone whose native language is not German should be allowed to revert to the older usage.

Rudolf Bultmann certainly employs the word "eschatology" in such a way that its connection with history-of-religions research has been preserved. It should be clear from these remarks on terminology, however, that it is not my intention to treat the whole problem of "history and eschatology." There are far-reaching hermeneutical, philosophical, and theological aspects to this problem as it is posed in Bultmann's Gifford Lectures.[3] Yet, however broad the scope of his work, Bultmann's existential interpretation presupposes a specific reconstruction of early Christianity.

At many points Bultmann has appropriated—perhaps too uncritically—the results of men like Wilhelm Wrede, W. Heitmüller, and Wilhelm Bousset in order to build on the foundation laid by

49

them.[4] As far as his understanding of eschatology is concerned, his debt to Albert Schweitzer seems to me quite evident. For Bultmann, that salvation is eschatological which ends everything earthly.[5] Eschatology is thus "the doctrine of the end of the world, of its destruction."[6] Jesus Christ is correspondingly *the eschatological event*, the action of God by which God has set an end to the old world. . . . The old world has reached its end for the believer." The stance of faith can be designated as liberation from the world. In a paradoxical way, Christian existence is simultaneously eschatological, unworldly, and historical.[7] But Schweitzer had already given the word "eschatology" a new meaning; it signified not simply the doctrine of the last things but rather an orientation of existence determined by the imminent end of the world. "The term 'eschatology' ought only to be applied when reference is made to the end of the world as expected in the immediate future, and the events, hopes, and fears connected therewith."[8] Behind Paul's expectation stands the idea "that Jesus Christ has made an end of the natural world."[9] When such statements are compared, it may be said that Bultmann has existentially interpreted Schweitzer's concept of eschatology.

By this assertion I in no way intend to minimize the many profound differences between Bultmann and Schweitzer. Exegesis was never really Schweitzer's strong suit. Before him, Johannes Weiss had demonstrated by means of careful exegesis the eschatological nature of Jesus' preaching concerning the kingdom of God. Basing his work on Weiss's findings, Schweitzer, with the single-mindedness of genius, made eschatology the key to a historical reconstruction of the life of Jesus and of the history of early Christianity. The presuppositions for this new understanding of eschatology were, however, already in place. They were provided when the world of Jewish apocalyptic was first made accessible to scholarship, about the middle of the last century.[10] To this extent it may be said—rather one-sidedly—that Bultmann's work on eschatology and history stands at the end of a period in the history of research that began when apocalyptic literature came to light.

THE IMPORTANCE OF THE QUMRAN TEXTS

To a certain extent research today is in a situation similar to that of a century ago. New source material for the history of Judaism and its eschatology has become accessible to us but has only partially been evaluated scientifically and theologically. In order to assess and evaluate correctly the material stemming from the caves near Qumran, it seems appropriate for me to work with a terminology least burdened by present-day debates. Thus my old-fashioned usage of terms.

The new material cannot easily be fitted into our current picture of Jewish eschatology. From W. Baldensperger to S. Mowinckel,[11] to mention only two names, a distinction has been made between a nationalistic expectation concerned with this-worldly redemption, and an apocalyptic expectation that is universalistic and transcendental. The Davidic Messiah is said to belong to the former inner-Jewish movement; to the latter belongs another figure, the heavenly Son of Man, alleged to have its roots in Iranian religion. In the Qumran writings we find a dualistic doctrine of two spirits, the prince of light and the angel of darkness, who oppose one another from creation to the end of the world. This dualism, however, has no corresponding apocalyptic, superhuman messianic figure. No trace can be found of the Son of Man. Rather, the eschatological persons named in the Qumran writings are officeholders within the Israel of the last days.

The two conceptions—the dualistic and the messianic—are not simply juxtaposed, however. The dualism takes on concrete form in an opposition between the sons of light and the sons of darkness, that is (in practice) between the members of the sect and its adversaries. The eschatological officeholders exercise their functions in the predestined final confrontation between the two groups. It is therefore permissible to elucidate the relationship between eschatology and history by focusing on the statements concerning these persons. There is all the more reason to do so, since in the New Testament, eschatology and history converge above all in Christology.

The views of scholars vary widely concerning the importance of the Qumran findings for the historical understanding of the Christological origins. A. Dupont-Sommer has interpreted the so-called Teacher of Righteousness as a Christ-figure prior to Christ. Others have attempted to explain the Christology of Hebrews or even the use of the title "Christ" in the Synoptics from the perspective of the Qumran doctrine regarding the priestly Messiah.[12] On the other hand, it has been maintained, one might even say apodictically, that the Qumran texts are thoroughly irrelevant to our understanding of the Christology of the early church.[13] This latter judgment, in my opinion, rests on sounder exegesis and sharper critical discrimination. Nevertheless, the purely negative assessment is not the last word on the subject. Today we must move beyond a direct comparison of isolated texts and concepts to a more structural approach. This necessity has been recognized by Krister Stendahl among others.[14] Bultmann saw this as well and observed that the most important analogy between the early Christian community and the Qumran sect is that each understood itself as the true Israel of the last days.[15]

Formerly, we possessed, on the one hand, a corpus of Jewish eschatological writings that were often difficult to date, about whose historical-sociological background we knew very little. On the other hand, we possessed (most notably in Josephus) a whole series of reports and notes about freedom-fighters and charismatics from the time of Judas Maccabeus to the time of Simon bar Kochba. However, the sources are almost completely silent regarding the grounding of the eschatological expectations within these liberation movements, the claims of the leading figures, and the way these expectations and claims were developed by interpretation of Scripture.

The findings at Qumran have placed us in a new position. Our picture of the messianic conceptions of pre-Christian Judaism is being enlarged and corrected. The necessity of comparing and contrasting the Qumran material with Jewish conceptions exhibited elsewhere frees us from our inherent tendency toward overhasty and uncritical examination of Jewish messianic ideas with a view to their relevance for Christology. It is of great importance that we are now quite well informed about the eschatological doctrines as well as about the sociological structures and history of one and the same movement. It has thus now become possible to study the relationship between eschatology and history within one community that was close to Jesus and to the early church both in time and in location. It can to some extent be demonstrated how history was interpreted in light of eschatology and, conversely, how traditional eschatology was transformed under the impact of history.

PERSONS EXPECTED TO COME

In the Scroll of the Rule, at the end of a series of legal prescriptions, it says: "And they shall be governed by the first ordinances in which the members of the Community began their instruction, until the coming of the Prophet and the Anointed [ones] of Aaron and Israel."[16] According to this, the legal ordinances are understood as interim laws that may not be altered during the pre-eschatological period. A similar mode of expression occurs several times in the Damascus Document.[17] It is known, however, from other sources as well: "until a trustworthy prophet should arise" (1 Macc. 14:41; cf. 4:46), "until a [the] priest with Urim and Thummim should arise" (Neh. 7:65; cf. Ezra 2:63), and "until he comes whose right it is" (Ezek. 21:27).

One may also compare the messianically interpreted oracle concerning Judah in Genesis 49:10: "Until he comes to whom it belongs." According to Qumran literature, Hosea 10:12 likewise belongs among such eschatological passages, being understood as "until he comes and teaches you righteousness" or "until the coming of the Teacher of Righteousness" (cf. CD vi, 11). In talmudic and post-talmudic literature, this text was applied to the return of Elijah.[18]

The eschatological interpretation of these biblical passages belonged in all probability to common Jewish exegetical tradition. However, in the text from the Rule (1QS 9:10f.), a prophet, a royal and a priestly Messiah are mentioned alongside one another. It has long been recognized that three figures are intended, and this has been subsequently confirmed by the citation of Deuteronomy 18:18ff.,[19] Numbers 24:15-17, and Deuteronomy 33:8-11 in a collection of testimonies.[20] These texts do not refer to precursors of the Messiah, a primarily Christian conception. Here they refer to contemporaneous eschatological officeholders.[21] It is probable that in this emphatic differentiation between the three offices lies a polemical allusion directed against their combination by the Hasmonean priest-princes. It is said of John Hyrcanus that he combined a prophetic gift with the sovereign and high-priestly offices.[22]

The expectation of all three figures was based on Holy Scripture; the scriptural bases, however, are employed quite differently in the three cases. Of the prophet we actually learn nothing beyond the fact that the prediction of the "prophet like Moses" was applied to him.[23] Among the Samaritans and perhaps in other circles, he stood in the center of expectation. Yet in later "normative" Judaism, the prophet as an independent eschatological figure has vanished. Perhaps for the enthusiasts the temptation was too great to play the role of prophet.

What is said in the Qumran texts about the Davidic Messiah, the anointed one of Israel, is almost exclusively a paraphrase and interpretation of well-known messianic prophecies, including Genesis 49:8-12, Numbers 24:15-17, and Isaiah 11.[24] Of particular interest is the clear proof that the promise of Nathan in 2 Samuel 7 was interpreted messianically in pre-Christian Judaism. This text must have had great significance for the beginnings of Christology as well as for the emergence and development of the entire expectation of the Messiah. The rabbis, however, avoid the text, perhaps because it could serve as a basis for the doctrine of Christ as the Son of God.[25]

The image of the Davidic Messiah in the Qumran texts is in essential agreement with the traditional picture (cf., e.g., Psalm of Solomon 17); the picture has been modified somewhat, however. In line with the priestly-theocratic conceptions once held by Ezekiel, the offspring of David is not called king, but "prince of the community." At the assembly, at the sacred meal, and even in the war of the last days he is associated with and even subordinated to the eschatological high priest.[26] This ordering reflects the community's structure.

The expectation of an Aaronic high priest in the last days in all probability must also have belonged to an older stock of eschatological ideas. It could be deduced from Zechariah (chaps. 2, 4, and 6) as well as from Jeremiah (33:17-22) that in the last days a Levitical priest would stand beside the Davidic ruler. Several texts could be applied to the eschatological high priest: the oracle concerning Levi in Deuteronomy 33:8-11, the promise to Phinehas of a perpetual priesthood in Numbers 25:11-13, and the saying concerning God's covenant with Levi in Malachi 2:4-8. This can be confirmed by rabbinic sources, although there the high priest of the last days remains a rather stereotyped figure.[27] It is strange, however, that in the Qumran writings these Old Testament texts are seldom employed, though the functions of the high priest are quite thoroughly described.[28] The actual cultic service, however, with its sacrifice and expiation rites, receives less emphasis than the coming high priest's commission, which is to offer prayers and thanksgivings in the assembly, at the common meal, and in the holy war, as well as to give instruction from Scripture concerning the will of God. In other words, the picture of the messianic prince is traditional, but that of the high priest is to a great extent an image projected into the future for which the activity of a leading priest within the Qumran community served as a model.

In the case of the historical Teacher of Righteousness, the relationship to the words of Scripture is of a different sort. His name comes from the passage already cited, Hosea 10:12 (cf. also Joel 2:23). In the Qumran writings these texts are not cited, however. Instead, a whole list of passages from the Prophets and the Psalms is applied to the teacher and his opponents. These texts were obviously not traditionally understood as statements regarding a future Teacher of Righteousness; rather, they were cited because they could be interpreted *ex eventu* as prophecies of the appearance and fate of the community's founder who bore this title.[29] The historical teacher was understood as the one who fulfilled the hope for a coming *mōreh ṣedeq*, and in light of his fate, many texts were reinterpreted as prophecies pertaining to him.

Critical examination of the texts yields no reliable basis for the hypothesis that the return of the historical teacher in the form of a priestly Messiah was expected.[30] Nevertheless, these two figures have several features in common. They bear the same names: "the priest," "Interpreter of the Torah," "Teacher of Righteousness."[31] To a great extent they share the same functions: teaching, interpretation of Scripture, prayer, thanksgiving, and leadership of the community.[32] Accordingly, one may not speak of an identity of persons, but of an identity of office.[33] The difference between the two is that while the historical teacher exercised his function at a time of eschatological tribulations, the messianic high priest will officiate during the eschatological war and at the time of salvation. All this implies that the images of the historical teacher and the eschatological high priest have influenced one another.

Some scholars have conjectured that the teacher was identified with the eschatological prophet.[34] There is, however, no textual basis for this hypothesis. It is not surprising that the expectation of the prophet diminished, since the task of a prophet in this environment would principally have involved inspired interpretation of Scripture and legal instruction, tasks that came to be assigned to the historical teacher and the eschatological priest. There remained for the prophet no particular function or importance.

Another hypothesis warrants careful consideration, namely, that during his lifetime, the teacher himself was regarded as a candidate for the high-priestly office and to this extent was an Aaronic *Messias designatus*.[35] Though presenting difficult problems, both historically (e.g., whether the *mōreh ṣedeq* was a legitimate Zadokite) as well as exegetically (above all, how the Damascus Document is to be interpreted),[36] such a hypothesis, if tenable, could provide answers to many questions.

Within this movement, which we may call Essene, eschatological conceptions were altered. In Judaism, what united the members of various communities with and distinguished them from other groups lay much more in the legal ordering of life than in theological doctrines.[37] In the Damascus Document, one Messiah of Aaron and Israel has developed from the two anointed ones of Aaron and Israel (the singular in the medieval manuscript from the Cairo Geniza may no longer be regarded as a scribal error, since it has been attested in a fragment from Cave 4).[38] The reformulation of eschatology reflects a change in the sociological structure. A division within the leadership of the community also appears to be lacking in the Damascus Document. The designations "priests," "Levites," and "sons of Zadok" are applied by means of spiritualizing exegesis to the first generation of the movement, its adherents, and the elect at the end of days.[39] In its messianic doctrine the duality of the priestly and princely offices is dropped. What is emphasized here is rather the chronological distinction between the former teacher and the coming Messiah of Aaron and Israel, who is probably called both "prince of the whole congregation" and "he who teaches righteousness."[40] This change may also have something to do with a cessation of hostility against the Hasmonean princes in the particular branch of the movement that is represented in the Damascus Document. Nothing is said here about the opponent of the Teacher of Righteousness.

THE INTERRELATIONSHIP OF HISTORY AND ESCHATOLOGY

Much more could be said about the interpretation of texts and historical details; I am principally interested, however, in what is illustrated by the details, namely, the correlation between the sociological structure and history of the communities and their eschatological interpretation of Scripture and messianic doctrine. Events and persons are understood in light of eschatological prophecies, and transmitted texts and concepts receive new explanations from events. Interpretations and reinterpretations are not merely subsequent additions; eschatological interpretations and reinterpretations must already have been formative factors in the events themselves.

The process of interpretation and reinterpretation, of historicizing and eschatologizing, was definitely not something peculiar to the Essenes; similar things occurred again and again. At the beginning of messianic doctrine both royal ideology as well as the peculiar history of David were already in place. It was probably expected of many a king of Judah that he would be a new David and by God's grace a king of salvation; but hopes were disappointed and projected further into the future. Deutero-Isaiah actualized these eschatological expectations, and his prophecies were partially fulfilled; however, they achieved their lasting significance as promises for a more distant future. What Haggai and Zechariah prophesied concerning the Davidic Zerubbabel and the high priest Joshua became the basis for the doctrine of the two anointed ones. In the Book of Daniel, older traditions are applied to the present and to the immediate future. Daniel then provided the basis for all subsequent apocalyptic. Though in the Maccabees we may not properly speak of eschatology as such (if we mean ideas that have to do with the end of the world), this era was in fact seen as one of fulfilled promises.[41] The Hasmonean priest-princes appear to have substituted for the legitimacy they lacked the assertion that because of their zeal for God their family was the genuine spiritual descendant of Phinehas.[42] With numerous variations, the same pattern must have been repeated in Zealot movements. The expectation of a Messiah ben Ephraim who falls in war is rooted in Scripture, but it reflected the fate of the leaders in the wars of independence, above all that of Bar Kochba.[43]

How completely it was possible for eschatological interpretation of Scripture to be bent in light of real events becomes strikingly clear in Josephus, who was able to apply the saying concerning the world ruler who would arise from Judah (Gen. 49:10?) to Vespasian.[44] An example from a much later period is the story of Sabbatai Zevi, who during imprisonment was converted to Islam. This led to the development of a doctrine of the necessity of apostasy by the Messiah. In this story Gershom Scholem has seen the most interesting parallel to the Christian doctrine of the crucified Messiah—quite correctly from the Jewish standpoint.[45]

The writings from the Dead Sea caves are thus suited to sharpen our picture of the complexity of Jewish doctrines concerning eschatological figures. The result of our brief overview may be stated as follows: The correlation between eschatology and history is by no means exclusively Christian or peculiar to the New Testament. Rather, expectations are repeatedly applied anew to the present situation, and eschatological texts and conceptions have undergone constant reinterpretation. Expectation of the imminent end, realized eschatology, eschatology in the process of realization, proleptic and inaugurated eschatology—all of these can be found, mutatis mutandis, in Judaism as well. The problem of the delay of the awaited end was only too familiar.[46]

What is new and unique with respect to Jesus is not the belief that the end and salvation are at hand or already present. Interest is not confined here to the mere "that"; of decisive importance are the "what," "how," and "who." Actual events, interpretations of Scripture, and eschatology are interwoven in early Christianity in approximately the same way as they were in the Qumran writings and into other branches of Judaism. But in the New Testament everything is altered because concern is focused on new and different events, specifically and exclusively on the name "Jesus Christ," a name in which the historical and the eschatological are inextricably interwoven.

SUMMARY: A WORKING HYPOTHESIS

The actual form of the relationship in the New Testament between historical event, eschatological doctrine, and reinterpretation of Scripture can be made clear only by detailed and penetrating studies. Yet I may be permitted briefly to sketch what I regard as working hypotheses.

1. The transference of the title "Messiah" to Jesus and the new meaning it received as a name of Jesus can be explained neither from the Jewish concept of the Messiah, nor from the preaching of Jesus, nor from belief in the resurrection as such. What was decisive was rather the historical fact that Jesus was accused as a messianic pretender and was executed as "King of the Jews."[47] This brutal fact led the early church to reinterpret christologically messianic texts and to read as messianic predictions texts not applied to the Messiah in Judaism.

2. The Easter events were for the disciples unexpected, yet they were real events. They were something to be interpreted; they were not themselves an interpretation of the significance of Jesus and his death.[48] The Easter events were interpreted with reference to the eschatological hope of the resurrection and the testimony of Scripture, again in quite diverse ways. All of eschatology had to be explained anew in light of the resurrection of Jesus Christ, which had already occurred, and indeed in a way unforeseen in Judaism.

3. The events of Jesus' death and resurrection led to a heightening of eschatological anticipation.[49] Paul's varied usage of the

formula "until so-and-so comes" may serve as an illustration. The one who is to come is identified with the one who died for us. In the interim more is involved than mere adherence to the legal formulations of a teacher: while giving thanks, the bread is broken and the cup is blessed in remembrance of Jesus, and thus the Lord's death is proclaimed "until he comes" (1 Cor. 11:26). But eschatological formulas can also be applied to the earthly appearance of Jesus in such a way that the Mosaic law itself is regarded as an interim decree: it was added for the sake of transgressions "till the offspring should come to whom the promise has been made" (Gal. 3:19).[50]

4. The appearance of the early Christian expectation of the parousia also belongs to the transformation of eschatology in light of history. Jews awaited the coming of the eschatological office-holders and, connected with that, the Messiah's assumption of power; some groups may have hoped for the heavenly enthronement of the Son of Man.[51] The idea of the parousia of the Savior in the sense of his coming from heaven to earth at the end of time, however, is not found in Jewish sources. In contrast, by its very nature the early Christian expectation of the parousia is the hope that the One who had already been on earth would come from heaven in power and splendor. It is therefore misleading to regard expectation of the parousia and of the impending end of the world as the point of departure, with the consequence that the delay of the parousia becomes the main problem in early Christian eschatology.[52]

5. In contrast to what often occurred in Judaism, the eschatological expectations that had been actualized through Jesus were not subsequently detached from his person to be bound up in altered form with new historical figures. As far as salvation figures were concerned, the constantly changing correlation between eschatology and history came to an end in the christological confession. The only variable is the expectation of the parousia, which could be revitalized again and again by historical events, as frequently occurred during New Testament times. Thus more radically than in Judaism, the Christian doctrine concerning the last things became a doctrine of the end of the world and of history.

6. With some variation in details, the New Testament transformation of eschatology is characterized by the tendency to relate all promises to Jesus (cf. 2 Cor. 1:20). Texts and titles that in Judaism had been distributed among various eschatological (and noneschatological) figures all served to attest the dignity and significance

of the one Christ. Neither the concentration of expectation upon Jesus nor the accumulation of all titles and testimonies associated with such expectation can be explained by the brute facts of Jesus' crucifixion and resurrection alone. This concentration presupposes rather the person and ministry of the earthly Jesus—even if he himself never laid claim to messianic dignity. No existing messianic category was adequate to him, yet he appeared with such authority that all the disciples' hopes focused on him.

7. What forms the central theme of biblical eschatology is not so much the end of the world and of history as the fulfillment of God's promises.[53] For the New Testament, Jesus Christ is an eschatological figure, and the events connected with his name are eschatological principally because through him the promises of God are fulfilled. In a historical description of New Testament theology, therefore, history of interpretation must receive its due.[54] This does not mean, of course, that New Testament Christology can be understood simply in light of the Old Testament. The Old Testament texts were available to the early Christians as they had already been interpreted in Judaism. Hellenistic and gnostic influences as well are not to be excluded. Then as always, exegesis was the means whereby contemporary ideas could be connected with sacred texts and traditions. Above all, we must observe that all texts and titles, concepts and myths that contributed to the interpretation of the history of Jesus were reinterpreted in the light of the events.

My attempt to shed new light on the relationship between eschatology and history from the Qumran texts has in a certain sense turned from the modern question concerning time, history, and eschatology back to the old schema, "promise and fulfillment." The theological problems have hardly been simplified, for the old doctrine of prophecy and fulfillment can no longer be reproduced in its classic form. It has become only too clear to us to what a great extent fulfillment always involves a reinterpretation of the promise; only in that way can it be understood as fulfillment.[55]

Behind Bultmann's work on the theme "history and eschatology" lies not only knowledge of history but also a hermeneutical program and a theological stance. My goal was much more modest; I wanted simply to make a few historical observations on the theme. Yet, if it is correct that Bultmann's view has in part been determined by a definite epoch within the history of New Testament studies, discussion with him may be carried on not only on the philosophical, hermeneutical, and theological levels. We must begin again and again with exegetical and historical study, conscious that it may be a long time before historical-critical analysis and theological interpretation are again brought together in as impressive a synthesis as Bultmann's.

Notes

[1]This essay is a revised form of a guest lecture given at the Universities of Utrecht and Heidelberg.

[2]K. Barth, *The Epistle to the Romans* (trans. E. C. Hoskins; London: Oxford University Press, 1933; 2d German ed., 1922) 314.

[3]R. Bultmann, *History and Eschatology* (New York: Harper & Brothers, 1957).

[4]Cf. my review of Bultmann's *Theology of the New Testament* in appendix A.

[5]R. Bultmann, *Jesus and the Word* (trans. L. Pettibone Smith; New York: Scribner's, 1934) 35.

[6]Bultmann, *History and Eschatology* 23.

[7]Ibid. 151 and 154. Cf. his *Theology of the New Testament* I (trans. K. Grobel; New York: Scribner's, 1959) 306, and "New Testament and Mythology," in *Kerygma and Myth* I (ed. H. W. Bartsch; trans. R. Fuller; New York: Harper, 1954) 29.

[8]A. Schweitzer, *Paul and His Interpreters* (trans. W. Montgomery; London: A. & C. Black, 1912) 228.

[9]A. Schweitzer, *The Mysticism of Paul the Apostle* (trans. W. Montgomery; New York: Macmillan, 1955) 54.

[10]Cf., e.g., A. Dillmann, *Liber Henoch* (Leipzig, 1851), and his *Das Buch Henoch* (Leipzig: Vogel, 1853); A. Hilgenfeld, *Die jüdische Apokalyptik* (Jena: F. Mauke, 1857).

[11]W. Baldensperger, *Das Selbstbewιsstesein Jesu im Lichte der messianischen Hoffnungen seiner Zeit* (Strasbourg: Heitz, 1888); S. Mowinckel, *He That Cometh* (trans. G. W. Anderson; New York: Abingdon, 1956); W. Bousset–H. Gressmann, *Die Religion des Judentums* (Berlin: Reuter & Reichard, 1926).

[12]A. Dupont-Sommer, *The Dead Sea Scrolls: A Preliminary Survey* (trans. E. M. Rowley; Oxford: Blackwell, 1952), and *The Essene Writings from Qumran* (trans. G. Vermes; New York: Meridian Books, 1962); H. Kosmala, *Hebräer–Esserner–Christen* (Leiden: Brill, 1959); G. Friedrich, "Beobachtungen zur messianischen Hohepriestererwartung in den Synoptikern," *ZTK* 53 (1956) 265–311.

[13]G. Jeremias, *Der Lehrer der Gerechtigkeit* (SUNT 2; Göttingen: Vandenhoeck & Ruprecht, 1963) 321.

[14]K. Stendahl, ed., *The Scrolls and the New Testament* (New York: Harper, 1957) 1–17.

[15]Cf. the preface to the third German edition of his *Theology*.

[16]1QS 9:10f. (Unless otherwise noted, all English translations of Qumran material are taken from Dupont–Sommer's *Essene Writings from Qumran.*)

[17]CD vi, 10f.; xii, 23f.; xx, 1. Cf. 4QPB 3f.

[18]L. Ginzberg, *Eine unbekannte jüdische Sekte* (New York, 1922) 303ff.

[19]More precisely, Exod. 20:21b, according to a text that agrees with the Samaritan Pentateuch. Cf. J. T. Milik, *Ten Years of Discoveries in the Wilderness of Judea* (SBT 26; trans. J. Strugnell; Naperville, Ill.: Allenson, 1959) 124 n. 1 (following Skehan); and further, 4Q158, frag. 6.

[20]4QTestimonia. R. Meyer (" 'Eliah' und 'Ahab,' " in *Abraham unser Vater: Festschrift für O. Michel* [Leiden: Brill, 1963] 356–68) would relate all three testimonies to the "Teacher of Righteousness." Given the general structure of the sect and its teachings, however, it is most improbable that the teacher was viewed as the bearer of the threefold office. Cf. Jeremias, *Der Lehrer der Gerechtigkeit*, and A. S. van der Woude, *Die messianischen Vorstellungen der Gemeinde von Qumran* (Assen: Van Gorcum, 1957).

[21]The three figures are basically contemporaneous, even if one assumes that the high priest or Elijah will already be present at the appearance of the Messiah. Cf., e.g., 4QF 1, 11 and Just. *Dial.* 8. In a similiar way the Messiah, Elijah, and the Prophet are each mentioned in John 1:20f., perhaps as bearers of the three offices. The conception of Elijah as the eschatological high priest is pre-Christian, attested for the time of John Hyrcanus by *Tg. Ps.-J.* Deut. 32:11. Cf. Meyer, " 'Eliah' und 'Ahab' " 356ff., and S. Schulz, "Die Bedeutung der neuen Targumforschung," in *Abraham unser Vater* 434f. (following Geiger).

[22]Josephus, *Ant.* 13.299; *J.W.* 1.68. Cf., e.g., R. Meyer, *Der Prophet aus Galiläa* (Leipzig, 1940) 60ff.; *TDNT* 6 (1968) 825f.

[23]In a still-unpublished text from Cave 4, the true prophet is to be recognized by the anointed priest. Cf. Milik, *Ten Years of Discoveries.*

[24]1QSb 5:20-29; 1QM 11:6f.; 4QPB; 4QT; 4QIsa; CD vii, 19f. Cf. on this van der Woude, *Die messianischen Vorstellungen*, though he has not systematically investigated the question of scriptural basis for Qumran doctrine concerning the Messiah.

[25]Cf. especially 4QFlor; in addition, 4QPB 2–4. From pre-Christian Judaism the following may be mentioned: Sir. 45:25; Ps. Sol. 17:4. From the New Testament Heb. 1:5; 3:2, 6; Rom. 1:3f.; Luke 1:32f.; 22:28-30; Acts 2:30; 13:22, 32ff.; Rev. 22:16; perhaps also Matt. 16:16-18; 22:41-44; Mark 14:57-62; John 8:35. Cf. A. van Iersel, *"Der Sohn" in den synoptischen Jesusworten* (Leiden: Brill, 1961); E. Lövestam, *Son and Savior* (Lund: Gleerup, 1961); S. Aalen, " 'Reign' and 'House,' " *NTS* 8 (1962) 215–40, especially 233–40. For the Old Testament, see G. von Rad, *Old Testament Theology* (trans. D. M. G. Stalker; New York: Harper & Row, 1962–65) I, 40f. and 318ff.; II, 45f. The question of age and original wording of the oracle of Nathan may remain open here, as well as its relationship to Psalms 89 and 132.

[26]1QSa 2:11ff. and 2:17ff.; 1QM 5:1 as compared with 15:4-6, etc. The mutilated texts 4QPB 4f. and 4QpIsa frag. D are perhaps similar.

[27]Material in Str–B IV, 462ff., 789ff.; Ginzberg, *Eine unbekannte jüdische Sekte* 340ff.

[28]1QSa 2:12-14, 19f.; 1QSb 2:24—3:21; 1QM 2:1ff.; 10:1—12:15; 15:4-6; 16:3—17:9; 18:5ff.; 19:11ff.

[29]Numerous examples in 1QpHab and the other commentaries, e.g., on Hab. 1:4, 13; 2:2, 4, 8, 15; Ps. 37:23, 32; also on Num. 21:18 and Isa. 54:6 in CD vi, 3-8. The analogy with the christological exegesis of early Christianity is obvious.

[30]Cf. J. Carmignac, "Le retour du Docteur de Justice à la fin des jours?" *RQ* 1 (1958–59) 235–48; Jeremias, *Der Lehrer der Gerechtigkeit* 275ff.

[31]"The Priest" is eschatological (1QSa 2:19; 1QM 10:2 [Deut. 20:2]; possibly 1Q22 4:8; 1Q29 5:2) and historical (1QpHab 2:8; 4QpPs 37 2:15). "Interpreter of the Torah" is eschatological (4QFlor 1:11; possibly 4QPB 5) and historical (CD vi, 7; uncertain: CD vii, 18). "Teacher of Righteousness" is historical (1QpHab 1:13, etc.; cf. CD i, 11; xx, 32) and eschatological (CD vi, 11).

[32]This becomes especially clear if we may attribute the Hodayoth to the Teacher— whether in part or in their entirety is in this respect a matter of indifference.

[33]Jeremias (*Der Lehrer der Gerechtigkeit* 283ff.) has demonstrated this with respect to the Teacher of Righteousness but has failed to draw the full consequences.

[34]Thus, e.g., van der Woude, *Die messianischen Vorstellungen* 186f., rightly criticized by Jeremias, *Der Lehrer der Gerechtigkeit* 296ff.

[35]Cf. D. Flusser, "Two Notes on the Midrash on II Sam. 7," *IEJ* 9 (1959) 99–109. According to 4QFlor 1:11, the Branch of David will appear at the end of days with the Interpreter of the Law. But it is highly questionable that the testimony collection was composed before the death of the Interpreter of the Law/Teacher of Righteousness.

[36]The interpretation of CD vii, 18–21 is controversial. In the interpretation of Num. 24:17, "scepter" is related to the "Prince of the Community" and "star" to the "Interpreter of the Law." This seems to reflect a doctrine of two anointed ones. But in what preceded, Amos 5:26f. is related to the early history of the sect. Thus the question is whether the sentence "and the star is the Interpreter of the Law coming to Damascus" refers to the future or to the past. Both are possible grammatically. But a reference to the past is supported both by the context and by CD vi, 7, where "Interpreter of the Law" clearly designates the historical teacher. These difficulties are most easily resolved by the hypothesis that CD vii, 10ff. draws upon traditional testimonies that go back to a time when the community still hoped that its teacher would become the high priest of the messianic age.

[37]Cf. M. Smith, "What Is Implied by the Variety of Messianic Figures?" *JBL* 78 (1959) 66–72.

[38]Milik, *Ten Years of Discoveries* 125 n. 3. A plausible explanation of the textual data is given by J. F. Priest, "*Mebaqqer, Paqid,* and the Messiah," *JBL* 81 (1962) 55–61.

[39]CD iii, 21—iv, 4. But elsewhere the distinction between priests, Levites, and laymen is maintained (CD x, 5f.; xiv, 3ff.).

[40]Cf. CD vi, 7-11; xix, 35—xx, 1. CD vii, 18-21 must also be interpreted in conformity with these texts. Cf. n. 36 above. By assuming a reinterpretation of older traditions, we can explain the apparently complicated teaching of the Damascus Document fairly simply. Only one messiah is expected, who will function as teacher (vi, 10f.; xii, 23), as ruler (vii, 20f.; xix, 10ff.), and—probably—as priest (xiv, 19). "Aaron and Israel" would then no longer mean priesthood and laity, but rather the priestly-Israelite community of the New Covenant. Cf. F. F. Hvidberg, *Menigheden af den nye Pagt i Damascus* (Copenhagen: Gad, 1928) 280f.

[41]Cf. especially 1 Macc. 14:4-15.

[42]1 Macc. 2:26, 54. Cf. W. R. Farmer, *Maccabees, Zealots, and Josephus* (New York: Columbia University Press, 1956) 178f.; and M. Hengel, *Die Zeloten* (Leiden: Brill, 1961) 168ff.

[43]Cf., e.g., Meyer, *Der Prophet aus Galiläa* 76–82.

[44]Josephus, *J.W.* 6.312f.; cf. 3.351-54, 400-402. See J. Blenkinsopp, "The Oracle of Judah and the Messianic Entry," *JBL* 80 (1961) 55–64.

[45]G. Scholem, *Major Trends in Jewish Mysticism* (3d rev. ed.; New York: Schocken, 1961) 307–10.

[46]Cf. A. Strobel, *Untersuchungen zum eschatologischen Verzögerungsproblem* (NovTSup 2; Leiden: Brill, 1961); J. Becker, *Das Heil Gottes* (Göttingen: Vandenhoeck & Ruprecht, 1964).

[47]Cf. my essay "The Crucified Messiah," chap. 2 above. F. Hahn (*The Titles of Jesus in Christology* [trans. H. Knight and G. Ogg; London: Lutterworth, 1969] 172–89) comes to a somewhat similar conclusion.

[48]I would support this statement, even if the story of the empty tomb were purely legendary. I doubt that it is, however, with Hans von Campenhausen; cf. below (p. 108 and chap. 2, n. 32).

[49]Cf. Stendahl, *The Scrolls*, 13ff.

[50]This text may be understood as an interpretive paraphrase of Gen. 49:10 (Heb): "Until he (the seed) comes, to whom (the promise belongs)." Similar interpretive paraphrastic quotations are found, e.g., in Rom. 3:20 and 1 Cor. 15:45. The use of the designation "offspring" for the Messiah in Gal. 3:16, 19 (cf. Gen. 13:15, etc.) is analogous to (and probably derived from) the messianic interpretation of "offspring" in 2 Sam. 7:12; cf. 4QFlor 1:10-12, 4QPB 4. The messianic interpretation of Gen. 3:15 (cf. 4:25 and 19:34) would also be a possible analogy if it is pre-Christian (cf. Str-B I, 958 n. 1; 26f.).

[51]For the outlook in the Similitudes of Enoch, cf. E. Sjöberg, *Der Menschensohn im äthiopischen Henochbuch* (Lund: Gleerup, 1946) 61ff.; P. L. Schoonheim, *Een semasiologisch Onderzoek van Parousia* (Aaltern: de Boer, 1953).

[52]In recent German scholarship this is done often and much too uncritically. Cf., e.g., E. Grässer, *Das Problem der Parousieverzögerung* (BZNW 22; Berlin: Töpelmann, 1957). F. Hahn (*The Titles of Jesus* 161–68, 284f.) also uncritically regards statements concerning the parousia as belonging to the oldest stratum of tradition and finds evidence for this even in Revelation and in the Lucan birth stories. English scholars have at least seen that the emergence of Christian expectation of the parousia poses a historical problem. Cf. T. F. Glasson, *The Second Advent* (London: Epworth, 1945), and J. A. T. Robinson, *Jesus and His Coming* (London: SCM, 1957).

[53]In his book *Jesus and the Word* (trans. L. Pettibone Smith; New York: Scribner's, 1934), Bultmann wrote: "The message of Jesus is an *eschatological gospel*—the proclamation that now the fulfillment of the promise is at hand, that now the Kingdom of God begins" (28). When in his later work Bultmann employs categories drawn from existential philosophy, this emphasis recedes in favor of a one-sided concentration on the end of the world and of history.

[54]This has to be emphasized against the tendency, common since Ernst Lohmeyer, to describe Christology by means of the individual christological titles. The tendency is to view each title as the bearer of a unique christological conception and even to distinguish a "paidology" or a "kyriology" or a "hyiology" from "Christology" proper. Cf. O. Cullmann, *The Christology of the New Testament* (trans. F. Filson; Philadelphia: Westminster, 1964); W. Kramer, *Christ, Lord, Son of God* (trans. B. Hardy; Naperville, Ill.: Allenson, 1966). On the basis of extant writings and Jewish analogies, we must assume, rather, that the conceptions were from the beginning very complex; they were shaped more by events and texts than by fixed concepts and preexistent ideologies.

[55]What G. von Rad has shown for the Old Testament in his *Old Testament Theology* is even more true of postbiblical Judaism and Christianity. On this problem see R. Bultmann, "Prophecy and Fulfillment," in *Essays Philosophical and Theological* (trans. J. C. G. Greig; New York: Macmillan, 1955) 182–208. Cf. in addition *RGG*, 3d ed., 6 (1962) cols. 1584–90 and the literature cited there.

4

The Crucified Messiah
and the Endangered Promises

THE NEW TESTAMENT EVIDENCE

"CHRIST DIED for our sins in accordance with the scriptures" (1 Cor. 15:3). This statement is part of the tradition that Paul had received and handed on when he first preached the gospel at Corinth. In his argument against some people who denied that there would be a future resurrection of the dead, Paul makes use of only the second part of the kerygmatic summary: Christ "was raised on the third day in accordance with the scriptures, and . . . he appeared to Cephas, then to the twelve," and so forth. The reference to Christ's death is included because it was an integral part of the traditional formulation. Paul presupposes that not only the resurrection of Christ but also his death "for our sins" was part of the gospel preached by Peter and the other early witnesses as well as by himself.

For the purposes of this article, the most important fact is that both parts of the formula include the phrase "in accordance with the scriptures" and that "Christ" is the common grammatical subject. To most Christians at Corinth, *Christos* may simply have been a second name or an honorific designation of Jesus, but both Paul and those who formulated the tradition certainly knew that the word meant "the Anointed One," that is, the Messiah. It is remarkable, however, that neither Paul nor the formula that he quotes states that Jesus is the Messiah. The identity of Jesus as Christ, the Messiah, is taken for granted, so that the term can be used to refer to Jesus. The title received its content from the person to whom it referred, more than from a preconceived notion of what the Messiah would be like. Jesus was the Messiah who had been crucified as "king of the Jews" but vindicated by God, who raised him from the dead. In view of messianic expectations, it is no wonder that most Jews found faith in a crucified Messiah to be offensive. As a zealous Pharisee, Paul had himself persecuted those who held this faith. Only a revelation of the risen Christ convinced Paul that he had been wrong and that Peter and the other disciples were right: Jesus was indeed the Christ, who had died and risen in accordance with the Scriptures.

In the letters of Paul the word *Christos* always refers to Jesus Christ, not to a general concept of the Messiah. It is in the Gospels and Acts that we find predicative statements of the type: "You (Jesus) are the Christ." Luke is aware of the etymological meaning of the title and represents Jesus as the Christ who was anointed by the Holy Spirit but who, like prophets and men of the Spirit before and after him, was rejected and had to suffer. This, however, happened according to the design of God, who vindicated the crucified Jesus by raising him from the dead. In Luke-Acts, the affirmation that Christ died and was raised in accordance with the Scriptures has been spelled out in the form of a proof from prophecy with two parts: (1) the Scriptures testify that the Christ had to suffer and rise from the dead and (2) Jesus is the Christ because he suffered and was raised (see, e.g., Acts 17:3). The argument is not purely rational, however. According to Luke 24:25-27 and 44-46 it was the risen Christ himself who opened the eyes of the disciples.

Neither the summary in 1 Corinthians 15:3ff. nor those in Luke 24 or Acts 17:2-3 refer to any specific texts. We know that Psalm 110:1 was among the passages that were supposed to speak about the resurrection of Christ, and we may assume that the song about the suffering servant of the Lord in Isaiah 52:13—53:12 was in the mind of the authors and their audience. The phrase "on the third day" is reminiscent of Hosea 6:2, and the rejection/vindication pattern had a basis in the saying about the rejected stone in Psalm 118:22. The interpretation of Psalm 16 in Acts 2:25-36 (cf. 13:35-37) illustrates how the proof from prophecy could be worked out in detail. Other examples might be added, but what passages like 1 Corinthians 15:3-4 and Luke 24:25-27 claim is not simply that some scriptural passages referred to the death and resurrection of (the) Christ, but that what had happened was in accordance with the entire testimony of the Scriptures, and thus with the will and design of God. The first disciples were convinced that the God of the fathers, who spoke through Moses and the prophets, had sent Jesus and vindicated him by raising him from the dead. Even the adversaries of Jesus had, unwittingly, carried out the counsel of God. The close correlation between what was written and what happened was a presupposition for the search for scriptural testimonies to Jesus as much as a result of exegetical efforts.

The basic conviction that the death and resurrection of Jesus had happened in accordance with the Scriptures had the double effect that the events were understood in light of the Scriptures, and the Scriptures were interpreted in light of the events. The procedure was not in itself any radical innovation. An interpretation of contemporary events and conditions in the light of the Scriptures and the corresponding actualizing interpretation of Scripture belonged to the essence of Jewish midrash as practiced both by exegetes at Qumran, who claimed that the hidden meaning of inspired texts had been revealed to them, and by the rabbis, who interpreted the texts according to hermeneutical rules. To a considerable extent, Christians took over Jewish exegetical methods and traditions along with the biblical texts themselves. What is new in the New Testament use of the Old is due to the new events, centering on the crucifixion of Jesus of Nazareth as an alleged "king of the Jews," much more than to any new exegetical approach.

The selection and use of scriptural texts varies a good deal from one New Testament author to another. The Book of Revelation contains no explicit quotations but uses biblical language and imagery in its prophetic message about the vindication of the crucified Messiah and his persecuted followers. The conviction that the Holy Spirit, who had spoken through the prophets, had also been given to Christians made a spontaneous use of biblical words and phrases all the more natural. It is, however, possible to discern some discrete patterns of exegesis.

Allegorical interpretation played a marginal role, but both persons and events and rituals of atonement and sacrifice were understood as prefigurations of Jesus and of the events connected with his name. Besides various forms of typology, however, we also find the pattern of prophecy and fulfillment, which occurs in several varieties, one typical for Matthew (e.g., 1:23), another for Luke-Acts (e.g., Luke 24:44). Jesus can also be supposed to be the speaking subject who talks in Scripture, using the first-person form. In some cases, this is best understood as a form of rhetorical personification, analogous to a literary dialogue or a drama: the biblical author, or the Holy Spirit who inspired him, not only talked about Jesus but formulated sayings that they attributed to him (see, e.g., Acts 2:25ff.). In other cases, the notion is rather that the preexistent

Christ himself is speaking (e.g., Heb. 2:11-13). In patristic writings, theophanies and angelophanies are interpreted as revelations of the eternal Logos, but in some New Testament passages the idea is rather that Old Testament witnesses saw the glory of the crucified Christ in advance (e.g., John 12:37-41). The specific notion of promises applies mainly to utterances that are explicitly attributed to God himself, who through his Word has committed himself to his people, to the patriarchs, and to the house of David. By sending Christ and raising him from the dead, God has kept his word and confirmed his promise (see, e.g., Rom. 15:8; 2 Cor. 1:19-20; Heb. 6:13-20).

This condensed survey intends simply to illustrate how biblical (i.e., Old Testament) passages were drawn into the story of Jesus Christ and, in a variety of ways, used in early Christian preaching and teaching. Reading and interpretation of the Scriptures made it possible for the disciples to come to terms with the scandal of the cross and to understand their own experiences at and after Easter as evidence that God had vindicated the crucified Messiah. The apologetic use of the proof from prophecy is, I think, a second move. Paul relied, at least to some extent, upon a tradition of christological exegesis in order to demonstrate that in Christ there was no distinction between Jews and Greeks and that those who belonged to Christ were no longer under the Mosaic law, while also maintaining that the law was holy and remained a part of the sacred Scriptures. The Epistle to the Hebrews uses traditional testimonies as building blocks for its elaborate exegesis, depicting Jesus as the high priest who brought an atoning sacrifice and entered the heavenly temple. As time passed, an increasing number of biblical testimonies to the crucified Christ were detected and became part of a continuous tradition. Even authors who were familiar with written Gospels used such testimonies to talk about Jesus and his passion. The Epistle of Barnabas, Justin's *Dialogue with the Jew Trypho*, and Irenaeus's *Demonstration of the Apostolic Preaching* provide classical examples.

Astonishing as it may be to us, words of the ancient Scriptures were used not only to explain the atoning and saving effects of the passion but also to describe the attitudes of Jesus himself (see, e.g., Rom. 15:3; 1 Pet. 2:21-25; and even Heb. 5:7-10). Apparently, early Christians read Psalm 22, Psalm 69, and other psalms of lamentation, probably also Isaiah 53, as accounts of the passion of Jesus before there existed any written passion story. The passion narratives of the Gospels are themselves colored by reminiscences from and allusions to the Psalms and other texts. Otherwise insignificant details were retained in memory because of a more or less striking coincidence with some biblical passages (e.g., Mark 15:23-24). The narratives are reticent about the physical pains of Jesus but highlight mockery and abandonment, like most psalms of lamentation, and are in fact influenced by them. We may conclude that the interplay between events and Scriptures shaped the memories, traditions, and interpretations of the death of Jesus from the very beginning.

THE CRITICAL AND HISTORICAL APPROACH

The early Christian use of the Old Testament Scriptures to tell the story of Jesus and talk about his death on the cross continued in an unbroken tradition until the time of the Enlightenment, in spite of many variations, different schools of interpretation, and occasional protests (Marcion!). For scholars, the history of this Christian, primarily christological, exegesis is a complicated and fascinating field of study that calls for constant comparison with Jewish interpretation of the Hebrew Scriptures. Much has been done in a series of monographs and articles, but there is still a good deal to do. The more I have worked in the field myself, the more I have been impressed by the work of the ancient Christian and Jewish interpreters. Once one has entered their world, one detects method and meaning as well as profound insights. To detect that, however, one must first realize that the aims and presuppositions, to a considerable extent also the tools and methods of the ancients, differed from those of the modern scholar, whether the latter deals with biblical texts themselves or with later Jewish and Christian use of them.

Employing the methods of biblical criticism, scholars search for the historical setting of the biblical writings and the sources and oral traditions that they may have incorporated, in order to understand what they meant to the original authors and the first audiences. This type of research has proceeded by trial and error but, on the whole, has been a formidable success, so that we today know a great deal more about the history of biblical times, and about the Bible itself, than did earlier generations. Critical scholars soon detected that New Testament and later authors frequently used Old Testament texts in a way that had little, if anything, to do with their original meaning. The use of the Hebrew Scriptures as historical sources led to the conclusion that the traditional Christian use represented an unhistorical Christianization. It could not have been otherwise. The New Testament authors had little interest in the original historical meaning. Their concern was what the Scriptures that God had inspired had to say to them and to their contemporaries (see, e.g., Rom. 4:23f.; 1 Cor. 10:11). We cannot expect historical exegesis to answer their questions.

From the Enlightenment onward, biblical scholarship has freed the texts from layers of interpretative traditions and made a fresh reading possible, for better and for worse. The classical apologetic argument, that Jesus was the Messiah because he fulfilled the messianic prophecies, simply does not work any longer. It presupposes that a Christian concept of "the Messiah" was first read into the Old Testament. A number of texts that Christians had used to talk about Jesus Christ did not at all relate to "the Messiah." Many texts that did pertain to "the Lord's anointed" had originally been royal psalms or promises to the Davidic dynasty and were only later understood as prophecies about a future Messiah. The more serious problem, however, was that historical research demonstrated a discrepancy between the messianic prophecies and the history of Jesus, both as it was told in the Gospels and as it was reconstructed by historians. The question of whether and in what sense Jesus had considered himself to be the Messiah became a controversial historical problem and has remained so.

Most representatives of historical criticism were at the same time Christian theologians who wanted to retain the unity of the Bible and the finality of Jesus Christ. They rightly refused to accept the view that Jesus had desired to be a royal Jewish Messiah but failed, a view that has little support in the sources and fails to explain the emergence of the Christian faith in the crucified Christ. The leading liberal scholars tended to read the Old Testament Scriptures as documents of the history of the religion of Israel, which had reached its peak and its goal in Jesus of Nazareth. The category "Messiah" was understood as a time-conditioned expression of his singular religious significance, which was mostly sought in his teaching, in his conduct, or in his inner life and unity with God, his Father, rather than in his death and resurrection. More often than not, this type of historical reconstruction implied an element of unhistorical modernization. Fundamentalistic efforts to prove the inerrancy and historical accuracy of the Bible, however, are both futile and sterile. Moderate, conservative scholars have tried to do justice both to historical research and to the classical Christian tradition, for example, by introducing concepts like progressive revelation and history of salvation and by insisting that Jesus as a matter of historical fact had a "messianic self-consciousness," anticipated his own death, and ascribed an atoning significance to it. The danger of this approach is that it easily becomes a compromise that only reluctantly embraces the methods of historical criticism and yet is so preoccupied with reconstruction of past history that it loses the more naive, but also more free and fruitful, creativity that integrated the Old Testament into the gospel story and into the proclamation and praise of Jesus Christ.

It is hard to deny that the historical study of the Bible has had a double, apparently self-contradictory result. On the one hand, it has confirmed that the New Testament is inseparable from the Old. Regardless of how much or how little early Christianity was open to influence from syncretistic, Greek, and Oriental sources, the sacred books of the Jews functioned as Holy Scriptures, not simply as a background. Reminiscences and interpretations of these Scriptures are woven into the passion narratives and the entire New Testament testimony to Christ in such a way that one cannot untangle the threads without destroying the design and the whole fabric. On the other hand, biblical scholarship has amply demonstrated that there is a gap between the New Testament use of scriptural texts and the original meaning of these texts in their own historical setting. The result has been an eclipse of the classical Christian use of the Scriptures, which had been practiced from the days of the apostles till the Enlightenment. What are the consequences? Is there any way out of the dilemma?

A DICHOTOMY?

At this point in our reflection, it is worth remembering that in worship, churches still draw upon the heritage of "precritical" Christian interpretation or its relics. Many hymns and spirituals are saturated with Old Testament language and imagery. The exegetical and homiletical tradition from the church fathers through the Reformers to great preachers in more recent times has not been completely forgotten. When an Old Testament text is read during the service, it is heard within a Christian context, and the same holds true for devotional reading. Over the course of history some texts have been Christianized. The Song of the Servant in Isaiah 53 is the most prominent but not the only example. We who are reared in the Christian tradition cannot but think of Jesus and his passion. The Book of Psalms provides a somewhat different example. In the biblical Psalms, both Jews and Christians find words for prayer, praise, and thanksgiving, and even for the cry from the depth of desperation. In Christian usage it has been customary to conclude a psalm with a doxology to the Father, Son, and Holy Spirit. Devotional use may be further enriched by some familiarity with the long tradition of christological interpretation of the Psalms and even more by the knowledge that Jesus himself, who shared our anxiety and agony, prayed to his Father with their words.

It is not necessary to add further examples, but it may be useful to recall that it is not only biblical texts that can take on new meanings in the course of their history. The meaning of a great work of literary or visual art is not exhausted by the conscious intention of the person who created it or the understanding of contemporaries. A classical work in particular takes on an existence of its own, not only calling forth manifold emotional reactions and ideational associations, but often taking on a meaning for new generations. The performance of an old drama is a creative act of art, and it is, for example, possible to stage a Greek tragedy in such a way that it addresses a contemporary conflict or problem. In a crisis, under a dictatorship or a military occupation, a text, biblical or not, may spontaneously be heard as a word that speaks to the actual situation and even as a reference to specific persons, to the delight of some and the annoyance of others. It is even more common that ancient stories take on a figurative or symbolic significance; the wide use of Ulysses and Exodus typology are sufficient examples. In the course of history a text may even permanently take on a fuller and deeper meaning than its author(s) intended, as has been the case with the declaration that "all men are created equal."

Under the influence of trends in literary criticism and general hermeneutics, the focus of biblical scholarship has to some extent shifted. The pioneers of biblical criticism were preoccupied with the sources that referred to historical events or reflected the history and the mentality of the ancient Israelites. Contemporary scholars more often pay serious attention to the ongoing tradition, collection, redaction, and shifting understanding of, for example, the stories about the patriarchs, the exodus, and the conquest of the promised land, or the beginnings of the monarchy. Even the laws, psalms, and prophetic oracles had a long history in the interval between their first origin—perhaps in a specific situation—and their present shape as parts of the canonical Scriptures. The process of reinterpretation did not start after the biblical books had received their canonical form and status; it already contributed to their formation.

The Christian use of the Scriptures can be understood as a continuation of this ongoing process of reinterpretation and as an extreme case of the more general phenomenon that texts may be filled with new meaning in the course of their history. As the Christian reading of the Scriptures was informed by the radically new faith in a crucified Messiah, the Christ Jesus, it also meant a new departure. The result was that the Hebrew Scriptures became the Old Testament of the church. This appropriation of the Jewish Bible by the sect of the Nazarenes and, later, by the churches of the Gentiles made an enormous impact upon later history and is itself of great historical interest. It has turned out to be a gross anachronism to read this Christian understanding back into the Scriptures themselves, considered an outcome of and sources for the religious history of ancient Israel and early Judaism. At the same time, it has become clear that in the devotional life of the Christian community, popularized treatments of Israelite religion in its Near Eastern context provide a poor substitute for the use of the Old Testament in the classical Christian tradition. The historian has no difficulty understanding and appreciating both the historical and the devotional approach; the question today is how far the church can live with a dichotomy between the two approaches.

Some knowledge about original settings and meanings can easily be incorporated into devotional reading. The crucial question, however, is a theological one. I may put it this way: Can we still with good historical conscience maintain that there is a close correspondence between God's action in Jesus Christ and God's intention as it was previously made known in the books of the Law, the Prophets, and the other writings? What is at stake is, in other words, the promises of God, more than the problem of specific messianic prophecies. The issue has traditionally been treated under the heading "promise and fulfillment." The problem with this formulation is that the crucifixion of Jesus would seem to contradict rather than to fulfill the promises of the Old Testament Scriptures, read within their own historical context. It may be more fruitful to adopt a somewhat different point of view and seek the correspondence between faith in the crucified Christ and the common biblical theme of God's endangered promises.

THE STORY OF GOD'S ENDANGERED PROMISES

Like the Hebrew Scriptures, the Gospels do not use any special word for "promise." Yet the concept of God's promises is present already in Mark's summary of the preaching of Jesus: "The time is fulfilled, and the kingdom of God is at hand" (1:15). The message that the kingdom of God is at hand is spelled out in a number of sayings and parables that have been preserved in the Gospels. The message implied that the time had come when God would do what he had promised. What happened in the ministry of Jesus was evidence that God had already begun to do so (see, e.g., Matt. 11:4-5). Jesus did not, I think, proclaim himself to be the Messiah; the Messiah was not expected to do so. Yet he acted and spoke with an authority that made both adherents and adversaries think that he might possibly be the Messiah who was to come, or a false pretender. If that had not been so, it would not be historically understandable that he was handed over to the Romans and crucified as an alleged king of the Jews. The death of Jesus meant that the disciples' hope that God would keep his promise, as it had been reaffirmed and restated by Jesus, was frustrated. That is both what the Gospels tell and what most likely happened.

The nature of our sources makes it much more difficult to say anything about what Jesus himself experienced. I do not think that the historian can say anything about Jesus' self-consciousness and his intentions apart from his actions and his passion. But I see no reason to doubt that Jesus intended to teach and to do the will of God and that he also discerned the will of God in what happened to him, even though that meant that he had to be accused, mocked, and crucified as an alleged king of the Jews. The evangelists, especially Mark, tell that Jesus was himself greatly distressed and in agony (Mark 14:32-36; 15:34). I do not claim to have solved the controversial question of the messianic self-consciousness of Jesus, but I know of no more satisfactory answer to it than the words from the hymn in Philippians 2: He "became obedient unto death, even death on a cross."

However that may be, the appearance of the risen Christ convinced the disciples that God had vindicated the crucified Messiah and, by implication, that God had confirmed his promises and done what he had said. The declaration of Psalm 110:1, "Sit at my right hand," is not by chance one of the most common and, I think, earliest testimonies to God's vindication of the crucified Messiah. The story of the passion and resurrection of Jesus is at the same time, albeit in a veiled form, the story of God's endangered promise and its reaffirmation. If we read the story from this perspective, we discern a climactic variation on a theme (or a "plot") that recurs in a number of stories in the Scriptures. Here I can only mention some of them.

The Book of Genesis tells how God promised Abraham that he would give him the land and a son and many descendants, but it also recounts how these promises were more or less constantly endangered. Abraham had to live as a stranger who acquired a piece of land only for a burying place. The promise of offspring was threatened on more than one occasion (see Gen. 12:10-20; chap. 21). Sarah was barren, and Abraham grew old. At the last trial it seemed that God would himself make his promise void, as he told Abraham to sacrifice Isaac, but the story concludes with the most solemn reaffirmation of God's promises (22:15-18).

As the story told in the Bible continues to unfold, the theme of God's endangered and reconfirmed promises reappears again and again. The story of the exodus provides sufficient examples, from the oppression of Israel in Egypt, the reluctance of Moses, and the constant murmuring of the people to the sin with the golden calf, the desire to return to Egypt, and death in the wilderness. The existence of Israel in the promised land is threatened equally by prosperity as much as by hostile attacks: "Jeshurun waxed fat, and kicked; . . . then he forsook God who made him" (Deut. 32:15). The history of Israel may be read as a story of how God remained faithful to his promises, even though these promises were constantly in jeopardy—more so because of the unfaithfulness and evildoings of his own people than because of its enemies (see, e.g., the summary in Deuteronomy 32 or Nehemiah 9).

The story of the nation was intertwined with the story of the monarchy. The promise to David and his house holds a key position in the Deuteronomistic work of history, but we are also told about David's great sin and all the troubles that threatened his reign. The power and the glory of Solomon are described with superlatives. Yet at the end, we learn, his politicking love of foreign women almost made the promise to David void and resulted in the division of the kingdom. From then on, the story of the endangered promises continues until the fall of Jerusalem, the destruction of the temple, and the end of the Davidic monarchy. After that, royal psalms and promises to the house of David became meaningful in a new way, as prophecies that one day God would raise up a new, righteous king and thus bring peace and salvation to his people. New messianic prophecies reaffirmed the promise.

The Bible recounts the history of Israel and Judah in a selective and highly stylized manner, but even when it mixes fact and fiction, it does so with a staunch realism, without any idealization. No other nation but Israel has recounted its own history with so much self-criticism; yet the books of the prophets contain oracles that even more severely and in greater detail castigate the kings and the people, its priests, and its prophets of bliss, for luxury, unrighteousness, oppression of the poor, false security, and lack of true faith. Amos and other prophets after him foretold the coming doom in such a way that the words of God that came to them would seem to make God's promises null and void. In their final redaction the prophetic books have been composed in such a way that the harsh words of judgment are followed by promises of a coming restoration. This blunted to some extent the cutting edge that the oracles of doom possessed in their original setting. The later emphasis upon God's reaffirmation of his endangered promises did, however, have some basis in the message of the prophets themselves (e.g., in the proclamation of Isaiah that a faithful remnant would be saved).

Many psalms that voice confidence in God's faithfulness in the midst of afflictions and agony may also be read as variations of the theme that I have here, in a shorthand fashion, called "God's endangered promises." The most obvious example is Psalm 89, a royal psalm to which early Christians did not fail to give attention. It is, however, not necessary to go into details. My general point has been that it is possible to read large portions of the Old Testament as a story about God's endangered and reaffirmed promises. It makes literary and theological sense to do so, and, if we do, even the New Testament use of the Old falls in line, much better than if we adopt a strictly historical approach. It was not only due to a more or less arbitrary reinterpretation and reapplication that the ancient formula maintained that Christ had died and been raised "according to the Scriptures." Both the way in which the early Christians read their Bible and the way in which they told about Jesus were informed by the basic conviction that God had vindicated the crucified Messiah and that, in doing so, he had reaffirmed the promises that he had given to his people as well as Jesus' own message that the kingdom of God was at hand. Borrowing a classic theological term, I dare to put it this way: The story of the crucified and vindicated Messiah is the recapitulation of the old and multifaceted story of God's endangered and reaffirmed promises.

This might have served as an edifying conclusion, but history continues and so must our reflections.

THE CONTINUATION OF THE STORY

The early Christians related the promises of God not only to the life, death, and resurrection of Christ but to their own experience as well. Inspired utterances, prophecy, glossolalia, and acclamations, as well as experiences of joy and exultation and of wisdom and power, were seen as evidence that God had poured out his Holy Spirit, as he had promised to do in the last days. When not only Jews but also Gentiles turned to Christ, this was further confirmation that the time of fulfillment had dawned. The Jews, however, to whom the promises belonged, generally rejected the apostolic preaching, a fact that compelled Paul to consider whether the Word of God might actually have failed (Rom. 9:6; cf. 11:1). By means of careful combination and interpretation of selected texts, Paul was able to show that what had happened conformed to the intention of God as set forth in the Scriptures, concluding that God's promise to his chosen people remained valid, even though the ways of God were inscrutable (Romans 9–11). Later Christian theologians came up with a much simpler solution, applying the promises of the Old Testament to Christ and the church, but all indictments of the sins of ancient Israel to the Jewish people. Testimonies to the crucified Messiah and testimonies against the Jews became two sides of the same coin.

The church was, however, also faced with an internal problem that some scoffers raised by saying: "Where is the promise of his coming? For ever since the fathers fell asleep, all things have continued as they were from the beginning of creation" (2 Pet. 3:4). We do not know how many Christians were frustrated and became skeptics because the promised parousia did not occur; most may have been satisfied with the answer given in 2 Peter. For centuries, the church of the crucified Christ endured persecutions, boasting of its martyrs. But when Constantine gave the church peace and a privileged position, the events were hailed as the dawn of a new age and a fulfillment of the promises. The church historian Eusebius of Caesarea was the most eloquent spokesman for this point of view. By and large, later historians of the church followed in his steps. Popular books on church history still tend to celebrate the triumph of Christianity and to gloss over the dark sides; it has become increasingly difficult to do so.

The Christian empire outlawed and extirpated pagans much more vehemently and consistently than the pagan authorities had ever persecuted Christians. Jews were tolerated but had to suffer legal discrimination and violent harassment. From the age of Constantine onward, theological controversies became entangled with state politics as well as with ecclesiastical politicking. The result was the separation of the churches outside the Roman Empire from those within it. Later followed the Arab conquest of countries where Christianity had flourished, and the atrocities committed by crusaders in the name of Christ and under the sign of the cross. The Eastern Byzantine Empire and the Roman papacy were two variants of Christian triumphalism. Reacting to ecclesiastical abuses, the Reformers with considerable agony trusted the promises of God and confessed that "one holy church is to remain forever." But the Reformation resulted in new divisions and wars among Christians. In state churches rank and class stratified the Christian community as much as the civil society. There is no need to continue the list of scandals that have tainted Christendom.

Some words must still be added about post-Enlightenment theological liberalism. The general trend was to abandon the argument from fulfilled prophecy in favor of a concept of Christianity as the universal and superior religion, in comparison with which paganism and Judaism represented inferior stages of religious development. No less than theological conservatism, however, this new version of Christian triumphalism could go hand in hand with political imperialism and economic exploitation, colonialism abroad, and racism at home. In retrospect we realize this, but only after two world wars and much criticism both from without and from within Christian churches all over the world. The Holocaust may be the most important single factor. While Christian theologians and churches cannot be held to be directly responsible for the lies and the crimes of the Nazis, they do carry an indirect responsibility because of what they had said, done, and tolerated. After Auschwitz it has become morally as well as historically impossible to continue the centuries-old practice of reading the Bible and the history of the church as if all promises and blessings belonged to the church while words of judgment pertained to the Jews.

If we face the dark aspects of the history of Christianity and the present state of affairs in the divided churches, the theme of this essay becomes a matter of existential concern. It has become difficult to harmonize the historical and social realities with the picture of the church as the people of the New Covenant, the holy temple of God, and the body of Christ. One may attempt to withdraw from the realities in favor of the concept of an invisible church, or an abstract essence of Christianity, or one among the many portraits of the "historical Jesus." But such options make it even more difficult to come to terms with the writings of the New Testament. These writings were addressed to young and oppressed minority churches, and we cannot expect them to speak directly to the problems, the social and political responsibilities, or the burdens of guilt that have been accumulated through centuries of history. In a strange way, however, the Old Testament Scriptures offer assistance in our present predicament. There we learn to read the story of the people of God as a story of losses as well as of gains, a story of corruption and reforms, of false security and lacking faith, the story of a rebellious people whom God in his mercy has not totally abandoned. Such is also the history of the church, a continuation of the story of God's endangered promises. Thus we can learn to look at the history and present reality of the church without becoming triumphant, but also without skeptical despair. God remains the sovereign Lord who castigates his people, but he remains faithful to his promises, which he reaffirmed by vindicating the crucified Messiah, Jesus of Nazareth. Would it be too much to say that the Old Testament in our day helps the church come to terms with its own identity and with the writings of the New Testament?

5

The Problem of
the Historical Jesus

THE HISTORICAL JESUS has become a problem for us. That does not
mean Jesus is primarily a problem. We have a direct impression of
Jesus as his figure encounters us in the Gospels, and for the simple,
believing Christian, this is enough. In life and death, believers may
set their hopes on Jesus as they learn to know him through the
Holy Scriptures. The *problem* of the historical Jesus first arises in
connection with critical reflection that asks what can be ascertained
about Jesus in a purely historical-critical fashion. The concept of
the "historical Jesus," as I use it here, designates Jesus as the object
of methodical, critical, historical research, and the picture of him
that can be drawn by such research. It is this historical Jesus who
has become a problem for us.

In the form in which it is posed today, this problem is a relatively recent one. Older Catholic and confessional Christianity was
certain that the Gospels, as canonical Holy Scriptures, give information about Jesus that is absolutely, historically reliable. The question was merely how the individual Scriptures could be brought
into complete harmony with one another. For rationalistic and liberal theology, the relation between the historical Jesus and the
Christ of church dogma became a problem, and it was the doctrine
of the church that was seen to be problematic, not the historical
Jesus. Liberal theologians assumed that the real picture of Jesus
could be reproduced by critical-historical research and that this
picture could serve as the basis for purification and renewal of
Christianity.

For present-day theology, however, it is precisely the historical
Jesus that has become a problem. A symptom of this is that our

time abounds with Jesus novels, while descriptions of Jesus' life that raise more scientific claims are written almost exclusively by outsiders and dilettantes. New Testament scholars know only too well how difficult the task is and how uncertain the attempts at solution are. The leading spirits among them content themselves with writing terse and sketchy descriptions in which, on the basis of their detailed research, they emphasize the elements that they regard as essential. Moreover, it is peculiar that the popularity of literature on the life of Jesus appears to be on the increase in the Catholic sector, while at the same time it has become suspect for German Protestantism, the classic sphere of research on the life of Jesus.

The problem involves not only the question of whether it is possible to give a scientifically founded and tenable description of the life of Jesus but also the question concerning the relevance of such a description for theology and the church. It is granted that such a description can be obtained only by means of the usual historical-critical method ("the profane scientific method," as it is sometimes put in theological circles). The methods employed, however, already prevent the recognition of what is essential for faith; namely, that Jesus Christ is the Son of God and the living Lord. It is understandable that some would question whether or not faith, the church, and theology should stick to that which is written in the New Testament, without troubling with the alleged historical Jesus of critical scholarship.

Today the uncertainty in the face of such questions appears to be very great. The following essay represents an attempt to contribute to the clarification of the historical and the theological problem.[1] First of all, the present state of the problem and its presuppositions in the history of research must be viewed somewhat more precisely.

THE HISTORY OF THE PROBLEM

The concept "the historical Jesus" as well as scientific research on the life of Jesus came into being in the period of the Enlightenment. The first presupposition for this study was the appearance of historical source criticism and the application of its methods to the Gospels, initially in a naive, rationalistic manner, later in a more methodical fashion. Albert Schweitzer in his *Quest of the Historical Jesus*, written with the single-mindedness of genius, has correctly pointed to a second presupposition: "When at Chalcedon the West overcame the East, its doctrine of the two natures dissolved the unity of the Person, and thereby cut off the last possibility of a return to the historical Jesus. . . . This dogma had first to be shattered before men could once more go out in quest of the historical Jesus, before they could grasp the thought of his existence."[2]

Liberation from dogma could now assume various forms. A few scholars went to work in a radical way and utilized the "historical" description of Jesus as a means of getting free from Christianity as such. That holds true for the pioneer of the German life-of-Jesus research, Hermann Samuel Reimarus. Strongly influenced by English Deists, he portrays Jesus as a political messianic pretender and his disciples as frauds. For such radicalism, however, he found relatively few disciples in the following century. The life-of-Jesus research, in its classic period of the nineteenth century, was mainly a gigantic attempt to break free from the christological dogma of the church and, at the same time, an attempt to maintain the religious singularity of Jesus. In carrying out this program, there were many possible variations on the sliding scale between strictly conservative and radical views. Differences could occur in the way in which Jesus' uniqueness was maintained. Rationalism especially emphasized the teaching of Jesus and his moral example. Later, Jesus' portrait and his God-consciousness assumed the center of the stage. For Ferdinand Christian Baur's research (carried on in the heyday of German idealism and from a Hegelian perspective), the decisive thing was that in Jesus the consciousness of the unity of God and humankind had first broken through. On the basis of this presupposition, the historical Jesus indeed became a problem; Baur himself saw in the speculative theology of German idealism a Gnosticism of a higher order. The problem was actualized by David Friedrich Strauss and his radical skepticism over against the historicity of the gospel tradition. Indeed, the solution of the problem for Strauss was given in advance by Hegelian philosophy: the essential thing is the Christ idea, the idea of God-manhood, realized in the total history of the human race. What Jesus as a historical person was or was not was assumed to be irrelevant.

This speculative theology rapidly drew to a close. The crisis called forth by Strauss led to an even more intensive preoccupation with the historical Jesus. Thereafter, life-of-Jesus research stood not only under the aegis of the struggle for freedom from dogma but also under that of the apologetic defense against Strauss. In the period of empiricism there was also the desire to erect a secure historical basis for Christian faith. It was assumed that the necessary basis in the sources had been found in the Marcan hypothesis and the two-source theory.

In contrast to rationalism and speculative theology, later liberal theology was more antimetaphysical and anti-intellectual. To be sure, Jesus' proclamation—of the fatherly love of God and the infinite worth of the individual human soul—could be strongly emphasized, but what was really decisive and unique was found in Jesus' personality, his religion, or his "inner life." Jesus lived in a unique relationship of sonship to God and thus made it possible for us as well to live in divine sonship of faith. Following upon such an evaluation of the person of Jesus, it was possible for a "liberal-positive" mediating theology to preserve a relation to the apostolic proclamation of Jesus as Savior and Lord. Liberal theology has been an influence within the Scandinavian churches chiefly in this mediating form.

In its more radical form, interest in the historical Jesus led not only to liberation from dogma but also to a break with the apostolic proclamation of the Christ underlying that dogma. That came sharply to light in the debate concerning Jesus and Paul, so intensively carried on at the turn of the century. Paul was represented as a second founder of Christianity, who replaced the simple teaching of Jesus with his complicated doctrine of redemption. Of course, this debate in its extreme form was quite senseless, as leading liberal theologians soon recognized; for the main features of the Pauline preaching of Christ already existed in the church before Paul. The real problem is not "Jesus and Paul" but, rather, "who was Jesus, and what has the church made of him?"

We would misinterpret the whole tradition of research if we failed to observe that a real piety was joined to this interest in the historical Jesus, his life, and his portrait. But we will have to agree with Albert Schweitzer's evaluation of the Jesus research of the nineteenth century that each epoch in theology rediscovered its own ideas in Jesus; "otherwise it could not endow Him with life." "But it was not only each epoch that found its reflection in Jesus; each individual created Him in accordance with his own character."[3] Modern religiosity gave rise not only to the quest of the historical Jesus behind and beyond the New Testament but also to the method by which the quest was carried out. This was candidly expressed by the otherwise critical and levelheaded Adolf Jülicher in the masterpiece of his youth: "I could not understand the Lord, and thus could not love him, if a Galilean spring, sunny days with an inspired view of high mountains, had not preceded his Easter-death in Jerusalem."[4] This contrast between the Galilean springtime and the dark days in Jerusalem was common to all presentations of the life of Jesus.

All the liberal biographies of Jesus shared the conviction of having in the historical Jesus an ally in their efforts to construct a modern theology and a broad-minded Christianity. Accordingly, the historical Jesus was modernized. This liberal Jesus-religion that wished to build on a historical Jesus freed from churchly dogma and isolated from the apostolic preaching has become an impossibility for us today. That same critical-historical research of the Bible, fostered by liberal theology, is responsible. It is to the unfading glory of this movement that it had the courage and the truthfulness to carry on a historical research that undermined its own dogmatic views.

The decisive blows against the liberal interpretation of the historical Jesus were already dealt at the turn of the century, though their effect only gradually became clear. The blows came from various sides. One of them struck at the sources for a presentation of the life of Jesus. In the Gospel of Mark some deletions had been made and were attributed to the theology of the church; otherwise it was thought to be a historically reliable source of the life of Jesus. However, Wilhelm Wrede in his *Das Messiasgeheimnis in den Evangelien* (1901) showed that this approach was fundamentally uncritical and unhistorical. The oldest Gospel, according to its basic structure, was already dogmatic, dominated by the conviction of Jesus' messianic secret. The significant thing about Wrede's book was, above all, its new methodological orientation. He put his finger on the sore spot: "Scientific research on the life of Jesus suffers from psychological conjecture."[5] A genuinely critical and historical treatment must abandon psychological hypotheses in order to study the extant sources in all candor, first of all as witnesses to the faith and theology of the evangelists and the communities in which they lived. From this standpoint, there was no longer any basic difference between Mark and John, and in respect to the gulf that had developed between Jesus and Paul, the Gospels were now to a certain extent removed from the historical Jesus and leaned toward the writings of Paul.

Julius Wellhausen's contributions to gospel research moved in the same direction. As a direct result of the radicalizing of criticism, he came to the conclusion in his *Einleitung in die drei ersten Evangelien* that "without his later influence in the community we can visualize nothing of the religious personality of Jesus. It always appears only in a reflection, broken by the medium of the Christian faith."[6] In our century the form-critical school has attached itself to Wrede and Wellhausen, although the form-critical method in itself does not need to be bound to this specific tradition of research, as some have incorrectly supposed. It has become a major concern of gospel research to understand the evangelical tradition in connection with its setting in church life. The function of the tradition and the interest of faith connected with it has determined the selection, formation, collection, and writing of the recollected words of Jesus and episodes from his life. The theology of the church, therefore, is not only a disturbing element that appeared subsequently and falsified the genuine picture of Jesus, but it was there from the very beginning and explains why any recollections about Jesus were retained in the tradition at all.

Another blow against the leading liberal theology came from the school of the history of religions. In this school there was opposition to the modernizing of primitive Christianity, which ought to be located within the framework of Hellenistic syncretism. Whereas the earlier liberal theology stressed the ethical sphere, now the specifically religious was more clearly featured; for primitive Christianity the uniqueness of Jesus lay not in his religious-ethical personality but rather in that he was the Redeemer and Lord of the community, its "cult hero." It was thereby made clear that for primitive Christianity the significance of Jesus was totally different from modern Christianity's evaluation of him.

When the need arose, radical gospel criticism and the religio-historical view of primitive Christianity could still be joined to a typically liberal picture of the historical Jesus, although in that case the historical connection between Jesus and primitive Christianity threatened to break completely. The attacks were also directed against the liberal picture of Jesus itself. Within liberalism Johannes Weiss raised the storm warning. In his *Predigt Jesu vom Reiche Gottes* he demonstrated that "the idea of the Kingdom of God in Ritschl's theology and in the preaching of Jesus are two very different things."[7] The message of Jesus was eschatological.

Albert Schweitzer proceeded further on this course. For Schweitzer, the kingdom of God in the preaching of Jesus was to be understood eschatologically, and "thorough-going eschatology" offered him the key for understanding Jesus' life. The dogmatic conception of his mission was not something added later; Jesus himself understood his life and suffering in the light of an eschatological dogmatic. In fact, less attention was paid Schweitzer's own attempt at solution than his settlement with the history of research "from Reimarus to Wrede." Contrary to the author's intention, the *Quest of the Historical Jesus* introduced a period of skepticism into this research. Schweitzer could maintain that the result of the life-of-Jesus research was negative.

> The Jesus of Nazareth who came forward publicly as the Messiah, who preached the ethic of the Kingdom of God, who founded the Kingdom of Heaven upon earth, and died to give His work its final consecration, never had any existence. He is a figure designed by rationalism, endowed with life by liberalism, and clothed by modern theology in an historical garb.[8]

> The study of the Life of Jesus has had a curious history. It set out in quest of the historical Jesus, believing that when it had found Him it could bring Him straight into our time as a Teacher and Savior. It loosed the bands by which He had been riveted for centuries to the stony rocks of ecclesiastical doctrine, and rejoiced to see life and movement coming into the figure once more, and the historical Jesus advancing, as it seemed, to meet it. But He does not stay; He passes by our time and returns to His own.[9]

The eschatological expectation is not the only aspect uniting Jesus with Judaism of the first century, however. That he was part of it has also become clear in many other connections. In this area, of course, scholars of another school have accomplished more than the liberals. The latter had generally presented *Die Predigt Jesu in ihrem Gegensatz zum Judentum* (W. Bousset, 1892), and had drawn a caricature of Pharisaism, a dark background for the portrait of Jesus' personality, which shone all the brighter. The school of the history of religions was primarily interested in primitive Christianity as a syncretistic religion and emphasized the influence of Oriental Hellenism. The conservative theologians showed a preference for the Jewish background in order to find a support for the historical credibility of the gospel tradition. It was hardly their intention to bring to light what was strange and ancient in the Judaism of Jesus.

Jewish scholars also took pains in a most profitable way to illuminate the Palestinian background of the gospel history. Influenced by Jewish emancipation and religious liberalism, they began research on the historical Jesus. The strange result was that liberal

Jews could draw an ideal picture of Pharisaism strikingly reminiscent of the liberal picture of Jesus. Even in Judaism, faith in God as loving Father, an emphasis on morality, and many other things could be found. It is not surprising that they made contact with the research on Jesus done by Christian theologians in order to utilize it to the advantage of reformed Judaism.[10] For this historical Jesus belonged to Judaism as one of its noblest figures, though a few prejudices and exaggerations on the part of his followers could explain why he became the founder of a new, non-Jewish religion. It also became clear to them that it was faith in Jesus as the crucified and risen Son of God that was at the heart of Christianity and that alone differentiated it from a reformed Judaism. Wellhausen expressed the same insight briefly, tersely, and somewhat brutally: "Jesus was no Christian; he was a Jew."[11]

In its attempt to discover the essence of Christianity in the "religion of Jesus," liberal theology (characterized by the slogan "back to the historical Jesus") had lost the historical ground beneath its feet. The lectures that Adolf von Harnack delivered on "What Is Christianity?" at the turn of the century were not the program for a new era but rather were the epilogue to an epoch in the history of theology that was fast coming to a close. The dilemma into which liberal theology had fallen was clearly seen by Wellhausen: "Without the Gospel and without Paul even Judaism would still have to cling to Jesus. . . . We cannot go back to him, even if we wanted to. . . . For if the Gospel were removed, the historical Jesus would be a very dubious and unsatisfactory substitute as a basis for religion."[12] Even Wrede, so it is reported, is supposed to have suffered from the discrepancy between the results of his research and the piety of liberal Christianity. But these men could not indicate a way out of the dilemma.

Albert Schweitzer found his way. His criticism of the modern liberal picture of Jesus was not simply the product of scientific research; it was the result of a reaction to his contemporaries who lacked the sense for the "elementary." Philosophically and religiously he found the solution in an ethical voluntaristic mysticism for which Jesus was, not the basis of religion, but indeed an enlivening and inspiring factor: "He comes to us as One unknown, without a name, as of old, by the lake-side, He came to those men who knew Him not. He speaks to us the same word: 'Follow thou me!' "[13] Obedience to this word led Schweitzer from academic theology to the forest of Africa. While his lifework attests to the power that can lie in liberal Christianity, it also raises the question of whether it can exist outside the shadows of a churchly Christianity. Schweitzer's intensely personal solution could not guide the further work of theology on the problem of the historical Jesus. How many seminal insights his conception contained was first made clear by the publication of his work *The Mysticism of Paul the Apostle*.

In the mainstream, little note was first taken of the theological crisis that resulted from the work of Wrede and Wellhausen, Weiss and Schweitzer, the school of the history of religions, and Jewish research on Jesus. Understandably, the consequences became clear only gradually. These scholars and schools of research were in part mutually opposed, and each of them could properly be criticized for their one-sidedness and exaggerations. Liberal theology disintegrated only after the First World War, but more because of studies on Paul and the Reformation than because of research on Jesus. This theological reversal would not have been possible, however, if New Testament research had not undermined the liberal Jesus-religion a few decades earlier.

Conservative theology had remained somewhat reserved over against the life-of-Jesus research. Hence, without concerning itself with the crisis in this research, it could continue working in the old way relatively undisturbed—more so in Scandinavian countries than in Germany. To a certain extent, these conservatives took a kind of morbid pleasure in the dissolution of liberal theology. For the most part, however, they were too preoccupied with defending the genuineness of New Testament Scriptures and traditions to have been able to make a decisive contribution to critical research on the life of Jesus.

There were also theologians of a conservative temper who combined a deep anchoring in biblical Christianity with an openness to the questions with which scholarship had to deal. Even before the problem of the historical Jesus had become critical, and when the life-of-Jesus research was still in full bloom, Martin Kähler had written his book *The So-Called Historical Jesus and the Historical Biblical Christ*. In it he pointed out a way that was to be significant for the future. Kähler stated that the foundation of faith cannot be scientifically reconstructed (and therefore the historical Jesus was hypothetical) but rather must be the Jesus Christ as proclaimed by the apostles in the preaching that established the church. The Gospels are not sources for the biography of Jesus, but rather are "sermons on the messiahship of the crucified," "passion stories with a lengthy introduction."

Upon publication, Kähler's book aroused lively discussion, but it had no decisive influence during his time and could be ignored

in favor of Schweitzer's *Quest of the Historical Jesus*. It had its real
effect only in our century, following the crisis in the life-of-Jesus
research. After the First World War Kähler's ideas were taken up
and further elaborated. Once more it has become clear to us that
Christian faith relates to the Jesus of Nazareth who is preached in
the apostolic proclamation as the crucified and risen Lord. What
gives the various New Testament writings their inner unity is not
a theoretical dogma, nor is it the inspiring impression of the personality of Jesus, but rather the gospel of the act of God in Jesus
Christ, in whom forgiveness of sins, righteousness, and life are
given to us. The message of the apostles is the proclamation of a
kerygma for which they are commissioned by the appearances of
the risen Lord. The resurrection of Jesus stands at the center of the
New Testament and cannot be removed from its place without a
resultant collapse. The recollections of the historical Jesus were
preserved, formed, and interpreted within the framework of the
proclamation concerning the risen Lord, and for Christian faith this
interpretation is the proper and legitimate one. Only by faith in
the apostolic gospel is it possible to hold fast to the unique religious
significance of Jesus. For a purely immanent, historical view he can
be unique only in that relative sense in which other great men may
be called unique. If liberal theologians wish to hold fast to the
unique significance of the historical Jesus in another and more
absolute sense, that is only as an aftereffect of ecclesiastical, dogmatic Christianity.

Reducing it to a brief formula, one may say that the life-of-
Jesus theology was superseded by a kerygmatic theology. To some
extent, a historical formulation of the question was now rejected:
The extant Gospels are the only things to which we must hold fast.
My honored teacher Ragnar Åsting said that the Gospels are "directed forward," bearers of a creative proclamation; we should believe them, instead of inquiring into the historical verifiability of
what is reported. Åsting was not the only one who tended to regard
the attempt to penetrate behind the Gospels to the historical Jesus
as a scientifically insoluble and unfruitful task, as well as a theologically illegitimate inquiry. This new kerygmatic-theological approach does not imply, however, that New Testament scholarship
has become a neo-orthodoxy free of problems instead of working
with serious historical questions. Both life-of-Jesus theology and
also kerygmatic theology appear in both ecclesiastically conservative and more radical forms. The question for debate is not merely
to what degree the old dogma of the church is a legitimate and

necessary interpretation of the apostolic kerygma, but also how the kerygma is to be interpreted today—the problem of demythologizing.

In spite of all its dependence on the older critical research, even Bultmann's existential interpretation must be viewed as a variant of the kerygmatic theology; it is concerned neither with the Christ-idea nor with the personality of Jesus as accessible to historical research, but rather with Jesus Christ proclaimed in the gospel. The debate on demythologizing, however, has shown that we cannot so quickly dispense with the problem of the historical Jesus. Already a certain reaction to a thoroughgoing kerygmatic theology appears to have set in. As Ernst Käsemann has recently pointed out, an interesting shift in fronts has come about; in reaction to Bultmann's radicalism, an attempt is being made to counteract a separation of kerygma from tradition.[14] In a most spirited manner, Ethelbert Stauffer has begun to advocate a renewal of the life-of-Jesus research on the basis of an inquiry into the historical context of the New Testament.[15]

It is impossible to return to the precritical evaluation of the Gospels as historical source documents. Archaeological discoveries and recent research may have invalidated radical critical hypotheses and strengthened trust in the tradition, but even if this should continue to an even greater extent, we will not be able to avoid reading the Gospels primarily as witnesses of the primitive church. It would be premature, however, to conclude from Kähler's theologically significant and exegetically fruitful ideas that the question concerning the historical Jesus should not be asked at all. To be sure, faith comes from preaching and is not dependent upon the historical-critical work of New Testament professors. It would be something quite different, however, to deny to scholars their work on historical questions or to oppose the use of methods that in themselves are completely profane but that are the only ones at the disposal of the historian. That the essence of Christianity cannot be found by a return to the historical Jesus does not mean that it would be senseless and improper to ask what we already know and are able to know about Jesus in a purely historical way. The fact that the problem is extremely difficult and its solution only approximate does not mean that we may simply abandon it. The curiosity that underlies all science will certainly lead to continually new treatments of the problem. If we theologians ignore this task, others will undertake it. Even if the question should be theologically irrelevant, it would remain legitimate. Scholarly ethos requires that we do not avoid it, but rather work at it in all sincerity, for God's law lies behind the scholarly ethos. The historical-critical concern with the problem of the historical Jesus is at least an honorable task that is subject to the distress and promise of every honorable profession, and to the Pauline *hos mē* ("as if not") as well.

THE HISTORICAL-CRITICAL PROBLEM

Objectively assured results can be reached only approximately, but that fact does not in itself distinguish Jesus research from other historical scholarship. Rather, the difficulties with which *all* historical science must grapple are especially perceptible in this area. All historical work is influenced by the presuppositions of historians, and they themselves are children of their own time. That becomes particularly noticeable when Jesus is made the object of historical research, and even historians can hardly deal with Jesus without being involved in a positive or negative way. It is worthy to question whether personal involvement is not a positive prerequisite for a scholar's attaining to any kind of historically fruitful results. To a certain degree, wishful thinking and subjective errors can be eliminated by methodological scientific work, when the will to know the truth is present. Scholars with different starting points cooperate and are able mutually to correct each other. For that reason also, it is not desirable that non-Christian scholars remain aloof from this work. In certain respects even antipathy can be illuminating. Jewish scholars, for instance, can have an acute sense for what is characteristic of Jesus.

Other difficulties for research on the historical Jesus lie in the nature of the sources. We have no documentary reports and no traditions concerning Jesus by his enemies or other contemporaries. Even the oldest extra-Christian references to Jesus appear to rest not on direct recollections but on encounters with Christians in Palestine or Rome. They may suffice to corroborate the historical existence of Jesus, but hardly more. Only on the basis of the New Testament writings are we able to construct for ourselves a real picture of Jesus. Of these the oldest were written about two decades after his death, and all aim at nourishing faith in him; none of them can be regarded as a neutral historical record. Once we recognize the nature of these sources, we will be more easily amazed at how much we still know of Jesus historically. A great part of the tradition consists of brief, pregnant expressions and characteristic episodes that are easily committed to memory. Very early, the tradition must have taken on a relatively fixed form in a milieu where it was customary to preserve recollections with great faithfulness. The interest of faith in the tradition about Jesus served not only to shape but also to preserve the tradition; flights of fancy were confined within narrower limits than is the case with the legends of the apostles.

Only by methodological, pure, and critical work can the received traditions be made useful for a historical description of Jesus. Personal and current views concerning what Jesus might have said or done should not be made a criterion in the evaluation of the material in question. The history of research has taught us what a dangerous source of error this can be. If we want to avoid all subjective arbitrariness, critical research on the Gospels becomes an extremely complicated work requiring the highest degree of precision. The extant Gospels are first of all to be studied and interpreted as literary wholes. Their interrelationship must be accurately examined, but even the relatively certain results of source criticism have only limited value for the historical question; we must acknowledge that the oral tradition existed alongside and subsequent to the first written records. It is quite possible that an older variant of the tradition may have been preserved in a secondary literary source.[16]

In addition to the literary investigation of the Gospels, we must consider the traditio-historical study of the small or smallest units of the tradition. In addition to the Gospels, material from later sources—for instance, quotations from the church fathers, textual variants, and fragmentary apocryphal gospels—has a significance that cannot be ignored. The new material that such sources provide is modest and of dubious value, but the subsequent history of the gospel tradition is illuminated, and from it the cautious scholar will be able to draw some conclusions regarding its earlier history. In further research, critical questions concerning the form, language, and substance are also to be observed. No single road leads to the goal; in spite of the very fruitful beginning of form criticism, the study of form has not yielded objective criteria for separating older from later traditions to the degree expected. The linguistic criteria, in their turn, point to old traditions where the original Semitic tongue shines through but do not allow any positive decision regarding the *ipsissima verba* of Jesus. Preference for one special method should be regarded as a calamity and, where possible, be replaced by the cooperation of a variety of specialists in various fields.

On the basis of numerous individual observations, a more comprehensive picture of the history of the tradition can be outlined. Though not absolute, certain statistical laws and regularities emerge that leave their imprint on the formation and transformation of the tradition. It is well known that the individual sayings and narratives have been relatively faithfully preserved, while the evangelists and the narrators before them were much freer in the collection and arrangement of the material. Within the individual sections of the tradition, greater freedom is exercised with respect to rendering introductory and concluding data than with regard to the central point. Among the different variants, agreement is greatest in the rendering of the words of Jesus, but the words have not been preserved because of any reverence for the antiquarian, but because they are words of the Lord to his community. Loosed from their original situation, the words have been used and construed in a new way, a factor that has affected not only their arrangement but also their formation. That can be most easily observed in the case of the parables.[17]

The goal of critical gospel research is to make clear the history of the tradition about Jesus within the church. With some certainty, moreover, distinction can be made between the core of the tradition and its later elaboration. It is much more difficult to find objective criteria that can determine whether the core of a tradition is authentic or secondary. It is theoretically possible that migrant sayings have been transferred to Jesus, that words of Jewish wisdom or utterances of primitive Christian prophets have been put in the mouth of the historical Jesus, but rarely can positive proof be adduced that such is really the case. Here, the total perspective of the scholar is decisive for an evaluation of the case in point, and not vice versa. That can easily be observed in Bultmann's *History of the Synoptic Tradition*, but also applies to scholars who, like myself, are inclined to think that on the whole the church did not produce the traditions about Jesus, but rather reproduced them in new and altered forms.

In no case can any distinct separation be achieved between the genuine words of Jesus and constructions of the community. We do not escape the fact that we know Jesus only as the disciples remembered him. Whoever thinks that the disciples completely misunderstood their Master or even consciously falsified his picture may give fantasy free reign. From a purely scientific point of view, however, it is logical to assume that the Master can be known through his disciples' words about him and their historical influence. On this assumption it is also possible to work methodically when an attempt is made to advance from the analysis of the gospel tradition to the description of the historical Jesus.

Even without a clear differentiation between pure history and later theology, the gospel tradition permits us to draw a very clear picture of what was typical and characteristic of Jesus. Cross sections of the tradition bring to the fore what was characteristic; for instance, his proclamation of the kingdom of God, his position toward the law, and his attitude toward various groups of people. Words and reports of differing form and genre, transmitted within various layers of the tradition, mutually illumine each other and yield a total picture in which there appears something that is characteristic of Jesus. Whether the historicity of individual words or episodes remains uncertain is consequently of less importance. The fact that these words and occurrences found a place within the tradition about Jesus indicates that they agreed with the total picture as it existed within the circle of the disciples.[18]

The cross-section method must be supplemented by drawing longitudinal lines leading from Judaism beyond Jesus to primitive Christianity. While the time when Zarathustra and Moses lived has long been the subject of debate, we know that Jesus was crucified under Pontius Pilate. The fixed starting point of all our knowledge about him is that he is the Crucified One, whom his disciples and, later, the community believed to be the risen Messiah. We also know that Jesus worked in Israel, that he was born and raised a Jew, that he was "born of woman, born under the law." The historical Jesus is to be found at the crossroad where Christianity and Judaism begin to separate from one another, although it has become clear that their paths parted in such a way that Christianity appeared as a new religion alongside Judaism.

From the oldest Christian sources we must work our way backward in the direction of Jesus. It is of great advantage that the most important groups of New Testament writings are independent of each other; Paul, the Synoptists, John, the Epistle to the Hebrews, and the others cannot be arranged into one straight line of development. Rather, each in its own way reflects the impression made by Jesus and the events connected with his name. Between the historical Jesus and the New Testament writings there are the Easter occurrences, but that does not alter the fact that the historian who works backward from the formulations of primitive Christianity toward the common starting point also approaches the historical Jesus. The investigation of the tradition lying behind the Gospels is the most important, but not the only part of this work.

On the other hand, we must view Jesus within the context of Palestinian Judaism. Everything that enlarges our knowledge of this environment of Jesus indirectly extends our knowledge of the historical Jesus himself. Since the results in this area are relatively certain, it is a very real question whether or not the insights gained here in the long run involve the greatest enrichment of our historical knowledge about Jesus. Only by saving the honor of the Pharisees has the unheard-of radicality of Jesus' words against the Pharisees really come to light. It is still not possible to estimate what the textual findings from the Qumran caves may yield; in any case they impel us to resume the quest of the historical Jesus. As never before we have the possibility of tracing the trends and ideas that, both positively and negatively, form the presuppositions for his ministry.

When, on the one hand, the historian works backward in this way from oldest Christianity to Jesus and, on the other, attempts to clarify the presuppositions of his appearance on the basis of Jewish sources, a fairly clear picture can be gained of the setting into which Jesus appeared and of the changes to which his ministry led. By this method it is also possible to insert the transmitted words and episodes into their original historical situation. Thus we can form an idea of what Jesus wanted to say to the Jews of his own time and can attempt to construct a historical picture of Jesus.

The historian's attempt to reconstruct the historical Jesus by the historical-critical method may be compared with the work of archaeologists who attempt to restore an old monument, of which only the foundation and a few scattered stones remain. They may try to draw sketches on paper in order to show how the structure probably looked. No one will deny them that, and it can be useful and necessary for their work. They mislead their readers, however, when they publish their sketch without calling attention to the place where exact knowledge leaves off, where they have good grounds for their reconstruction, and where they have drawn freehand. When they find the precise spot where one or a few of the scattered stones originally lay, it means more in the long run than such reconstructive attempts. Similarly, it is permissible to write a description of the historical Jesus, but hypotheses may not be advanced as exact scientific results. If there is an element of genius in the hypotheses, as in Albert Schweitzer's case, then they may give important impulse to further research. But over an extended period an expansion of our exact knowledge of primitive Christianity and of Judaism in Jesus' time means more for our historical knowledge of Jesus than many books about his life.

Historical studies can only approximately achieve exact results. This general truth is most particularly to be observed in regard to the problems associated with the Jesus research. Whoever has to fix an uncertain chronological datum, such as the year of origin of a work, is seldom in the position of finding new arguments which allow one to make a completely accurate decision. One must begin by establishing the *termini a quo* and *ante quem* and, on the basis of these two limits, try to approach the precise point of time. Even the more involved historical problems will, *mutatis mutandis*, have to be dealt with in a similar way. As far as Jesus is concerned, the scholar must search for what can be established without question, even in the face of great historical skepticism. Radical criticism has a necessary function here. The rule is that an individual piece must be demonstrated to be genuine. Genuine transmission concerning Jesus is established only when the "tradition, for various reasons, can be neither derived from Judaism nor attributed to primitive Christianity."[19] This radical criticism and its results may not be dogmatized, but it is one necessary heuristic principle among others. Whatever is discovered in this way is only a critically assured *minimum*.

On the other hand, the total tradition concerning Jesus must be taken into consideration. In its totality it is theology of the church, but at the same time it is also in its totality a reflex of Jesus' activity— a *maximum* that contains everything of importance for our historical knowledge about Jesus. To delineate this maximum more precisely is a problem for the solution of which Stauffer's "iron rule" applies: *In dubiis pro tradito.*[20] The ongoing task is to narrow the gap to the highest degree possible between the maximum of tradition and the critically assured minimum in order to approach more closely to the historical Jesus. The chief reason why the older life-of-Jesus research became sterile and scientifically unfruitful might have been that it set out too directly and rashly toward its goal. Today, facing a renewed interest in Jesus research, we will again have to be on our guard against committing the same error.

Although we are still far removed from the desired degree of exactitude, we may construct a reasonably clear picture of the manner of Jesus' appearance as well as of the content of his proclamation and his teaching, and of the impression that he made on the adherents and opponents among his contemporaries. The sources do not permit us to say much regarding his inner life, since they were not interested in it. The open question is whether we may detect only characteristic features or whether it is possible to give a scientific description of the life of Jesus founded on objective arguments. That a biography of Jesus cannot be written is a truism today. We cannot even write the history of Jesus' development within the period of his public ministry. The contrast between the Galilean spring and the subsequent period of defection and opposition is not sufficiently attested to in the sources, as Albert Schweitzer correctly emphasized. But Schweitzer's own theory, which did not proceed from the beginning but rather from the climax of Jesus' public life, found the key for understanding the history of Jesus in the delay of the parousia at the time the seventy were sent out (Matt. 10:23) and rested on an entirely arbitrary combination of the sources.

The difficulty of the task does not mean, however, that it would be senseless to work at it. One point in the life of Jesus is unconditionally established: his death. A historically tenable description of the life of Jesus would be possible only in the form of a description of his death, its historical presuppositions, and the events preceding and following it. In other areas it has proved a fruitful method to begin with a very definite event and from it to throw light on the preceding and following periods. In our case this could be the only practicable way because of the nature of the sources. Kähler's statement "passion stories with a lengthy introduction" is important not only for the proper interpretation of the Gospels but also for their use as historical sources on the life of Jesus. Historical considerations of a more general character point in the same direction. In the historical development that led to the rise of Christianity, the death of Jesus is the axis on which everything turns. "Without his death he would not have become historical at all," said Wellhausen.[21] Historical research must begin with the death of Jesus if it wishes to illumine the life of Jesus and the preaching that followed.

Of course, a historical description of the death of Jesus remains a most difficult and complicated task. No doubt the Gospel reports at this point, and only at this point, are rather detailed, coherent, and to a certain degree even chronologically arranged. The interest of the evangelists, however, lies in describing Jesus' death as the saving event and the basis of the New Covenant, and not in presenting it as a world historical phenomenon with certain historical causes and effects. Before written Gospels existed, the oldest passion narratives that Christians read were such Old Testament texts as Psalm 22, a practice that can often be traced in the Gospel accounts. One must be extremely cautious about employing them in the service of historical reconstruction.

In other respects as well, our historical knowledge is extremely limited. The debate over the Sanhedrin's authority to levy the death sentence, a debate that still has not been settled, provides one example. It is also questionable how much of rabbinic penal law can be traced back to the time of Jesus. Even in the instances where it is possible, the gain is dubious. For we must reckon with the possibility that the trial of Jesus may have been conducted according to the rules of Sadducean legal practice—if, indeed, there was any intention of conducting a trial against Jesus according to regular juridical forms, which is equally uncertain. The motives that induced the Jewish authorities and Pilate to proceed against Jesus are very difficult for us to detect. Despite the existing difficulties, however, the attempt should be made to begin with the death of Jesus and, utilizing every means of historical methodology available, to study the remaining problems of Jesus' life. There will always be much that remains doubtful, but we may be confident that research that works energetically in this direction will attain more certain results than the previous life-of-Jesus literature was able to attain.

In any case, it is clear that what we know with certainty about the life of Jesus is that it ended on the cross. That end must be kept in mind in the attempt to understand the preaching and teaching of Jesus. An obvious weakness of many descriptions of Jesus— as a very pious, very humane, and somewhat harmless teacher— lies in the fact that it is not understood why high priests and Romans had any interest in the execution of this man. The end of Jesus' life helps to sharpen our understanding of why Jesus' existence, his preaching of the Sermon on the Mount, for example, was a challenging claim to authority. We must observe the same in the exposition of the parables; in many instances the real meaning becomes clear only when we keep in mind how, in veiled form, they express the decisive meaning Jesus attributed to his own mission.[22] Accordingly, no one can maintain that historical research has access only to the preaching of Jesus and not to his life. Rather, we must state that a historical understanding of his preaching can be attained only when it is seen in connection with his life, namely, with the life that ended on the cross.

THE THEOLOGICAL PROBLEM

In spite of all the problems and difficulties, the inquiry into the historical Jesus is a legitimate and a fruitful task. The more difficult question is whether this work is also of significance for faith, for the church and theology. The problem becomes clear at this point when we presuppose, hypothetically, that it would be possible to give a scientific description of Jesus' life in the form of a presentation of his death and the events preceding it. The goal would be to reach such a degree of scientific objectivity that everyone, regardless of presuppositions of faith, would have to admit that everything happened in just this way and no other. Not only the external course of Jesus' life would be illuminated, but also a series of factors influencing it. The nature and content of Jesus' preaching would also come into consideration as important elements that unleased opposition to him. It is probable that Jesus not only foresaw his own death but actually ascribed to it a vicarious significance and saw in it a necessary presupposition for the coming of the kingdom of God. For the historian, such ideas of Jesus' would be one factor among others illuminating the course of Jesus' life. In this light, it would be understandable why Jesus did nothing to avoid the threatening danger but, through his purification of the temple, seemed to provoke the intervention of the high priests.

In any case, the Christian faith and the church would have only limited interest in such a presentation of what actually occurred, even if it could be stated with a high degree of historical probability. What alone is decisive for faith and the church—namely, that Jesus' death was a dying *for us*—would not appear at all in the historical description of the causes and effects of his death. The historian *qua* historian can say nothing concerning the events that really took place—that God showed his love to us, that while we were still sinners, Christ died for us. The believing community might even disregard the historical description of Jesus' death and his previous life for the sake of holding to the Gospels and the rest of the New Testament writings. Once more it would be clear to the church that only the resurrection of Jesus from the dead and the witness of the Holy Spirit through the apostles disclose the meaning and the significance of Jesus' death and his previous life. The church, therefore, maintains that in the New Testament and nowhere else is it revealed who Jesus really was—without being required to contest the results of historical science.

Faith is concerned neither with the immanent effects of Jesus' death nor with an evaluation of his personality. Jesus' life and death have their significance in and with the message that God raised him from the dead. But in contrast to the life and death of Jesus, his resurrection cannot be made an object of historical research. Only the Easter faith of the disciples is accessible to the historian, the origin of which can be illumined only to a certain degree. Good reasons can be advanced for the fact that the tradition of the empty grave is historical in essence, as von Campenhausen has recently shown.[23] Even if it were proved beyond every doubt, however, the historian would still find only an empty grave and no risen Savior. The possibility of some kind of a misunderstanding or an inexplicable accident would remain. Similarly, the revelations of the risen Lord to Peter and to the disciples can be explained as visions or hallucinations. And even if it could be proved that no psychological explanation suffices, the possibility of a parapsychological interpretation remains, and we would not be one step nearer the Christian faith, which praises God for the fact that he has begotten us anew to a living hope through the resurrection of Jesus Christ from the dead.

Whoever knows what historical research is and what the resurrection of Jesus from the dead means cannot suppose that one is able to prove the resurrection by historical arguments. That Jesus of Nazareth is the Son of God who died for us and rose from the dead is visible only to those who believe in him. Objective, historically scientific arguments are not decisive where belief and unbelief are concerned. The decisive factor lies, rather, in the personal relation to the apostolic message of the Crucified and Risen One, the Son of God, our Lord. Faith arises from the grace that is given us to believe in this gospel. The emphasis of kerygmatic theology that faith comes through preaching and that it is relatively disinterested in a historical Jesus is not simply an escape from an acute crisis in the life-of-Jesus research, but actually rests upon a proper knowledge of what the Christian faith is.

That faith is *relatively* uninterested in the historical-Jesus research does not mean that it is *absolutely* uninterested in it. To draw this conclusion would be a kerygmatic theological Docetism, or even a denial of faith in God as Creator, under whose worldly rule even the historian does his or her service as a scholar. The fact that Jesus can be made an object of historical-critical research is given with the incarnation and cannot be denied by faith, if the latter is to remain true to itself.

The Jesus research, with its more or less debatable results, has at least made it clear that Jesus was really a true man with human individuality, belonging to a definite time and a definite milieu. The message of the New Testament that *this* man is the Son of God, the Word become flesh, can be neither proved nor refuted by the Jesus research. One thing has become clear, however: incarnation signifies not only the assumption of an abstract human nature by the godhead but that the Word really became flesh, concrete, human history. By making this more clear, historical research has helped to clarify the offense of the Christian message and the possibility of its scandal. Because of this, Jesus research has triggered offense and inner conflict from which many difficulties for Christianity have arisen and may still arise. Still, this has not made it any more difficult to have a living faith—at least not more difficult than in the first period of the church, when there was still an immediate remembrance of Jesus as a man among men. The possibility of offense was not less for the contemporaries of Jesus, for whom the foolishness and the offense of the cross were not yet tempered by traditional symbolism, than for us who today can make him an object of historical research. By clarifying the problem, historical research helps us to hear the word of the Master with new joy: "Blessed is he who takes no offense in me." Whoever in anxiety over Christianity wishes to keep critical-historical research away from Jesus should ask themselves whether or not, in reality, they are seeking to avoid the possibility of the offense and the inner conflict in which faith must live in this world.

In any case, the life-of-Jesus research has this negative relevance, that it uncovers the possibility of the offense. The question is whether it has or at least can have positive significance. A tendency toward a negative answer can be observed not only in such representatives of kerygmatic theology who would hold simply to the canonical Gospels but also in a radical critic such as Rudolf Bultmann. In the case of the existentialist interpretation of the New Testament, it is only of consequence that Jesus lived, that he died on the cross, and that this message is proclaimed as the saving event to be grasped in the obedience of faith. Faith as an existential attitude is not supposed to be interested in the question of the *how* of Jesus' life. The understanding of faith may not be interpreted as objective knowledge and a basis for discerning between dogmatic mythologoumena and demonstrable historical facts.

Therefore, kerygmatic theology in this form does not lead to indifference regarding the historical-critical question but, rather, points to the fact that radical historical criticism can be pressed into the service of a definite theological conception. Criticism itself is a theological function, since it clarifies the fact that faith cannot hold to a historically unequivocal picture of Jesus' personality and that a "messianic consciousness" cannot be demonstrated as an observable phenomenon.[24] Faith has no historical security, but only the assurance given by the word of preaching. The Gospel of John is for Bultmann the chief Gospel, not in spite of his regard for it as completely unhistorical, but precisely because he regards it as unhistorical. In it Jesus is described "not as a reliably attested person in the past, but in such a way as he is always present in the word which proclaims him in the power of the Spirit."[25] In such a way the significance of Jesus becomes clear for faith.

It is important to understand that historically mediated knowledge can create no security for faith. Conversely, it is important to understand that much that is unhistorical may be in the Gospels without the need for faith to feel itself seriously endangered. The existentialist interpretation carried out consistently signifies not only a demythologizing but also a dehistoricizing of the New Testament.[26] This dehistoricizing of the New Testament is an ultra-Pauline extreme, conditioned by existentialist philosophy that does not do justice to the Gospels. Though the Gospels may be proclamation and witness, it would be contrary to the intention of the evangelists to declare inquiry into the historicity of the narratives as irrelevant. In all philosophical naïveté it may be regarded as natural and normal that even the present-day believer shares the interest of the evangelists in preserving reliable information concerning the shape and actions of the Lord and Savior's earthly life.

This interest may lead us astray. For example, when the history of Jesus is interpreted by means of improper historical categories, or when a false and illusory security is sought, errors may result. As a warning against this possibility, the Pauline refusal to know Christ after the flesh retains its abiding justification. The necessity of this critical corrective, however, does not mean that positive interest in the history of Jesus is objectionable per se. Without seeking a false historical security, Christians may rejoice when historical research not only brings inner conflicts for faith but shows that the historically demonstrable facts of Jesus' life are not unambiguous proofs, but are indeed visible signs to faith that Jesus was the one the New Testament proclaims him to be. When the *how* of the life of Jesus is declared to be theologically irrelevant, the incarnation of the Word threatens to become a paradox devoid of content. We must raise the question whether or not the dehistoricizing existentialist interpretation leads to an avoidance of the possibility of offense lying in the concrete history of Jesus and thus fails to see his hidden glory.

To require that the Jesus research should establish the glory of Jesus by means of objective arguments would be the demand for a sign on the part of an unbelieving generation. On the other hand, we must openly admit that it would be fatal theologically if the result of this research would be the establishment of an irreconcilable opposition between the historical Jesus and the witness of the New Testament to Christ. Even Bultmann cannot avoid it; theologically he is not so disinterested in the question concerning the historical Jesus as it might appear from some of his statements. That Jesus' preaching must be interpreted as a call to decision—in such a way that he, as bearer of the Word, signifies the demand for decision[27]—is a necessary presupposition for Bultmann's interpretation of the New Testament. It follows that the preaching of Jesus, after his death, could only be taken up in the form of a message concerning the saving deed of God in Jesus Christ calling to decision—not in the form of a literal reproduction of his sayings or of a biographical description of his life.[28]

Bultmann calls attention to the fact that the Jesus research is theologically questionable and dangerous when it results in interpreting the historical Jesus in categories that originate elsewhere and that are not appropriate to him: for example, when he is presented as a teacher of timeless ideas, a personality, a charismatic miracle worker, or a religious hero. The use of such categories is conditioned by the respective presuppositions of the scholar, however, and is not a necessary result of historical inquiry; the inappropriateness of such presuppositions is proved by the continuing research itself.

In view of the historical source, it is now pertinent to ask whether it is or is not permissible to describe the historical Jesus merely as the bearer of the Word that calls for decision. It must be the object of historical research, whenever possible, to eliminate all modern categories in order to ascertain how Jesus was understood by his contemporaries and how he himself wanted to be understood. Such research will best serve theology and the church when it limits itself to this task with complete impartiality. (The historian has access only to an interpreted history of Jesus, not to the *nudum factum* of the *Verbum Dei incarnatum*, which Stauffer supposes he is able to illuminate by research into the historical context of the New Testament.)

Even a scholar who does not share Bultmann's existentialist interpretation will agree with him that the relationship between the historical Jesus and the preaching of his apostles is not a problem that threatens theology to the extent it appeared to at the turn of the century. At first it appeared that the radical gospel criticism and the history-of-religions school would lead to an unbridgeable gulf between Jesus and the church. Hence, it is understandable that some proceeded to deny the historical existence of Jesus. Theologically, the most important result of Albert Schweitzer's grand conception was that it pointed a way out of this dilemma. The eschatological message and expectation bind Jesus and primitive Christianity into unity.[29] Jesus proclaimed the nearness of the kingdom of God; indeed, as we express it today in our correction of "thoroughgoing eschatology," he preached that in and with his own mission, his word and work, God's kingdom was already breaking in. The primitive community and Paul share the same expectation, but their place in the eschatological history of salvation is different. Neither a proof of the difference between Jesus' preaching and the teaching of his apostles (from the standpoint of the history of ideas) nor a proof of their connection (from the standpoint of the history of their development) can really lead us anywhere.

On the basis of the presuppositions common to Jesus and the primitive church, it is unlikely that the disciples, after Jesus' death, preached the message of salvation in the same form in which Jesus himself preached it. Between Jesus and the primitive community there lie his death and resurrection as decisive events: Jesus is appointed to the position of messianic ruler, in which he shall some day be revealed; those who call upon his name now already assemble themselves as the *ekklēsia* of God in the new time of salvation. Jesus research thus leads us to this alternative: Either the events of Easter and Pentecost are the preliminary fulfillment of Jesus' eschatological promise, or this promise, which lay at the heart of his message, remained unfulfilled. In the case of this latter alternative, the inspiring impressions emanating from him have to classify him among the messianic pretenders of Judaism.

Accordingly, we might say that instead of isolating the historical Jesus from the apostolic gospel and the church, the historical research has enabled us to see them in their unity. The question today is whether we may proceed still further and establish a direct connection (in the sense that the historical Jesus himself intended the church). A whole series of investigations has shown what a great role church, worship, sacraments, and the like have played in primitive Christianity. There have also been attempts to show that all this must have been rooted in the earthly life of Jesus. In the more recent Swedish theology, but not only there, much was accomplished in this direction in the last decades. Anton Fridrichsen has pointedly remarked: "Everything that Jesus does and says points toward that goal, His *ecclesia*."[30] With such an emphasis, kerygmatic theology takes on the form of a new ecclesiology in which the neglect of the historical Jesus, on the one hand, and its positive interest in grounding the church's Christology and sacraments in this historical Jesus, on the other, seem to contradict each other.

To what degree this view of the church may correctly appeal to the results of New Testament research is still debatable on many points. The methodological difficulties are very noticeable here. Wherever we see in the Gospels a direct agreement with the Christology and the community life of the primitive church, the critical question arises as to whether or not such ideas were only subsequently dated back into Jesus' earthly life. And yet, the christological interpretation of the resurrection appearances and the subsequent formation of the church can hardly be understood if the words of Jesus had not already paved the way for both the Christology and the ecclesiology of the primitive church. Therefore, in such questions it is extremely difficult to attain, negatively or positively, any certain results; the classic example of this is the ever-fluctuating debate concerning the word of Jesus to Peter in Matthew 16. In other instances, such as the choosing and sending out of the Twelve or the words of the Lord's Supper, we may assume with a greater degree of certainty that the words concerned go back to Jesus himself. As far as Christology is concerned, not only the post-Easter proclamation of the disciples but also the fact of Jesus' crucifixion proves how easy it was to assume that he himself intended to be the Messiah, even though he did not proclaim himself publicly as such. The consciousness of authority inherent in his preaching and his total attitude over against the Jewish authorities and persons points in the same direction.

It is natural for the church to be interested in what can be rendered probable on this issue, but historical research never proceeds beyond probability. The certainty of faith rests upon the proclaimed gospel and not upon what science does or does not have to say concerning Jesus' messianic self-consciousness. Likewise, the certainty of belonging to the church of God relies on the fact that by his death Jesus gained a people for God's own possession, and not upon arguments that the ministry of the historical Jesus had the formation of a church as its goal.

The "new ecclesiology" has avoided a danger that threatens other forms of kerygmatic theology—namely, the danger of disengaging the gospel from real history, the danger of kerygmatic-theological Docetism. Instead, another danger threatens. It would be not only scientifically suspect but also theologically fatal if interest in the historical Jesus should limit itself to rendering it probable that Jesus' own work aimed at his *ekklēsia*. Fridrichsen is essentially correct in asserting that the unity of the New Testament can be affirmed only when Jesus is seen in unity with the church and not in categories of personalistic idealism.[31] The danger in such a formulation is that this unity (between Jesus and the church) could be understood as an identity by which Jesus Christ is dissolved into the church, into its proclamation and dogma, its cultus and office.

Thus it is also a theological necessity to keep the question concerning the historical Jesus alive and open, at least for the reason that the independence of Jesus over against the church must be maintained. Jesus already exists before and outside of the church's proclamation; he may be absorbed neither by the existential here-and-now of the kerygma nor by the tradition and the church. This independence of Jesus is not to be understood as an isolation of Jesus, as was the case with the "back to Jesus" slogan. It does mean, however, that Jesus is present not only in the church and its proclamation but also—first and foremost—in that he stands over against the church in sovereign freedom. Research on the historical Jesus must continually refer to this independence. It does so simply and primarily by recalling the basic, historical fact that Jesus was a Jew, "sprung from the seed of David according to the flesh." Through Jesus the church is bound to the Scriptures of the Old Testament and to the sacred history of Israel. That the church is the legitimate successor of the people of God of the Old Covenant cannot, however, be proved with historical exactitude. The people of Israel continued to exist alongside the church in the midst of many sufferings that were often inflicted upon them by the believers in Christ, but Christ is an Israelite according to the flesh, and research on the historical Jesus makes this explicitly clear to us. For the church this fact signifies a continual warning against ecclesiastical self-sufficiency and self-confidence. Paul was aware of this (see Romans 11), but the church after him has only too often forgotten it.

Not only the fact that Jesus belonged to Israel but also the nature of his historical influence within Israel constitutes a warning against that form of self-contented ecclesiasticism. The preaching and the appearance of Jesus attest to his deep unity and solidarity with his people, the people of God. In this solidarity, however, he appears as a man whose word and work are a judgment upon all

Jewish ecclesiasticism; temple worship, scriptural erudition, pious practice, the basic attitude of those who trust in the privileges of the people of God—nothing is spared. This Jesus who chastens and reprimands the people of God is the Lord of the church, in whom we believe. This is made unmistakably clear by research on the historical Jesus and has certain necessary consequences, namely, that even the church of the new people of God stands under his judgment and under the reprimand that proceeds from him: the living Lord who is none other than he who once lived in Israel, the historical Jesus. When the church is unconcerned about the historical Jesus, this will only too easily lead to its ignoring his warning against all ecclesiastical self-sufficiency. Already in the case of the evangelists, and especially in Matthew, we can observe how Jesus' warning words of judgment to the Jews have received a new addressee and serve as a warning to the members of the new community (cf. Matt. 7:22ff. with Luke 13:25ff.).[32]

To be indifferent to the concrete, earthly history of Jesus for the sake of principles leads to the danger that kerygma will not be related to the concrete, everyday life of humans, but only to an abstract understanding of existence or only to the sacred realm of the church. The preacher stands basically in the same post-Easter situation as the evangelists and is bound to the interpretation of the history of Jesus by the apostolic proclamation transmitted in the New Testament. Still, the preacher must be allowed to go back to the alleged original meaning of a word—a process analogous with the procedure of the evangelists—in order to proclaim it, in view of the post-Easter situation and the change of audience, as a word of the Lord to the community of his time. Because of the special authority already ascribed to the words of the Lord in the New Testament, we cannot regard the question concerning the historical genuineness or nongenuineness of a word as completely irrelevant for theology.[33] Yet, for preaching and dogmatic reflection this question becomes actual only in the cases where there is no real agreement of a word with the central kerygma; then, when objective historical criteria suggest that there is no authentic word of Jesus, we will more easily be able to disregard the word.

A dogmatic answer to the question of the theological relevance of Jesus research has not been given; rather, several viewpoints and observations have been stated. I think that this must be the case if scientific research on the historical Jesus is neither of fundamental significance nor totally irrelevant for faith and the church. Neither the historical-critical nor the theological problem of the historical Jesus is to be answered definitively, so that we could ever dispense with it. This problem signifies an element of unrest for the church, but this unrest is salutary and should remind us that Jesus is Lord of the church and that the church may not make itself lord over Jesus. To the question Who was Jesus? the church answers with its praising confession. The church will not go astray because of the alleged results of the life-of-Jesus research. It also would be true not to its confession but rather to pride if it were to declare itself on principle disinterested in the work of sober historical research.

It can be temporarily beneficial to New Testament research to leave behind attempts at historical reconstruction in order to work at other tasks in which there are greater possibilities of obtaining fruitful and certain results. But we cannot on principle, or for any length of time, ignore the problem of the historical Jesus. Even scholars who stand within the church and who would serve the church by their work cannot allow themselves to be ordered by ecclesiastical courts regarding the results they must obtain. Indeed, New Testament scholars will be interested in a cooperative effort with colleagues in systematic theology because they can make clear whether, with the historical methods necessary for such work, they have also appropriated a definite historical and ideological tradition that is not appropriate for the investigation. We should neither expect nor desire that the church's preaching and dogmatic reflection be built on the uncertain ground of research on the historical Jesus. Rather, we should retain an openness and truthfulness toward this research. We must expect of dogmatic work in Christology that it not avoid the problem of the historical Jesus but have a concern for a better solution than the historical life-of-Jesus theology and the dehistoricizing kerygmatic theology.

Notes

[1]This essay originally appeared in a collection of lectures entitled *Rett lære og kjetterske meninger* (Oslo, 1953). The revised German draft still gives evidence that the essay was written also for nontheologians, which accounts for a certain breadth and scope in presentation.

[2]A. Schweitzer, *The Quest of The Historical Jesus* (trans. W. Montgomery; New York: Macmillan, 1948) 3.

[3]Ibid. 4.

[4]A. Jülicher, *Die Gleichnisreden Jesu* I (Tübingen: Mohr, 1910) 144.

[5]W. Wrede, *The Messianic Secret* (trans. J. C. G. Greig; Greenwood, S.C.: Attic, 1972) 6.

[6]J. Wellhausen, *Einleitung in die drei ersten Evangelien* (Berlin: Reimer, 1905) 114.

[7]J. Weiss, *Predigt Jesu vom Reiche Gottes* (Göttingen: Vandenhoeck & Ruprecht, 1982) v (ET, *Jesus' Proclamation of the Kingdom of God* [Philadelphia: Fortress, 1971]).

[8]Schweitzer, *Quest* 396.

[9]Ibid. 397.

[10]Gösta Lindeskog has written the history of this research in *Die Jesusfrage im neuzeitlichen Judentum* (Uppsala, 1938). Cf. also *Judaica* 6 (1950) 190–229, 241–68.

[11]Wellhausen, *Einleitung* 396.

[12]Ibid. 115.

[13]Schweitzer, *Quest* 401.

[14]Cf. E. Käsemann, *Essays on New Testament Themes* (trans. W. G. Montague; Naperville, Ill.: Allenson, 1964) 15ff.

[15]E. Stauffer, "Der Stand der neutestamentlichen Forschung," in *Theologie und Liturgie* (ed. L. Henning; Kassel: Johannes Stauda, 1952) 35–105. Cf. his *Jesus and His Story* (trans. R. Winston and C. Winston; New York: Knopf, 1960).

[16]Cf. my essay "Die Passionsgeschichte bei Matthäus, *NTS* 2 (1955–56) 17–32 (translated as "The Passion Narrative in Matthew," in *Jesus in the Memory of the Early Church* [Minneapolis: Augsburg, 1976] 37–51).

[17]Joachim Jeremias, *The Parables of Jesus* (trans. S. H. Hooke; New York: Scribners, 1955) 20–28.

[18]Julius Schniewind's remarks in "Zur Synoptikerexegese," *TRu* 2 (1930) 129–89, are still of value, and particularly his discussion of "longitudinal" and "cross-section exegesis." On the questions of method, cf. also C. H. Dodd, *History and the Gospel* (London: James Nisbet, 1938).

[19]Käsemann, *Essays* 37.

[20]Stauffer, "Der Stand" 93.

[21]Wellhausen, *Einleitung* 115.

[22]Here, the starting point of C. F. W. Smith, *The Jesus of the Parables* (Philadelphia: Westminster, 1948) 17, is correct: "Jesus used parables and Jesus was put to death. The two factors are related and it is necessary to understand the connection." On the exposition of the parables, cf. also my essay "The Parables of Growth," *ST* 5 (1951) 132–66 (in *Jesus in the Memory of the Early Church* 141–66).

[23]Hans Freiherr von Campenhausen, *Tradition and Life in the Early Church* (Philadelphia: Fortress, 1968) 42–89.

[24]Cf. R. Bultmann, *Faith and Understanding* I (ed. and trans. R. W. Funk and L. P. Smith; New York: Harper & Row, 1969) 206.

[25]R. Bultmann, *Theology of the New Testament* I (trans. K. Grobel; New York: Scribner's, 1951) 165f.

[26]On this cf. my review article, appendix A in this volume.

[27]Bultmann, *Theology* I, 8.

[28]Cf., e.g., Bultmann, *Faith and Understanding* I, 237f.

[29]Cf. especially Albert Schweitzer, *The Mysticism of Paul the Apostle* (trans. W. Montgomery; New York: Macmillan, 1955) 113–15, 389–96. In addition, cf. also Rudolf Bultmann, "Jesus and Paul," in *Existence and Faith* (ed. Schubert M. Ogden; New York: Meridian Books, 1960) 183–201.

[30]A. Fridrichsen, *This Is the Church* (ed. Anders Nygren et al., trans. Carl C. Rasmussen; Philadelphia: Muhlenberg, 1952) 22.

[31]Anton Fridrichsen et al., *The Root of the Vine* (London: Dacre, 1953) 60.

[32]Cf. Jeremias, *Parables* 25–28.

[33]On this question cf. W. Michaelis, "Notwendigkeit und Grenze der Erörterung von Echtheitsfragen innerhalb des Neuen Testaments," *TLZ* 77 (1952) 398–402.

6

Sources of
Christological Language

The State of the Question

THE TOPIC of my presidential address is a variation of a theme with which generations of scholars have dealt. The discussion has often centered on the relationship between christological doctrine and the historical Jesus, between the gospel of Jesus and the gospel about Jesus. There has also been an ongoing debate about Jewish and Greek components in the New Testament writings that identify Jesus both as the promised Messiah and as the eternal Logos. The debate continued even when scholars learned to distinguish between the classical Greek tradition and Hellenism and between the ancient religion of Israel and what was called *Spätjudentum*—a misleading but convenient term. As more source materials have become available, explanations of the background and origin of Christology have multiplied. An early example of this would be Lobeck's *Aglaophamus*, followed by Gfroerer's *Jahrhundert des Heils*.

The publication of Jewish apocalyptic literature had a great impact on scholarship. Jesus was assumed to have understood himself as the transcendent "Son of Man" rather than as the national Messiah (G. Baldensperger, A. Schweitzer, etc.). Even Paul's Christology could be explained as deriving from a Jewish concept of the eschatological redeemer, into which Jesus' earthly life, death, and resurrection had been inserted (W. Brueckner, W. Wrede). More often, representatives of the history-of-religions school, from H. Gunkel onward, explained Pauline and Johannine Christology as products of Hellenistic religious syncretism, influenced, for example, by the mystery religions, with their dying and rising gods.

Apocalyptic and syncretistic explanations were combined by Wilhelm Bousset, who in his *Kyrios Christos* distinguished between

113

early Jerusalem Christianity, which expected the coming of Jesus as the Son of Man, and pre-Pauline Hellenistic Christianity, which worshiped him as *kyrios*. In his historical reconstruction of early Christianity, Rudolf Bultmann followed in the steps of Bousset. The major difference was that Bultmann paid less attention to the analogy to the worship of Oriental gods as cult heroes and, more than Bousset, emphasized the gnostic Redeemer-myth, which, with critical variations, Christians transferred to Jesus. It would not be an overstatement to say that Bousset and Bultmann, more than any other scholars, have set the stage for the debate concerning the origins of Christology in my own generation. That is not to exclude contributions by the debate that developed in the first part of this century in Paris between scholars such as Alfred Loisy, Charles Guigneber, and Maurice Goguel. Perhaps Couchoud, one of the last and most intelligent advocates of a purely mythological explanation of Christology, should also be mentioned. The results of these scholars did not differ so very much from those of their radical German colleagues. But while the German debate largely centered upon the historical genesis and the theological interpretation of New Testament Christology, the approach of the French scholars was, in another intellectual context, similar to the socio-historical approach of Shirley Jackson Case and other members of the "Chicago school" in the United States.

Since the days of Bousset and Bultmann, or of Loisy and Goguel, our picture of early Christianity has become increasingly diversified. The shift was adumbrated in works of Walter Bauer and Ernst Lohmeyer. More recently, theories about concepts, models, and myths that influenced early Christology have become increasingly diversified, as a comparison of the works of Ferdinand Hahn and Reginald Fuller with those of Bousset and Bultmann reveals. Each of the major christological titles is investigated, and all of them turn out to be complex; three layers of tradition are distinguished: Palestinian Jewish, Hellenistic Jewish, and Gentile Christianity. Other scholars, such as Helmut Koester, prefer to distinguish among different types of tradition or, as Koester puts it, "four primitive Gospels"—that is, the cross-resurrection kerygma, sayings of Jesus, stories about Jesus as a divine man, and revelations from the risen Lord. A number of studies deal with the Christology of the hypothetical logia source (Q); others find traces of conflicting Christologies in extant New Testament writings. The discovery of the Dead Sea Scrolls and of the Nag Hammadi library have called widely accepted theories about the Son of Man and the gnostic redeemer into question while simultaneously suggesting new possibilities. Some also make new suggestions on the basis of familiar data. Charles Talbert, for example, places Christ among the "immortals" (and the "eternals"); Morton Smith writes about "Jesus the Magician," using magical papyri as a major source of comparative materials.

During the last three decades, new source materials have enriched the debate, fresh questions have been posed, methods have been refined—yet no scholarly consensus has emerged. That is no cause for astonishment, for theories about the background and origin of Christology have always been controversial. But today the theories have become so numerous and so complicated that it is difficult to know even what to discuss and about what to disagree. The present state of the question concerning sources of christological language calls for a comprehensive survey and for some critical reflection. It is an impossible task, not least for a single lecture, but the honor of being elected president of the Society for New Testament Studies has given me the requisite audacity, not to say hybris, to forge an attempt.

Approach

The state of the question might call for criticism of current methods. We might question the value of parallels, for example, or the limitation and propriety of causal explanations in historical research. It would also be possible to discuss what might be learned from other disciplines and approaches, for example, linguistic or philosophical semantics, social science, anthropology, literary criticism, and even structuralism. A mastery of some of these disciplines would certainly have sharpened my analytical tools. I have not adopted any specific method or terminology, however, but wish rather to offer some reflections as a New Testament scholar who has been at the game for quite some time, and who has in the process acquired some awareness of what is taking place. I have chosen to speak about christological language because this term is both more comprehensive and more neutral than terms such as "christological doctrine" or "kerygma." "Christological language" is shorthand for what those who believed in Jesus after his death said about him, as well as for the ways in which they spoke about him.

Scholars have thoroughly investigated the vocabulary of christological language, especially the titles of Jesus. By comparison, only sporadic attention has been paid to a systematic description of the syntax of christological language, beginning with questions concerning what roles various designations of Jesus play in Greek sentences and concerning possible semantic transformations of these sentences. To take the simplest example, even equative clauses that state what or who Jesus is can have several meanings, depending upon the context. "Jesus is the Christ" can mean that Jesus is the Christ and not Elijah or one of the prophets; it can also mean that he and no one else is the Christ.

Before attending to the question whether christological titles are interchangeable or express different conceptions, we should observe how they are used. Jesus is identified as Christ, the Son of God. He is also acclaimed as Kyrios. We never encounter, however, a statement that Jesus *is* the Son of Man. (Ignatius says that he was *a* son of man.) Attention to syntax proves, among other things, that christological titles were not all of the same order. It can also help overcome the tendency to treat Christology in isolation from theology and from actual life. New Testament authors frequently insert a reference to Jesus, for example, in the form of a prepositional phrase or a subordinate clause, while speaking about something else, thus providing warrants for their arguments or exhortations. Such passing references may tell us as much about the significance of Jesus for the actual life of early Christians as do thematic statements about who he was and what he did and experienced. I should also add that talk about Jesus, like other forms of speech, has not only a vocabulary and a syntax; we can also observe larger units of composition, which often follow more or less conventional patterns and can be analyzed in terms of style and form. I need not say more about this topic, since form-critical analysis of kerygmatic summaries, confessions, hymns, stories about Jesus, and the like is a well-cultivated field. My topic is not the vocabulary, syntax, and composition but the sources of christological language.

When I speak of "sources," I do not wish to suggest the image of remote sources from which a number of small streams flow, later merging to form a wide river. No such causal nexus can do justice to the way in which early Christology took shape. I prefer to visualize the sources as springs from which people draw water. In other words, the sources are linguistic resources—words, phrases, forms, and patterns of composition—that existed prior to their use in speaking about Jesus. The approach is synchronic more than diachronic. The following sketch offers a description of data more than a causal explanation, but it does not preclude some reflection on the genesis of Christology.

The sources of christological language may be classified according to several criteria. One can distinguish among various linguistic, geographical, cultural, and religious environments; chronological criteria are also possible. One can also arrange the materials according to various titles for Jesus or according to forms of discourse and literary genres. For the purpose of this survey I have chosen a different set of categories. My question is simply this: To what extent did Christian speech about Jesus have analogies and precedents in what was said about different types of persons and beings? Using this approach to classification, we can identify at least four major types of sources for christological language: (1) language about the Messiah and other eschatological figures; (2) language used about men of God and heroes of various types; (3) language used to speak of heavenly intermediaries and agents; (4) language used to speak of God. Since the data are familiar, it will be sufficient to comment briefly on each of these categories.

FOUR MAJOR CATEGORIES

Eschatological Figures

Jewish eschatological expectations were fluid. Some texts spoke only of God's redemption of his people, others about an angelic agent. An anointed king from the house of David was almost certainly the most popular figure, but there were also hopes for the coming of a prophet like Moses, for the return of Elijah, for a legitimate high priest, and for other figures as well. A number of biblical passages contained promises that referred to, or could be read as referring to, one or another of these figures. Selection and interpretation of these passages, however, were open to considerable variation; several figures could be juxtaposed or identified with one another. There is little, if any, evidence for pre-Christian use of the word *Māšîaḥ* (or *ha-māšîaḥ*) as a technical term for the Davidic Messiah. Nevertheless, there is little doubt that the title "the Anointed" identified Jesus as the person to whom the promises to David and his offspring applied. *Christos* soon became a second, honorific name of Jesus, but this fact attests that the designation of Jesus as the Anointed One must have been current already in the Aramaic period, prior to the beginnings of the mission to Greek-speaking Jews and Gentiles.

In order to speak about Jesus as the Anointed, early believers used and interpreted messianic prophecies like Nathan's oracle in 2 Samuel 7, the prophecy of Isaiah 11, as well as Psalms 2, 89, and 110. Statements about the prophet like Moses in Deuteronomy, about the messenger of good tidings in Isaiah 42 and the suffering servant in Isaiah 53, about the pierced one in Zechariah 12, and about the Son of Man in Daniel 7 were also interpreted and used as statements about Jesus the Messiah. In short, early Christian use of messianic language is both selective and cumulative. Other groups, like the Qumran covenanters, preferred other selections, combinations, and interpretations. What is amazing is the degree to which the image of Jesus the Christ diverges from all known variants of "messianic" expectations. It is true that early Christians did use elements from Daniel 7 or Isaiah 11 to talk about the parousia of Jesus. But the title "the Christ" is as a matter of fact only rarely associated with the work of Christ at his second coming. Terms like *parousia, epiphaneia,* or "the day of the Lord" do not derive from traditional messianic language. The hope for the parousia of Jesus was not simply a hope that in the near future Jesus would act as the Messiah (or Son of Man) was expected to. It was rather a hope that Jesus, the crucified Messiah, whom God had vindicated by raising him from the dead, would soon be publicly vindicated over against his enemies and redeem those who had put their hope in him.

Early Christians quite consciously used what tradition had said about the Messiah to speak about Jesus. But this does not mean that they transferred any given concept to him. They used biblical and current messianic language to say things about Jesus that had never been said about any Jewish eschatological figures or about any messianic pretender or eschatological prophet. This should be kept in mind as the other sources of christological language are considered.

Men of God and Heroes

This is a comprehensive category with many subspecies. I have used the terms "men of God" and "heroes" because both terms are rather vague. The vagueness of this category is intentional; by employing these terms I wish to indicate that both Jewish and Gentile figures come into play here. Perhaps it would have been

better to use even more ambiguous terms such as "holy men" or
homo religiosus, provided that these terms do not evoke connotations
of personal piety but rather designate persons who possess a religious vocation, who inspire awe and fascination, and who may
evoke feelings of respect as well as animosity.

This broad category includes sacred kings and charismatic leaders, sages and prophets, thaumaturges and magicians, saints and
martyrs. The term *theios anēr* has been widely employed in recent
debate, but its usefulness has also been contested (Carl Holladay).
Talbert prefers to speak about "the immortals." Much of what is
told about Jesus has analogies in stories about other men of God
and legendary heroes. He is depicted as a teacher of wisdom and
interpreter of the will of God, as a prophet, a charismatic leader
who called others to follow him, a miracle worker and exorcist.
Many heroes and men of God had to suffer trials and adversity,
some even a violent death. The death of the seven brothers under
Antiochus Epiphanes was considered to have been vicarious, and
we also hear about God's vindication of his righteous servants (e.g.,
Wisdom 1–5). Stories relating the miraculous birth of divine men
and "immortals," the disappearance of their bodies after death,
postmortem appearances, their assumption to heaven and instal-
lation in some heavenly office were also told. As random examples
I may mention Hercules and Romulus, Alexander, Augustus, and
Apollonius of Tyana. Jews hesitated to call a man *theios* or to speak
about his apotheosis, but Enoch, Elijah, and, according to some
traditions, Moses were taken up to heaven and continued their
ministry in new forms.

No other type of source material provides as many parallels
to the story of Jesus. The problem is that the analogies are so
numerous and so diverse. Several New Testament authors draw
their portrait of Jesus in analogy and contrast to the life of Moses.
The Fourth Gospel, Matthew, Luke-Acts, and Hebrews do so, each
in a particular manner. Hebrews combines the Moses typology with
a Melchizedek typology; other types and analogies were employed
as well, including Isaac, Joseph, David and Solomon, the son of
David, Elijah, and Jonah. For the most part, however, it is difficult
to trace stories about Jesus or statements of Jesus as a man of God
to any particular source. The history of religion is full of holy men
and legends, which have various features of family resemblance in
common. Jesus' contemporaries must already have had the impression that he was "a man of God," a *homo religiosus*, but that he
did not quite fit into any of the known categories. Later, the story

of Jesus would be told in the form of a narrative about a man of God. But the evangelists used the genre to make it clear that Jesus was not to be categorized as one among many men of God.

Heavenly Intermediaries

To proceed from heroes and men of God to heavenly agents of God is akin to moving from a swamp where water puddles crop up here and there back to firm ground where springs are easily located. Jesus can be identified as the Word (*logos*), the Image (*eikōn*) and the Effulgence (*apaugasma*) of God, as well as the mediator of creation and of revelation and redemption. The principal texts are well known: the prologue to the Fourth Gospel, the hymn in Colossians 1:15-20, and the opening verses of Hebrews; also 1 Corinthians 8:6, Philippians 2:6f., and Revelation 3:14. It is generally recognized that such christological statements make use of a type of language once employed to speak about Wisdom and other hypostatized attributes and manifestations of God. Traces of "Wisdom Christology" are also present in statements about the risen Christ as the agent of God's action. Some Synoptic and several Johannine sayings of Jesus (e.g., "Come to me, all who labor . . ." [Matt. 11:28]; "He who eats my flesh . . ." [John 6:56]) make use of a type of language earlier attributed to Wisdom (e.g., Matt. 11:28-30; John 4:14; 6:35, 37; 7:37). I hardly need add that this type of language was of special importance for the later formulation of the dogma about Jesus as the eternal Son and Logos, the second divine person or hypostasis. This is the most "dogmatic" category.

From Justin Martyr, probably even Hermas, orthodox Christians spoke about Jesus as an angel. Old Testament angelophanies were taken to refer to appearances of the eternal Logos. No New Testament author explicitly speaks about Christ as an angel or as the angel or archangel. The Book of Revelation, however, transfers angelic attributes to the risen Christ (e.g., Rev. 1:13-16—cf. especially Dan. 10:5f.). Moreover, the risen Jesus is, like an angelic prince, represented as the heavenly Paraclete, the intercessor or witness, the priest in the heavenly sanctuary, and vice-regent at the right hand of God. He is the revealer of mysteries and bearer of the divine name (cf. Exod. 23:21 and the notion of the highest angelic prince as the "lesser YHWH"). There are also angelological precedents for the terminology of descent and ascent, as well as for the sudden appearances and disappearances of the risen Christ in the Easter stories. To my knowledge, we have no comprehensive study to replace W. Lueken's *Michael*, but there seems to be increasing agreement that angelology is one source of christological language.

The notion of gnostic redeemer myths as possible christological models warrants brief comment here. The Nag Hammadi texts have confirmed the existence of non-Christian gnosis and of gnostic redeemer figures. But the theory of R. Reitzenstein concerning a pre-Christian model myth of the "redeemed Redeemer," which Bultmann took over and refined, has not been confirmed. It would rather seem that various men of God, primeval heroes, or heavenly intermediaries could be represented as revealers of saving gnosis. As far as I can see, the most specific gnostic elements—the split in the deity and the distinction between an inferior agent of creation and the mediator of saving revelation—are likely to have emerged in the second or late first century in connection with a revolt of heterodox Jews against the strictly monotheistic representatives of emerging normative Judaism (A. Segal). Neither the New Testament authors nor their opponents presuppose a split of this type. It is therefore unlikely that first-century Christians took over some features of a full-blown gnostic redeemer myth and eliminated others. The gnostic transmutation of heavenly intermediaries (Wisdom, Logos, Eikon, the secondary manifestations of the deity, and the supreme angelic prince) provides illuminating analogies but not sources for christological use of the same concepts. To some extent, the gnostic texts may also teach us something about pregnostic use of terms or about esoteric exegesis of the early chapters of Genesis. To that extent (to give just one example), Bultmann's collection of evidence for a Logos concept less philosophical than Philo's may well remain relevant.

Language about God

According to orthodox dogmatics, Jesus is true God and true man. Ignatius of Antioch already uses the noun *theos* in reference to Jesus quite frequently. The same usage occurs in the New Testament, but only in relatively few and late passages. Transfer of language about God to Jesus, however, is discernable at a much earlier stage. The most obvious example is the frequent application of Old Testament passages about the Lord (i.e., God) to Jesus, the Kyrios. As L. Cerfaux has pointed out, Paul usually employs *kyrios* as a reference to God when he explicitly quotes a passage and may have checked the quotation. The christological reference is more common in loose quotations and allusions. Pre-Pauline usage is attested in common phrases like "the day of the Lord," "the name of the Lord," "the word (spirit, glory, or table) of the Lord." The transfer cannot have occurred without some reflection, especially since at least some early Christians are likely to have used Greek Bible manuscripts in which the written text had some form of transliteration of the Tetragrammaton. The hymn in Philippians 2 attests to the belief that God bestowed the name that is above every name (i.e., the Tetragrammaton) upon Jesus at his exaltation (Phil. 2:9; cf. Rev. 19:12). The Fourth Evangelist interprets Isaiah's vision of the King, YHWH Sabaoth, as a vision of the glory of the crucified Jesus (John 12:41). The notion that the Tetragrammaton or other names of God could, in some biblical texts, refer to the agent of God has analogies in angelological and gnostic texts, as well as in Philo. It is no longer possible to maintain that statements about YHWH can have been transferred to Jesus only by Christians who used solely the Septuagint Bible.

The use of "God language" to talk about Jesus is by no means limited to the use of *theos* and *kyrios*. The Book of Revelation designates Jesus as "the King of kings and Lord of lords" and as "the first and the last" (Rev. 19:16; 17:14; 1:17; 2:8, 13). It is impossible to go into further details on this point, though this particular issue merits further consideration. The standard works on New Testament Christology fail to deal adequately with the theological source of christological language. The same attributes, intentions, and actions can be ascribed to God and to Christ, and faith and hope, fear and love can be directed toward Christ as well as toward God. Only the Fourth Gospel deals quite explicitly with the relationship between the Father and the Son, stressing their unity and the identity of their actions. But even in other writings, theological and christological utterances condition one another in a variety of ways. What early Christian authors have to say about God's essence and attributes only seldom takes the form of general statements. They speak much more about how God in Christ has acted in his sovereign might, faithfulness and justice, mercy and love. Even a number of Jesus' parables are best understood on the assumption that they refer to God's way of acting, while at the same time explaining and defending Jesus' own attitude and actions.

My four categories are not exhaustive. I have not included examples of language used about Jesus with analogies in language used about pagan deities (e.g., the acclamation *heis kyrios*). Furthermore, there is a residuum of historical references (e.g., to the cross) and metaphors without close analogy in what was said about persons belonging in any of the four categories. Most of what the early Christians said about Jesus, however, can be subsumed under at least one. Some of the key christological titles contain components drawn from more than one, for example, "Son of God" as designation of the Anointed, the righteous man, the Logos, or an angel.

The four categories must also not be viewed as rigid types. There was some overlapping already in pre-Christian usage. "The prophet" is one type of a "man of God" but can also be an eschatological figure. Elijah was expected to return, to officiate in heaven, or to appear as a helper. "Son of David" has messianic connotations, but may also suggest some analogy with Solomon's wisdom and magic power. A man of God may be taken up to heaven and transformed into what Greeks would consider a divine, Jews an angelic, being. The reports about the elevation of Enoch in Jubilees 4 and in the Ethiopic, Slavonic, and Hebrew books of Enoch illustrate the growth of such traditions. There were Greek stories about gods who appeared in human form, and also some evidence that some Old Testament figures could be regarded as angelic princes who had descended to earth and appeared in human form (Jacob/Israel in the apocryphal Prayer of Joseph, probably Melchizedek in 11QMelch). As already mentioned, names of God (Tetragrammaton or Elohim, *theos* and *kyrios*) can, in some contexts, be taken to refer to the highest angel, to the Logos, or to powers of God. Judged by the standards of rabbinic orthodoxy, a "high" Christology was just one more example of the heresy of those who said that there were two powers in heaven (Segal). Yet even if we find transitions from one type to another, or fusions of several types, there is no full analogy to the fusion, or synthesis, of the categories such as we find in christological language.

OBSERVATIONS AND REFLECTIONS

History and Myth

The main point of my cursory survey has been to demonstrate the diversity of source materials that have to be taken into consideration. Early Christology is too complex to be explained by theories of adoption or adaptation or by the combination of a limited series of models or myth. Proposals include the Suffering Servant and the Son of Man, Oriental Kyrios-deities of dying and rising gods of the mystery religions, the gnostic redeemer, or the *theios anēr*. In several cases, the desire to find a model for Christology in the history of religions has contributed to the reconstruction of the model. Theories about a comprehensive pre-Christian myth that was attached to a Jesus who never existed are the most obvious, but not the only examples.

If the term "myth" is to be applied, one would have to speak about the mythopoetic creativity of early Christians, who thought and spoke about Jesus as about a divine person and thereby created a new myth of the crucified and vindicated Messiah, the Son of God. Like other myths, the myth of the crucified Messiah is attested in several versions; but that is a natural result of mythopoetic creativity. Nor is the interplay between history and myth anything unique to Christian dogma. Mythology has been defined as the use of this-worldly terms to speak about the transcendent. More recent scholarship prefers to view mythology as a way of speaking about the ultimate meaning of cultic actions, historical events, and social realities. The history of religions provides analogies, not only to many components of christological language, but also to an interplay in which mythological language was adapted to new realities and historical events gave shape to new myths. Examples would range from sacred kingship in the ancient Near East to charismatic kings and emperors (Alexander and Augustus), to "religious entrepreneurs" in late antiquity. As the term "myth" carries with it pejorative connotations, we may also speak about an interplay of history and eschatology in early Christianity, about a process in which Jesus was "theologized" and "theology" (in the broad as well as in the narrow senses of the word) was, in a new way, related to historical events.

Forms of Discourse

The various christological titles express only to a limited degree different concepts that can be traced back to diverse sources. There is also some correlation, but no complete correspondence, between the types of sources and units of speech that can be distinguished form-critically. Miracle stories were told about Jesus as a prophet and man of God. In the sayings tradition he appears as a sage, a teacher who with authority announces the will of God. Missionary preaching centered on the proclamation of the crucified and risen Christ. Christ appears as the heavenly mediator of revelations in literary apocalypses and perhaps also in some forms of prophetic speech. References to Christ as the mediator of creation have their principal setting in hymns and hymnlike commemorations used in parenetic contexts. Coordination of God and Christ frequently occurs in formulas of greeting and blessing, occasionally also in statements about judgment. The transfer of statements about God to Jesus is most easily observed in scriptural quotations and allusions, but interpretation of Scripture was also an important setting for arguments about Jesus as "the Anointed."

If we turn to individual authors, we observe that each exhibits individual preferences while drawing little or not at all from some of the main types of sources. There are few, if any, traces of traditional messianic language in the Johannine epistles; the confession that Jesus is the Christ apparently means that the heavenly Christ, the Son of God, is identical with Jesus, not that Jesus is the Messiah of eschatological expectations. Paul considers the sayings of Jesus as normative rules, and he must have known traditions about his miracles, but in his letters he rarely represents Jesus as a "man of God." The Apocalypse calls Jesus the "faithful witness" and represents him as the slain lamb who has been vindicated and who soon will vindicate his persecuted followers, but otherwise the "man of God" category is even less prominent than in the letters of Paul. Luke, by contrast, makes use of the etymological meaning of *Christos* and depicts Jesus as a man who was anointed by the Spirit to heal and to preach (Luke 4:18-19); as God's anointed he also had to suffer (Luke 24:26, 46). Luke stresses that it was the God of the fathers who raised his servant Jesus and seems to avoid christological statements that might give monotheistic Jews and God-fearers the impression that Christians were "two-powers heretics." Even in Luke-Acts, however, we find examples of the transfer of God language to Jesus (e.g., Acts 2:21). In general, all the individual authors draw from more than one of the main categories of sources; they differ in their emphasis and in the way they select, combine, and use the various types of language.

It is unlikely that things were much different in the earliest years, from which we have no literary evidence. In order to get back to pre-Pauline Christianity, we must rely on formal units of tradition in Paul's letters. But it would be incorrect to conclude that the earliest Christians spoke about Jesus in stereotyped ways. I would suppose that they used a less-stereotyped language than we find in the written texts. There is no evidence and little reason to think that there ever existed communities that possessed a pure form of Christology, characterized by the use of language from one of my four types of sources, or by one type of preaching and one christological title.

The one possible exception would be the tradition of sayings of Jesus, as contained in the "logia source," in the Gospel of Thomas, and in the sayings (*rhēmata*) incorporated into the Johannine discourses. According to all of these traditions, salvation depends upon response to the words of Jesus—hearing, believing, or understanding. The title "Christ" is seldom if ever used, and the christological language differs from that of the Pauline and pre-Pauline kerygmas. The sayings tradition may well represent a special type of preaching and teaching, carried on by itinerant apostles and prophets who continued the type of mission that began during Jesus' lifetime. There is no proof, however—and to me it seems rather unlikely—that there ever existed communities that knew only this type of preacher and this type of discourse about Jesus.

Traces of Historical Developments

Interest in sources for and influences upon early Christology has mostly been tied to attempts to reconstruct the origin and early development of christological doctrine. A diachronic approach is, of course, legitimate, and in many instances it is indeed possible to distinguish between secondary and more primitive layers of tradition and between earlier and later uses of titles and terminology. For several reasons, however, it has turned out that an attempt to integrate such observations into a comprehensive pattern of development faces greater difficulties than previous generations of scholars assumed. It has become increasingly clear that the diversity within first-century Christianity must have been considerably greater than is apparent from the differences among those writings that eventually were included in the New Testament. Various trends must have existed simultaneously and even in the same areas.

Another complicating factor is that we have no direct sources for the most seminal stage of development, the period before the genuine letters of Paul, which already presuppose the existence of a highly developed christological language. Paul's thought and speech may to some extent have changed over the years, but I see no reason to doubt that the faith that he preached was in substance identical with the faith that he had once persecuted. Martin Hengel is right, I think, in maintaining that the most important development of Christology must have taken place within a remarkably short period of time. The evidence that we possess indicates that Paul and Peter disagreed about the consequences to be drawn from faith in Jesus Christ, not about christological doctrines. There is little reason to doubt that the type of preaching that centered on the crucifixion, resurrection, enthronement, and future coming of Christ can be traced back to Peter. In retrospect, the overall picture is clear: the main line of development seems to have passed from Peter through Barnabas and Paul to the churches of Gentile Christians at the end of the first century; but the details of that picture must have been considerably more complex. The Johannine tradition is likely to have developed within a sectarian group of Christian Jews. The appearance of the Fourth Gospel in its present form, however, marks the point at which this special current flowed into the mainstream of Petrine Christianity. In different ways, nearly all New Testament writings draw some line separating true from false teaching. Furthermore, both apocryphal gospels and second-century writings such as the Shepherd of Hermas are likely to draw upon traditions that go back to the first century.

In order to integrate data and observations into a comprehensive scheme of historical development, scholars need some generalized theory. Some such theories, which do not necessarily exclude one another, have at times been widely accepted. F. C. Baur operated with a dialectical pattern of opposing trends that found their resolution in a more comprehensive synthesis. The generations after Baur tended to reckon with a more unilateral development, an ongoing process of Hellenization, a shift from eschatology to ontological and protological categories (due to the lapse of time and the delay of the parousia), and an increasing tendency to think and speak about Jesus as about God. Each of these theories, or some combination of all of them, can fairly easily be applied to the general development from the beginnings of Christianity to Nicene and post-Nicene orthodoxy. They might also receive support from observations of what has happened or usually happens to movements with which early Christianity can be compared. Hellenization of Near Eastern religions was almost a universal phenomenon in the time of the Roman Empire. Regardless of time and place, the history of cults and chiliastic movements founded by or centering on a charismatic leader provide at least partial analogies to the social history of Christianity and the concomitant adaptation of doctrines.

All of this may be granted and could be spelled out in detail, but such general schemes do not provide criteria precise enough to allow for the arrangement of the varieties of christological language used by the New Testament authors into any clear diachronic sequence. With respect to my four major categories, one might assume that Christians initially spoke about Jesus as a man of God and a messianic figure, and only later, at a more developed stage, applied language used about heavenly mediators or about God himself to Jesus. Such an assumption, however, has no basis in the extant sources, in which heterogenous terms and phraseology are used contemporaneously and are often combined in the same documents. It is not unreasonable to assume that the earliest stage might reveal a similar situation, had we unmediated access to the sources.

The distinction among Palestinian, Hellenistic Jewish, and predominantly Gentile environments for early Christianity retains some heuristic value, but it does not yield precise criteria for construction of separate strata in the formation of Christology. Greek was spoken in Palestine, Aramaic outside of Palestine, and geography was by no means the sole, or even the most important, factor as far as the degree of Hellenization was concerned. Various, more or less similar trends existed both in Palestinian Judaism and in the Diaspora, and even within early Christianity it is more likely than not that there were crosscurrents (e.g., between Jerusalem and Antioch). The Gospel of Matthew presupposes a predominantly Jewish environment, yet it is dependent on Mark's work, which does not. The composition of at least one Jewish–Christian gospel in Hebrew or Aramaic confirms that the influence could go from "Hellenistic" back to Palestinian Christianity, not merely the other way around.

As for the types of christological language, it is obvious that the portrayal of Jesus as a charismatic prophet or exorcist included features that must have been more familiar to a non-Jewish than to a Jewish audience (e.g., John 2:23-25). By contrast, the accusation that Jesus was guilty of blasphemy because he, a man, made himself God is likely to be rooted in an inner-Jewish conflict between Johannine sectarians and their adversaries (cf. John 5:18; 10:33).

Like the process of Hellenization, the lapse of time and the delay of the parousia conditioned the long-range development of Christology. The first generation of believers did not only expect Jesus to appear in glory in the near future but also understood his first coming, death, and resurrection as eschatological events that inaugurated the realization of God's ultimate design for his people and his world. From the second century onward, attention focused much more upon the preexistence and incarnation of Christ, and the ascension of Jesus was understood as a return to heavenly glory rather than as a messianic enthronement. Even in this respect, however, the development was not unilateral. The hope for the imminent parousia could be revived again and again, and the use of messianic language could be reactualized and adapted to new settings, as in the writings of Luke and Justin. At an early stage, eschatological categories left room for the notion of preexistence. The New Jerusalem existed already in heaven, the kingdom had been prepared for those who were to inherit it, the blessings were already stored in the heavenly treasury, and so on. Even in pre-Christian Judaism the idea of an existence in heaven prior to appearance on earth was not exclusively used in an eschatological context. As the incorporation of God's wisdom, the Torah had been present with God before it was revealed on Mount Sinai (e.g., Sir. 24:23). We also find statements to the effect that God had made Moses beforehand, or the patriarchs, ready to appear on the stage of history when the time had come. Regardless of whether or not the notion of a preexistent Messiah is attested in pre-Christian Judaism, the possibility of ascribing an "eschatological preexistence" to Jesus did exist, even at the initial stages of christological doctrines (cf. R. G. Hamerton–Kelly).

Thinking in terms of eschatology, early Christians stressed that the crucified Jesus had been vindicated and enthroned as Messiah, Lord, and/or Son of God. This "adoptionist" language, however, did not imply that Jesus, prior to his exaltation, was merely a human agent of God. He was thought of, rather, as the Coming One (*ho erchomenos*—e.g., Matt. 11:3), who had already come in accordance with the plan and the promises of God, although his contemporaries had failed to recognize his true identity. What happened later was not simply a shift from adoptionist to incarnational language but rather that these two ways of speaking about Christ became mutually exclusive options when they were no longer held together within an eschatological framework.

Both Hellenization and the shift from eschatology to a metaphysical ontology went hand-in-hand with an increasing tendency to "theologize" Jesus. Christology originated as an answer to the question of the true identity of the prophet Jesus of Nazareth. The problem was turned around when it had become a dogma that the Son was of one being (*homoousios*) with the Father, as the second person of the Holy Trinity. Then it became difficult to explain the unification of the divine and the human nature in the incarnate

129

Jesus Christ. It would nevertheless be misleading to conceive of the historical development as a trajectory that led from a "low" to a "high" Christology; more appropriate would be a comparison of Christology with an index of prices, or charts of temperature in the spring—gradually, both prices and spring temperatures increase, but there are many ups and downs, and often a significant gap between the maximum and minimum on any given date. Some examples may illustrate what I mean. The Christology of Paul is higher than that of Luke/Acts, and the Christology of the Pastoral Epistles appears to be lower than that of Colossians and Ephesians.

What is more important, but less frequently observed, is that God language is often transferred to Jesus in references to the day of the Lord and the glorious epiphany of Jesus, who is to send out his angels to gather the elect, or to be the impartial judge of the living and the dead (e.g., Mark 13:27; 2 Cor. 5:10; Eph. 6:8-9; 2 Thess. 1:7-9; Rev. 2:23; 22:12; cf. 2 Clem. 1:1 and see T. F. Glasson, J. A. T. Robinson, and R. Aus). Dyadic formulas like "God the Father and our Lord Jesus Christ" have antecedents in Old Testament passages such as Exodus 14:31, "They believed in the LORD and in his servant Moses," and Psalm 2:2, ". . . against the LORD and his anointed." Applied to God, the Father, and the risen Christ, however, the dyadic formula became an expression of a "binitarian" faith. In a similar way the designation of God as the "God and Father of our Lord Jesus Christ" has ancient antecedents in references to Yahweh as the personal God of particular individuals. Christians, however, believed that God had demonstrated who he was by raising Jesus from the dead and bestowing all manner of blessings in Christ, and they inferred that God had been the God and Father of Jesus Christ already before he created the world (see Eph. 1:1-4; 1 Pet. 1:3-4, 18-21). The Jewish conviction that God had always been the God of Israel and the God of Abraham, Isaac, and Jacob makes it unlikely that Christians ever thought that God had become the Father of Jesus Christ at any particular point in time.

When Christians required an intellectual clarification of the relationship between God the Father and Jesus Christ, the Son of God, the language used of heavenly intermediaries proved most helpful, since it made it possible to maintain both the unity and the distinction between the two objects of faith and worship. The level of reflection was much lower in the first century than in later controversies about christological and trinitarian doctrine, but both "Wisdom Christology" and the representation of the risen Christ as God's heavenly vice-regent are already attested in the letters of

Paul. The language that allowed for the articulation of faith in Jesus in such terms was present both in the Palestinian environment as well as in the Jewish diaspora. It is quite possible, however, or even likely, that terms and scriptural passages referring to God were transferred to Jesus before it became customary to apply the heavenly-mediator category to the ascended and—later, I would think—to the preexistent Christ, and even to the earthly Jesus.

From the very beginning, faith in Jesus as the risen Christ contained elements that led beyond available analogies, including esoteric Jewish and Samaritan doctrines about the highest angelic prince (L. Hurtado, H. Odeberg). The difference is due not so much to the terms and concepts employed as to the manner and context in which they were employed. The attitude of the early Christians toward Jesus was more like their attitude toward God than toward any *deuteros theos* (second god) figure attested in mystical trends in contemporary Judaism. Valid arguments against Bousset's sharp distinction between Palestinian and Hellenistic Christianity were raised soon after the appearance of his *Kyrios Christos* (e.g., by L. Brun). The likelihood is that Christians in Jerusalem as well as in Antioch called upon the name of Jesus and praised him, performed exorcisms and healings in his name, or even addressed short prayers to him (see especially 1 Cor. 16:22, *marana tha*). The experiences at and after Easter, the Christophanies, and the experience that the Holy Spirit had been poured out upon believers do not suffice to explain the consequences of the events. The events themselves required interpretation, and the interpretations given them were conditioned by the impression that Jesus had made upon his adversaries, who accused and crucified him, and upon the disciples, for whom the Easter events became evidence that God had vindicated the crucified Messiah. Even before Easter, however, the religious attention of the disciples must have been focused upon Jesus. For them, the call to repentance was virtually identical with the call to listen to Jesus and follow him. Before any explicit Christology emerged, sayings and actions of Jesus had identified him in terms of the coming kingdom of God.

The Use of Christological Language

The question whether christological language, titles, and concepts can be traced back to Jewish, Greek, or syncretistic sources has turned out to be more complicated and less important than was once supposed, both by scholars who favored a syncretistic derivation and by those who tried to trace as much as possible back to Jewish origins. Hellenism and Judaism were not separate worlds. There were crosscurrents, and there was a common climate in which related religious trends assumed different forms within particular religions—pagan, Jewish, or Christian (Segal).

For students of christological origins it is especially important to realize that it matters relatively little how far christological language and ideas can be traced back to Old Testament writings as these are read by historians of Israelite religion. What matters are the Sacred Scriptures common to Jews and Christians as they were or could be interpreted in the first century. As Sacred Scriptures, they provided materials, warrants and backing, inspiration, norms and limits for what the early Christians said about Jesus Christ. Two aspects are of special importance. First, exclusive biblical monotheism was not called into question but remained the rule for the use of christological language, even for mythopoetic creativity and for the incorporation or rejection of ideas that stemmed from other sources. The formation of a redeemer myth within the framework of exclusive biblical monotheism was not without problems, however. It occasioned not only Jewish polemics but inner-Christian controversies as well. The trinitarian dogma was not simply the result of an increasing deification of Jesus; it was also an attempt to safeguard biblical monotheism.

The other aspect is hardly less important. Even Christians of Gentile origin learned to understand that as the Christ, Jesus was the Redeemer of God's people, not simply the savior of individuals or the cult hero of religious associations. This fact was important not only for ecclesiology but also for the social history of Christianity and, for better and for worse, for the relation between Christians and Jews, as well as for large segments of world history.

Several works on the origins of Christology speak about sources and influences in a manner that evokes the image of a complicated watershed—say the Mississippi water basin, in which water from innumerable sources runs through creeks and streams and finally comes together in the mighty river. It might be wise to exchange this image for the notion of a "language game," to use the term of Wittgenstein. Consider the game of chess. The pieces may be made from various material and possess a more or less artistic shape. One may study variations in form, or even the social conditions and forms of warfare that prevailed at the time in which the game originated. Even play strategy itself may vary, from a more romantic to a more scientific approach, and so on. What really matters, however, are the rules of the game. They allow for innumerable moves, so that one game of chess is never like any other. But if the basic rules are changed, it becomes a different game. In a somewhat similar way, it matters little whether the components of christological language are of Jewish or syncretistic, ultimately perhaps of Greek, Babylonian, or Iranian origin. What matters are the rules.

It is possible, I assume, to detect rules that more or less universally apply to all forms of religious and mythical language. As I have pointed out, very important rules for christological language were given in the Scriptures Christians received from the Jews. Yet the life, death, and resurrection of Jesus changed the rules. Whatever was said about God, or about the world and human existence in it, about sin and salvation, ethical conduct and matters of church, had to be related to Jesus in some way, or at least not contradict the rule of faith in Jesus Christ. Yet there may be room for a variety of Christologies that differ from one another as much as various games of chess, some of which are worth remembering, others not.

Concluding Reflections

The study of christological language has often suffered from oversimplification. Some comparative material has been stressed to the exclusion of other, whether the emphasis has been upon the Jewish or the syncretistic sources. Attempts to discover concepts, models, or myths that would help to explain the origins of Christology have often influenced the historical reconstruction of the model myth (e.g., the Son of Man or the "redeemed Redeemer"). Another methodological fallacy has involved the gathering of heterogenous data and the construction of a generalized ideal type (e.g., the *theios anēr*, the immortals, dying and rising gods, or the righteous sufferer) and the subsequent positing of abstract types and patterns as causal factors. I do not deny that such attempts can be illuminating; many such explanations contain some degree of plausibility. The problem is that there are too many of them, all of which cannot be true. In that respect, we may say that the study of christological origins has suffered from overexplanation as well as from oversimplification. The time may have come to lower the scientific claims for all causal derivations of Christology and to distinguish between available sources and causal factors.

I am inclined to propose that early Christians spoke about Jesus as they did because they had something to say about him and used available linguistic sources to say it. This starting point does not render the source for comparative material, parallels and sources, irrelevant. As far as possible and practicable, we should give heed to all analogies. Only by using analogies are we able to make meaningful utterances and understand what other people are saying, even though there are endless possibilities for saying things that have not been said before. The linguistic capacity of the early Christians was conditioned, and limited, by the linguistic tools and rules of their environments. They used the language, or languages, of the first century, including mythopoetic language, when they expressed their faith in Jesus—otherwise they could not have communicated with outsiders, or with one another.

New Testament scholarship is in a state of transition. That is always the case, but the themes and the constituency of this international meeting of biblical scholars indicate that the truism applies today more than ever. In the coming generation, the focus of scholarship may possibly shift from sources and influences to the structure, the literary use, and the sociological function of christological language (Keck). It is also possible, even likely, that the interest will not center upon Christology to the same extent as it has in my generation. There are some signs that the strange neglect of how the early Christians spoke about God will not be perpetuated. And after all, first-century Christians, including the New Testament authors, did not only speak about Jesus to proclaim a kerygma or to set forth a Christology. They referred to Jesus when they talked about many other matters and used "christological language" to do a number of things: to praise God, to give thanks and pray, to bless and, occasionally, to curse, to exhort and to give advice, and so forth. An increasing awareness of the manifold uses of what I have, in shorthand fashion, termed "christological language" will also give new shape to the hermeneutical problem. But the purpose of this address has not been to formulate a program for the future but simply to give one person's perspective on questions that have been at the center of New Testament studies in my generation.

Bibliography

Aus, Roger D. "Comfort in Judgment: The Use of the Day of the Lord and Theophany Traditions in 2 Thess. 1." Ph.D. diss., Yale University, 1971.

Baldensperger, Guillaume. *Die messianisch-apokalyptischen Hoffnungen des Judenthums*. Strasbourg: Heitz & Mendel, 1903.

Bauer, Walter. *Orthodoxy and Heresy in Earliest Christianity*. Ed. R. Kraft and G. Krodel. Philadelphia: Fortress, 1971.

Baur, F. C. *The Church History of the First Three Centuries*. London: Williams & Norgate, 1878–79.

Betz, H. D. *Lukian von Samosata und das Neue Testament*. Berlin: Akademie, 1961.

Bousset, Wilhelm. *Kyrios Christos*. Trans. J. E. Steely. Nashville: Abingdon, 1970.

Brueckner, W. *Die chronologische Reihenfolge, in welcher die Briefe des Neuen Testaments verfasst sind*. Haarlem, 1890.

Brun, Lyder. *Paulus und die Urgemeinde*. Giessen: Töpelmann, 1921.

Bultmann, Rudolf. *Theology of the New Testament*. 2 vols. Trans. Kendrick Grobel. New York: Scribner, 1951–55.

Case, Shirley Jackson. *Jesus: A New Biography*. New York: Greenwood, 1968.

Dahl, Nils A., and Alan Segal. "Philo and the Rabbis on the Names of God." *JSJ* 9 (1978) 1–29.

Daniélou, Jean. *Gospel Message and Hellenistic Culture*. Trans. J. A. Baker. Philadelphia: Westminster, 1973.

Fossum, Jarl. *The Name of God and the Angel of the Lord*. Tübingen: Mohr, 1985.

Fuller, Reginald. *The Foundations of New Testament Christology*. London: Lutterworth, 1965.

Gfroerer, August F. *Geschichte des Urchristentums*. 3 vols. Stuttgart: Schweigerbart's Verlagshandlung, 1838.

Glasson, T. F. *The Second Advent: The Origin of the New Testament Doctrine*. London: Epworth, 1945.

Goguel, Maurice. *The Birth of Christianity*. Trans. H. C. Snape. New York: Macmillan, 1954.

———. *Jesus the Nazarene—Myth or History?* Trans. F. Stephens. London: T. Fisher Unwin, 1926.

Hahn, Ferdinand. *The Titles of Jesus in Christology*. Trans. H. Knight and George Ogs. New York: World, 1969.

Hamerton–Kelly, R. G. *Pre-Existence, Wisdom, and the Son of Man: A Study of the Idea of Pre-Existence in the New Testament*. Cambridge: Cambridge University Press, 1973.

Hengel, Martin. *Between Jesus and Paul*. Trans. John Bowden. Philadelphia: Fortress, 1983.

Holladay, Carl. *Theios Anēr in Hellenistic Judaism*. Missoula, Mont.: Scholars Press, 1977.

Hurtado, Larry W. *One God, One Lord*. Philadelphia: Fortress, 1988.

Juel, Donald. *Messianic Exegesis*. Philadelphia: Fortress, 1988.

Keck, Leander. "Toward the Renewal of New Testament Christology," *NTS* 32 (1986) 362–77.

Knox, John. *Christ the Lord: The Meaning of Jesus in the Early Church*. Chicago: Willette, Clark, 1945.

Koester, Helmut, and J. M. Robinson. *Trajectories through Early Christianity*. Philadelphia: Fortress, 1971.

Lohmeyer, Ernst. *Das Urchristentum*. Göttingen: Vandenhoeck & Ruprecht, 1932.

Loisy, Alfred. *The Origins of the New Testament*. Trans. L. P. Jacks. London: Allen & Unwin, 1950.

Moxness, Halvor. *Theology in Conflict*. Leiden: Brill, 1980.

Odeberg, Hugo. *Third Enoch; or, The Hebrew Book of Enoch*. New York: Ktav, 1973.

Robinson, J. A. T. *Jesus and His Coming: The Emergence of a Doctrine*. London: SCM, 1957.

Schweitzer, Albert. *The Quest of the Historical Jesus*. New York: Macmillan, 1961.

Segal, Alan F. *Two Powers in Heaven*. Leiden, Brill, 1977.

Smith, Morton. *Jesus the Magician*. New York: Harper & Row, 1977.

Stauffer, Ethelbert. *New Testament Theology*. Trans. John Marsh. New York: Macmillan, 1956.

Talbert, Charles. "The Concept of the Immortals in Mediterranean Antiquity." *JBL* 94 (1975) 419–36.

Wetter, G. P. *Charis: Ein Beitrag zur Geschichte des ältesten Christentums*. Leipzig: Hinrich, 1913.

Wrede, Wilhelm. *Paul*. Trans. E. Lummis. Boston: American Unitarian Association, 1908.

7

The Atonement:
An Adequate Reward
for the Akedah?

BY THE ATONEMENT, I here understand the death of Jesus interpreted as a divine act of redemption, regardless of the specific terminology used by various writers. The Akedah means what in Christian tradition is called the sacrifice, and in Jewish tradition the binding of Isaac (ʿaqedat yiṣḥāq), as interpreted in the haggadah. Similarities between the atonement and the Akedah have long been observed. Modern discussion of the relationship between the two traditions began when Isidore Levi in 1912 argued for the independence and priority of the Jewish lore.[1] The immediate reaction was slight, but after World War II the theme was taken up by a number of scholars, including H. J. Schoeps,[2] H. Riesenfeld,[3] and E. R. Goodenough.[4] S. Spiegel has published a brilliant analysis of Akedah traditions up to the twelfth century C.E., originally in Hebrew and recently translated into English by Judah Goldin; the introduction to his study conveys important insights into the general nature of haggadic interpretation.[5] Later studies by G. Vermes[6] and R. Le Deaut[7] have concentrated upon early traditions, with special attention to the various versions of the Palestinian Targum. Even patristic and iconographic materials have been gathered.[8]

It is reasonable to assume that the most relevant sources have been (fairly well) exhausted by these studies. Levi's work has been supplemented and modified at a number of points, but his main thesis concerning the independence of the Jewish tradition has been confirmed. Reactions to the Christian doctrine of the atonement may have stimulated the development of the haggadah, but only as a secondary factor. Much more open is the other problem, namely, to what extent and in which ways the Akedah served as a model for early Christian understanding of the atonement. The number of parallels would be hard to explain without the assumption of some kind of relationship, and yet the New Testament texts are elusive. The few explicit references to the sacrifice of Isaac do not deal with the atonement,[9] and passages that deal with the atonement may be more or less reminiscent of the Akedah but never make the allusion explicit.[10] This is the case even in Romans 8:32, where the formulation "he who did not spare his own Son but gave him up for us all" is obviously reminiscent of Genesis 22, as has been recognized by exegetes from Origen onward.[11] Why did Paul use a phrase drawn from the story of Abraham's sacrifice of his son in order to speak about the death of Christ? An answer to this question would illuminate the way in which the atonement was first related to the Akedah. The results may remain conjectural, but an exploration is worth attempting.

In Romans 8:32 the allusion is unambiguous, but Paul in no way draws it to the attention of his readers. They might perfectly well understand what he had to say in this context without being aware of the biblical phraseology. In fact, a number of commentators pass it over in silence.[12] If the allusion is recognized, it may simply call for an emotional response: No gift can be greater than that of Abraham, who did not withhold his only son! One can hardly object when C. K. Barrett notes the allusion but writes, "Paul makes no serious use of it."[13] Adolf Jülicher even issued a warning: "The words of the poet do not provide materials for critical exercises."[14] Yet, research starts with curiosity, and I wonder whether there might not be more behind the biblical phraseology than what is apparent in the context of Paul's letter.

The form of Romans 8:32 is that of a syllogism; if the protasis is valid, the apodosis must follow. Within its present context, the passage reminiscent of Abraham's sacrifice therefore functions as a warrant for the certitude of full salvation. As to its content, the passage runs parallel to Romans 5:8-9 and 5:10, where we have the more regular form for a conclusion a fortiori, with *pollō mallon*.[15] The formulations are open to variation, but Paul can assume that there is agreement upon the protasis and, quite likely, that such formulations were familiar to Christians at Rome. The same holds true also for the famous *hilastērion* passage in Romans 3:24-26, to which the other passages on the atonement refer back. In general, while Paul drew new and radical consequences, his basic affirmations concerning the person of Christ and the event of atonement conform to accepted statements of kerygma, creed, and liturgy.[16]

In his commentary on Romans, O. Michel has argued that Romans 8:32a is based upon some fixed form of preaching.[17] He finds the use of first person plural to be typical of confessional style and points to the creedlike relative clauses in v. 34 as well as to the analogous passages in Romans 4:25 and John 3:16. Even the linguistic form favors the assumption that Paul's formulation is based upon tradition. Whereas *ouk epheisato* corresponds to the Septuagint, *tou idiou huiou* does not, but rather is an independent rendering of the Hebrew text.[18] Paul is likely to have commented upon the traditional formula not only by appending the apodosis but also by adding *pantōn* to the current phrase *hyper hēmōn* in the protasis. Thus he stresses a main theme of his letter, at the same time achieving a rhetorical correspondence between *hyper hēmōn pantōn* and *ta panta hēmin*. The latter phrase probably refers to nothing short of the eschatological inheritance promised to Abraham and his offspring.[19] Persons familiar with the Genesis texts and their early Christian interpretation may have realized that Paul's cryptic allusion indicated the possibility of scriptural backing for what he wrote.

If Paul's formulation in Romans 8:32a is not created ad hoc, it is no longer sufficient to assume a loose and not very serious use of biblical phraseology. In recent years a number of scholars, representing various schools, have proved that the New Testament use of Scripture presupposes much more conscientious exegetical work than we were formerly inclined to think.[20] The formulation in Romans 8:32a is likely to go back to some kind of midrashic interpretation. The exegetical pattern must have been one of correspondence: as Abraham did not spare his son, so God did not spare his own Son. The question is how this correspondence was understood. According to a predominant, now somewhat fading mood, one would immediately think of the analogy between type and antitype. And certainly it was possible to find a typological relationship between the "binding of Isaac" and the death of Christ.[21] But typology cannot be made the general principle of early Christian hermeneutics, and the statement in Romans 8:32a relates to the conduct of Abraham and not to the suffering of Isaac. It is unlikely that Abraham's act of obedience was ever considered a typological prefiguration of God's act of love.[22]

The text of Genesis 22:16-17 suggests a different type of correspondence, that of act and reward. "By myself I have sworn, says the LORD, because you have done this, and have not withheld your son, your only son, I will indeed bless you. . . ." A homiletic exposition or paraphrase of this promise may well have been the original context of the passage now found in Romans 8:32a. God rewarded Abraham by corresponding action, not sparing his own Son, but giving him up for us (i.e., the descendants of Abraham), and thus he indeed blessed Abraham and promised to bless all nations in his offspring. A homiletic interpretation of this type is not a pure conjecture. It is attested by Irenaeus: "For Abraham, according to his faith, followed the commandment of the Word of God, and with ready mind gave up his only and beloved son, as a sacrifice to God, in order that God might be pleased to offer His beloved and only Son for all his offspring, as a sacrifice for our salvation."[23] In the Armenian version the idea of reward is even more explicit; it speaks of Abraham as the one "who also through faith asked God that for the sake of humanity (= philanthropy?) He might reward him for his son."[24] The language used is not derived from Romans 8:32, and the reference to Abraham's offspring points to a Jewish–Christian origin of the paraphrase. Is it conceivable that Irenaeus cites a later version of the haggadah from which Romans 8:32a was drawn?[25]

The passage in Irenaeus does not provide more than late and therefore uncertain evidence in favor of a conjecture that I would have dared to venture even without it: the allusion to Genesis 22 in Romans 8:32a is best explained on the assumption that it is derived from an exposition in which the atonement was understood as an "adequate reward" for the Akedah. Obviously, the adequacy should not be understood in terms of quantitative equivalence but as an exact correspondence of quality. In fact, this is how the rule "measure for measure" was applied both in Judaism and in early Christianity.[26] Some early Jewish adherent of the crucified Messiah may have taken Genesis 22 to imply that God, who judges those who judge and shows mercy upon those who act with mercy, rewarded Abraham's sacrifice by offering up his own Son. If this view was actually held, it would provide a most satisfactory explanation for Paul's otherwise cryptic reference in Romans 8:32. Caution forbids us to postulate that Paul's statement may not be explained otherwise. The conjecture would gain credibility if we could prove (1) that the understanding of the atonement as a reward for the Akedah conforms to some trend in contemporary haggadah, (2) that the hypothesis is supported rather than contradicted by other evidence in Paul's letters, and (3) that it would be in harmony with our general knowledge of pre-Pauline Jewish Christianity. In all three respects I regard the evidence as favorable to the conjecture.

I

In Jewish traditions, Isaac was early regarded as a model for suffering martyrs,[27] but there is little, if any, evidence that he was ever seen as a prototype of the Messiah.[28] In several texts, however, God is said to remember the Akedah and therefore to rescue the descendants of Isaac on various occasions, from the exodus to the resurrection of the dead.[29] Both the daily sacrifices in the temple and the blowing of the shofar at Rosh Hashanah make God recall the Akedah.[30] References in prayers offer features of special interest. The kernel of the tradition may be a simple prayer that God might remember the binding of Isaac to the benefit of Israel.[31] This was often spelled out in terms of an "adequate reward." In the Palestinian Targums a prayer is attributed to Abraham, with the following conclusions: "I have done Thy word with joy and have effected Thy decree. And now, when his [Isaac's] children come into a time of distress (ʾaktā), remember the binding (ʿăḳēḏāh) of Isaac, their father, and listen to their prayer, and answer them and deliver them from all distress."[32] Here the point of correspondence is that God might listen to Israel's prayers, as Abraham listened to God's word.

A version of the haggadah on the prayer of the patriarch, attributed to Rabbi Johanan, includes a reference to Genesis 21:12, "Through Isaac shall your descendants be named." When God, in spite of this promise, told Abraham to offer Isaac as a burnt offering, Abraham could have made a retort. But he suppressed his impulse and asked God to act likewise: "Whenever Isaac's children enter into distress, and there is no one to act as their advocate, do Thou speak up as their advocate."[33] That is, as Abraham made no retort, so God should make no retort. Another variation of the motif is found in the Zikronoth, part of the additional prayer for Rosh Hashanah: "Consider [literally, 'May there appear before Thee'] the binding with which Abraham our Father bound his son Isaac on the altar, suppressing his compassion in order to do Thy will. So let Thy compassion suppress Thine anger (and remove it) from us."[34] It is not necessary here to discuss the relationship between legends and liturgy or to mention all variants. What is important may best be summarized in Spiegel's statement: "It may be surmised that all these variations originally had one feature in common: a parallelism between Abraham's conduct at the Akedah and the conduct expected in return from God."[35]

The parallelism is also attested outside the Akedah prayers. R. Benaiah, third-generation Tannaite, said that at the exodus the waters were cleft because Abraham cleaved the wood.[36] From later sources we hear similar comments: "As Abraham bound his son, so the Holy One, blessed be He, tied the princes of the pagans above."[37] Due to Abraham's worship, the descendants of Isaac were found worthy to worship at Mount Sinai, and the exiles will be reassembled to worship in Jerusalem.[38] "On the third day" the dead will be raised up because of the "third day" of Father Abraham.[39] His ten trials were rewarded by the ten plagues in Egypt, and they may serve as a compensation when the Ten Commandments are broken.[40] The playfulness of such interpretations should not be overlooked, nor should the basic principle of "adequate reward." The same principle can also be applied to other chapters of Abraham's story, as in a homily on Genesis 18, where it is explicitly stated: " 'And the Lord went before them by day' (Exod. 13:21). This is to teach you that with what measure a man metes, it is meted out to him. Abraham accompanied the ministering angels . . . (Gen. 18:16), and God accompanied his children in the wilderness. . . . (Exod. 13:21)." A similar correspondence is found with regard to supply of water, bread, meat, shelter, attendance, and protection.[41]

None of this material is older than Paul, but all of it illustrates a tendency (well established in the tannaitic period) to relate the history of Israel to the story of Abraham, including the Akedah, by application of the principle "measure for measure." Yet at the crucial point—Abraham's offering of his son—the principle was not applied in non-Christian Judaism. Only an interpreter who believed the crucified Jesus to be Messiah and Son of God could dare to follow the trend consistently to its bitter end, saying that as Abraham offered up his son, so God offered up his own son for Isaac's children.

II

Apart from Romans 8:32 the clearest Pauline allusion to Genesis 22 is found in Galatians 3:13-14. Verse 14a, "That . . . the blessing of Abraham might come upon the Gentiles," is a paraphrase of Genesis 22:18, "And in your offspring shall all the nations of the earth be blessed." The expression "the blessing of Abraham" is taken from Genesis 28:4, and "in Christ Jesus" has been substituted for "in your offspring."[42] It is also likely that the notion of substitution in verse 13 is related to Genesis 22. Here too there is a conscious interpretation in the background. In Deuteronomy 21:23 it is stated that a hanged man is accursed. This might be taken to exclude faith in a crucified Messiah, but the passage could be turned into an argument in favor of the Christian faith if "a man hanging on a tree" was compared with "a ram caught in a thicket" (Gen. 22:13). Thus the crucified Jesus was understood to be the lamb of sacrifice provided by God. Here there is an element of typology; but the ram, rather than Isaac, is seen as a type of Christ.

The allusions to Genesis 22 in Galatians 3 are all contained in verses 13a-14. These verses must be a fragment of pre-Pauline tradition. By his comment in verse 14b Paul identifies the blessing of Abraham with the Spirit, given as a down payment even to Gentile believers. Thus he makes the fragment bear upon the Galatian controversy but blurs the distinction between "us," the Israelites, and the Gentile nations. Moreover, Paul interprets redemption from the curse of the law to imply freedom from the law itself. The phrase "Christ redeemed us from the curse of the law" by itself suggests no more than liberation from the curse inflicted by transgressions of the law, in analogy with Daniel 9:11. According to the pre-Pauline tradition the Messiah, through his substitutionary death upon the cross, redeemed the Israelites from the curse brought about by their transgressions. As a consequence of Israel's redemption the blessing of Abraham would come upon the Gentiles in Abraham's offspring, the Messiah Jesus. The fragment must be of Jewish-Christian origin. Most likely it is derived from a midrash on Genesis 22.

Without considering possible connections with the Akedah, a number of scholars have argued that Paul makes use of traditional formulations in Romans 3:24-25.[43] Others have proposed that the passage alludes to Genesis 22:8, "God will provide himself the lamb for a burnt offering."[44] It is philologically possible to translate *hon proetheto ho theos hilastērion* as "whom God appointed (designed, purposed) to be an expiation."[45] There is some difficulty in that we have no evidence that *protithesthai* was ever used to render *yirʾeh* (Gen. 22:8) or the *y rʾh* of 22:14.[46] The twofold theory, that Paul cites a tradition of Jewish-Christian origin in which the atonement was related to the Akedah, would help explain several features in the text of Romans 3:24-26. The use of the term *hilastērion* has its closest analogy in *dia . . . tou hilastēriou (tou) thanatou autōn* (4 Macc. 17:22), where the vicarious death of the Maccabean martyrs is seen as an imitation of Isaac. The blood of Isaac is mentioned as early as Pseudo-Philo; redemption, mostly the prototypical redemption from Egypt, is related to the Akedah.[47] The phrase *en Christō Iēsou* may well be of pre-Pauline origin on the assumption that "in Christ Jesus" is a paraphrase of "in your offspring," as in Galatians 3:14a.[48]

Considerable problems have been caused by the phrase *dia tēn paresin tōn progegonotōn hamartēmatōn*. This has often been taken to mean God's tolerant "passing over" sins in the past, but a number of exegetes take *paresis* as a synonym for *aphesis*. They generally assume that *dia* with accusative is in the sense of *dia* with genitive. Thus, the clause would state that God's righteousness was manifested through the forgiveness of past sins. The rare word *paresis* is, however, attested to mean legal nonprosecution, dropping of a case.[49] There is no reason why it should not be used in the same sense in Romans 3:25. The sins were committed in the past, in the generations between Isaac and Christ. That the prosecution was dropped, however, is the negative counterpart of providing for expiation and does not refer to tolerance in the past. I would propose the following translation: "Whom God designed to be an expiation . . . by his blood, in order to manifest his righteousness, because the prosecution of the sins committed in the past was dropped in the forbearance of God, so that his righteousness might be manifested in the present time."[50] This interpretation is favored by the analogy with Romans 8:31ff. There the allusion to the Akedah is followed by the question, "Who shall bring any charge against God's elect?" As God, who did not spare his own Son, is the one who justifies, the case has been dropped, and there will be no prosecution. Somewhat analogous also are the Akedah prayers in which God is asked not to make any retort to the children of Isaac and not to listen to their accusors, but to speak up as their advocate.[51]

This interpretation also makes clear the meaning of the clause *eis endeixin tēs dikaiosynēs autou* becomes clear. It does not refer to a justice that requires either punishment or expiation, or to righteousness as a gift of God, or even to God's covenantal faithfulness.[52] The phrase is best understood in analogy with Romans 3:4f., "That thou mayest be justified in thy words. . . ." Providing for an expiation, God manifested his righteousness; that is, he vindicated himself as being righteous, doing what he had said.[53] This he did in spite of Israel's sins in the past, because in divine forbearance he dropped the charge against them. In the original context of the fragment, it would have been clear that the manifestation of God's righteousness especially implied that he kept his oath to Abraham (Gen. 22:16-18). Thus, the fragments of ancient tradition preserved in Romans 8:32, Galatians 3:13-14, and Romans 3:25f. concur not merely by using a phraseology vaguely reminiscent of the Akedah but also in interpreting the atonement as the fulfillment of what God promised by a solemn oath to Abraham after the sacrifice of Isaac.[54]

In the Pauline Epistles all passages reminiscent of the Akedah seem to reproduce traditional phraseology.[55] Paul's own interest in the story of Abraham is focused at other points. The understanding of the atonement as reward for the Akedah might even seem to run contrary to Paul's point of view—indeed, to an extent that would exclude his incorporating fragments of a tradition that expressed this idea. Yet, on closer examination, the theory of dependence is confirmed rather than disproved. Stressing that the atonement excludes the *kauchēsis* (of the Jews), Paul goes on to argue that not even Abraham had anything of which to boast.[56] His reward was given *kata charin* and not *kata opheilēma*. (It is not denied that he was rewarded!)[57] Concentrating upon interpretation of Genesis 15:6, Paul avoids any direct reference to Genesis 22, even where we might have expected one.[58] As it would not have been difficult to argue that the trial was a test of Abraham's faith, Paul may have avoided doing so for the sake of simplicity.

Paul's use of the ancient Jewish–Christian tradition implies a critical interpretation, sharply formulated in the statement "There is no distinction."[59] Yet Paul did not contradict the old tradition but incorporated it in a new context. He recognized "Jew first" to be a principle of divine economy and reckoned both "the oracles of God" and "the fathers" among the privileges granted to the Israelites.[60] Even when the order was reversed, Gentiles believing the gospel and Jews rejecting it, Paul insisted that the Israelites were "beloved for the sake of their forefathers."[61] At the end of his letter to the Romans, Paul summarized in words that fully conform to the Jewish-Christian interpretation we have been tracing, "Christ became a servant to the circumcised to show God's truthfulness, in order to confirm the promises given to the patriarchs, and in order that the Gentiles might glorify God for his mercy."[62] Both direct and indirect evidence from Paul's letters supports the conjecture that he was familiar with Jewish–Christian interpretation of the promises given to the fathers, especially in Genesis 22:16-18.

III

It has been surmised, and may today be generally accepted, that to the earliest churches in Judea the ministry, death, and resurrection of Jesus were believed to bring redemption to Israel, according to the Scriptures. The effect upon the Gentile nations was considered a further consequence, and an object of eschatological hope rather than of missionary efforts.[63] In this respect my tentative results simply add support to the scant evidence that this really was the case. And if my arguments are correct, they provide information about another important matter: there existed a specifically Jewish–Christian "doctrine of the atonement," more explicit than has often been assumed on the basis of Acts. The death of Jesus upon the cross was interpreted as fulfilling what God had promised Abraham by oath: As Abraham had not withheld his son, so God did not spare his own Son but gave him up for Isaac's descendants. As the sacrifice, provided by God, he expiated their former sins. Vicariously he was made a curse to redeem them from the curse caused by their transgressions of the law, so that even the Gentile nations might be blessed in the offspring of Abraham, the crucified Messiah Jesus. That God in his great mercy rewarded Abraham by acting as the patriarch did at the Akedah would thus seem to be part of fairly coherent early Jewish–Christian theology, in which the crucifixion of Jesus was interpreted in the light of Genesis 22.

The fragments surmised to be contained in Paul's letters to the Romans and the Galatians cannot belong to the very beginnings of Christian doctrine. The interpretation of Genesis 22 presupposes that Jesus was identified not only as the Messiah but was also predicated Son of God, in accordance with 2 Samuel 7:14 and Psalm 2:7. By way of analogy, not only "offspring of David" but also "offspring" of Abraham was taken to refer to Jesus as the Messiah. Yet the interpretation must be early, because it would seem to have been germinal to the phrase "God gave his Son,"[64] and possible to the designations of Jesus as "the only Son" and "the lamb of God."[65]

The use of Genesis 22, attested by the texts we have considered, presupposes some familiarity with haggadic traditions as well as with the biblical text.[66] It is not possible to assume, however, that current ideas about the vicarious suffering of Isaac were simply taken over and applied to the passion of Jesus.[67] Like the biblical story, the New Testament allusions emphasize the conduct of Abraham and the promise of God. If the motifs had been directly transferred from Isaac to Christ, one would have expected more emphasis upon the voluntary submission of the former, as in the haggadah. In many respects it would seem better to regard the early Christian interpretation of Genesis 22 as an independent parallel rather than as derived from Jewish Akedah traditions. What the earliest Jewish Christian traditions presuppose is not so much any special features of the haggadah as the general spiritual climate of Midrash. It cannot be characterized better than in the words of Judah Goldin: "That conviction lies at the heart of Midrash all the time: The Scriptures are not only a record of the past but a prophecy, a foreshadowing and foretelling, of what will come to pass. And if this is the case, text and personal experience are not two autonomous domains. On the contrary, they are reciprocally enlightening: even as the immediate event helps make the age-old text intelligible, so in turn the text reveals the fundamental significance of the recent event or experience."[68] Without alteration this statement might also be applied to early Christian use of Scriptures.

Early Christian use of Scriptures was not differentiated from contemporary Jewish Midrash by some new hermeneutic. The methods of interpretation remained much the same, with variations in branches of the primitive church and Judaism. What caused a basic difference was new events and new experiences. For Judaism, the story of the binding of Isaac provided help in understanding that the God of the fathers allowed the sufferings and death of faithful Jews in the days of Antiochus Epiphanes and later. The same story helped followers of Jesus deal with the scandal of the cross, understanding what had happened as an act of God's love and a manifestation of his righteousness. For centuries the interpretation of Genesis 22 was a part of the controversy between Christians and Jews, and even the common use of scientific methods has not quite brought the controversy to an end. It is interesting, and may be important, to realize that the earliest Christian interpretation antedates the controversy. Close correspondence rather than competition between the Akedah and the atonement was stressed probably to the extent that the redemption by Christ was seen as an adequate reward for the binding of Isaac.

Notes

[1]I. Levi, "Le sacrifice d'Isaac et la mort de Jesus," *REJ* 64 (1912) 161–85.

[2]H. J. Schoes, *Paulus* (Tübingen, 1959) 144–52 (ET, *Paul* [Philadelphia, 1961] 141–49). Cf. *JBL* 65 (1946) 385–92.

[3]H. Riesenfeld, *Jésus transfiguré* (Copenhagen, 1947) 86–96.

[4]E. R. Goodenough, *Jewish Symbols* (New York, 1953–69) IV, 172–94; cf. IX, 71–77; XII, 68–71, etc.

⁵S. Spiegel, *The Last Trial* (trans. Judah Goldin; New York, 1967). The original essay appeared in *Alexander Marx Jubilee Volume* (New York, 1950).

⁶G. Vermes, *Scripture and Tradition in Judaism* (Leiden, 1961) 193–227.

⁷R. Le Deaut, *La nuit pascale* (AnBib 22; Rome, 1963) 133–208 and "La présentation targumique du sacrifice d'Isaac et la soteriologie paulineienne," in *Studiorum Paulinorum Congressus Internationalis Catholicus* II (Rome, 1963) 563–74. Cf. *RSR* 49 (1961) 103–6. Cf. also F.–M. Braun, *Jean le théologien*, vol. 2, *Les grandes traditions d'Israel* (Paris, 1964) 179–81, and R. A. Rosenberg, "Jesus, Isaac, and the 'Suffering Servant,' " *JBL* 84 (1965) 381–88.

⁸Cf. D. Lerch, *Isaaks Opferung, christlich gedeutet* (Tübingen, 1950); I. Speyart van Woerden, "The Iconography of the Sacrifice of Isaac," *VC* 15 (1961) 214–55; Spiegel, *Last Trial*, xi.

⁹Cf. James 2:21f.; Heb. 11:17f.; cf. 6:13f.

¹⁰Cf. Rom. 3:24f.; 4:25(?); 8:32; 1 Cor. 5:7(?); Gal. 3:13-14; Eph. 1:3-6f.(?); John 1:29; 1 Pet. 1:19f.; Rev. 5:6(?).

¹¹Origen, *Hom.* 8; *MPG* 12, 208. Cf. Lerch, *Isaaks Opferung*, and Speyart van Woerden, "Iconography."

¹²E.g., Jülicher, Lietzmann, Dodd, Schlatter, Nygren, Leenhardt.

¹³C. K. Barrett, *A Commentary on the Epistle to the Romans* (London, 1956) 99, cf. 172.

¹⁴A Jülicher, *Die Schriften des Neuen Testaments* II (2d ed.; Göttingen, 1908) 280.

¹⁵On the parallelism between Rom. 5:1-11 and Romans 8, cf. my "Two Notes on Romans 5," *ST* 5 (1951) 37–48 (repr. in *Studies in Paul* [Minneapolis: Augsburg, 1977]). Today I would not argue so strongly that Romans 1–8 should be divided into 1–4 + 5–8 rather than into 1–5 + 6–8. The sections 5:1-11 and 5:12-21 function both as conclusions of what precedes and as introductions to what follows.

¹⁶Cf., e.g., R. Bultmann, *Theology of the New Testament* I (New York: Scribner's, 1951) 78–86, 124–33, etc.; A. M. Hunter, *Paul and His Predecessors* (2d ed.; London, 1961).

¹⁷O. Michel, *Der Brief an die Römer* (MeyerK, 10th ed.; Göttingen, 1955) 184.

¹⁹*Ta panta* is related to the cosmic outlook in Romans 8, especially vv. 17-23 and 35-39. For the promises to Abraham, cf. Gen. 12:7; 13:14-17; 22:17f.; 26:3-5; etc., and the interpretation implied in passages like Rom. 4:13; Gal. 3:16-18; and 4:7. Cf. especially Zahn and Michel, *Römer*.

²⁰It may here be sufficient to mention names like Dodd, Daniélou, Daube, Doeve, Stendahl, Lindars, Ellis, Vermes, Gerhardsson, and Borgen.

²¹Barn. 7:3; Melito, *Paschal Homily* 59 (431), 69 (499), frag. 9. Cf. J. Daniélou, *Sacramentum futuri* (Paris, 1950) 97–111. Vermes finds that "the Akedah merely prefigures the redemption by Christ" (*Scripture and Tradition* 220), and Le Deaut still tends to subsume all New Testament allusions to Genesis 22 under "l'aggadah typologique propre à la perspective chrétienne" (*Nuit pascale* 203).

²²Not even John 3:14 would be a real analogy.

²³Iren. *Adv. Haer.* 4.5.4. A fragment of the Greek text is preserved: *Prothymōs ton idion monogenē kai agapēton* (+ *huion?*) *parachōrēsas thysian tǭ theǭ, hina kai ho theos eudokēsē hyper tou spermatos autou pantos ton idion monogenē kai agapēton huion thysian paraschein eis lytrōsin hēmeteran.*

²⁴"Qui et advocavit per fidem deum quoniam (*vel ut*) pro humanitate pro filio retribuit (*vel retribueret*) ipse" (Latin translation by Mercier in *Irénée de Lyon, Contre les heresies, livre IV* [ed. A. Rousseau; Paris, 1965]).

²⁵In fact, Irenaeus seems to draw upon old traditions. Thus, Isaac is seen as a prototype for Christians who are to carry their cross, rather than as a prefiguration

of Christ. In the present context the "Word of God," whose commandment Abraham obeyed, is the preexistent Logos, but originally it may have been God's *memra*. Elsewhere Irenaeus has certainly preserved interpretations of "presbyters" and even fragments of Hebrew-Christian midrash; cf. N. Brox, *Offenbarung, Gnosis, und gnostischer Myth bei Irenaus von Lyon* (Salzburg/Munich, 1966) 83 n. 103 and pp. 150–57, with literature.

[26]Matt. 7:1f.; Luke 6:37f.; *m. Soṭa* 1:7-9, etc. Cf., e.g., H. Ljungman, *Guds barmhärtighet och dom* (Lund, 1950) 25–30.

[27]Cf. 4 Macc. 7:14, 13:12; 16:20. Isaac's willingness is also stressed by Josephus (*Ant.* 1.232) and Pseudo-Philo (*Ant. Bibl.* 32:3; 40:2). Cf. Vermes, *Scripture and Tradition* 197–204. This emphasis does not diminish the role of Abraham, who is a model for the mother of the seven brothers in 4 Maccabees.

[28]Riesenfeld, *Jésus transfiguré* 86–96, argues to the contrary, on the basis of a very broad use of the term "Messiah."

[29]The evidence is conveniently summarized by Vermes, *Scripture and Tradition* 206–8. Of special interest is an exegesis of Ps. 79:11 (and 102:21), according to which the one in fetters ʾasîr) and close to death (*tĕmûtâ*; cf. Jastrow, *Dictionary* [New York: Pavdes, 1950], s.v.) is Isaac, whose children God will set free. This interpretation is presupposed already by R. Joshua (ca. 100 C.E.), who makes God speak to Isaac with the words of the psalm (*Mek. R. Simeon* Exod. 6:2 [ed. Hoffmann, p. 4]). Cf. *Pesiq.* 31 (or 32), ed. Buber 200 b (in spite of Vermes, *Scripture and Tradition* 207 n. 6).

[30]Vermes, *Scripture and Tradition* 208–14.

[31]Cf. *Tg. Lev.* 22:14; Le Deaut, *Nuit pascale* 171f.

[32]*Tg. Neof.* Gen. 22:14. The other versions differ only on minor points; cf. Le Deaut, *Nuit pascale* 154, 163–69.

[33]*y. Taʿan.* 2:4, 65d, in Spiegel, *Last Trial* 90. Cf. the various texts treated by Spiegel on pp. 89–98. R. Johanan lived in the third century, but the contrast between Gen. 21:12 and Genesis 22 is already stressed in Heb. 11:18.

[34]Text in, e.g., *The Authorized Daily Prayer Book* (ed. J. H. Hertz; New York, 5709/1948) 882. The additions in parenthesis are taken from Goldin's translation of Spiegel, *Last Trial* 89. Cf. also *Gen. Rab.* 56:10, translated by Goldin in ibid. 90.

[35]Spiegel, *Last Trial* 93.

[36]Gen. 22:3—Exod. 14:21. *Mek. be-Shallah* 4, on Exod. 14:15 (Lauterbach I, 218).

[37]R. Haninah, fourth-generation Amora, *Gen. Rab.* 56:5.

[38]Gen. 22:5—Exod. 24:1—Isa. 27:13. *Lekah Tob*, p. 98.

[39]*Gen. Rab.* 56:1. Cf. Spiegel, *Last Trial* 109–16, regarding nn. 36–39.

[40]*Exod. Rab.* 15:17; 44:4.

[41]*Mek. be-Shallah* 1, on Exod. 13:21 (Lauterbach I, 184f.). The further references are to Gen. 18:4; Num. 21:17; 18:5; Exod. 16:4; 18:7; Num. 11:13; 18:4; Ps. 105:39; 18:18; Exod. 12:23. The text as a whole is inspired by Ps. 105:39-42. For the principle of adequate retribution, cf. already Wis. 11:15ff.; 15:18ff.; etc.

[42]Cf. Gal. 3:16 and 19; Acts 3:25f.

[43]Cf. Bultmann, *Theology* I, 46; E. Käsemann, *Exegetische Versuche und Besinnungen* I (Göttingen, 1960) 96–100 = *ZNW* 43 (1950–51) 150–54; J. Reumann, "The Gospel of the Righteousness of God," *Int.* 20 (1966) 432–52.

[44]Thus Schoeps, *Paul* 146, following G. Klein, *Studien über Paulus* (Stockholm, 1918) 96. Cf. Le Deaut, "Présentation targumique" 571f.

[45]Cf. Rom. 1:13; Eph. 1:9. This interpretation has been defended quite apart from the question of allusion to Genesis 22; cf. C. Bruston, "Les conséquences du vrai sens de hilastērion" *ZNW* 7 (1906) 77. Cf. also J. H. Moulton and G. Milligan, *The Vocabulary of the Greek New Testament* (2d ed.; London, 1915) 554.

⁴⁶But cf. the use of '*izdammen*, *yizdammen*, or *yibḥar* in the Targums; Le Deaut, *Nuit pascale* 157f., 171.

⁴⁷Cf. Ps.-Philo *Ant. Bibl.* 18:5, "Pro sanguine eius eligisti istos." See also n. 29 above.

⁴⁸Thus a solution is provided for a problem felt by J. Reumann, "The Gospel," 40–42. Is Gen. 22:18 reflected also in *ho eulogēsas hēmas . . . en Christǫ* (Eph. 1:3; cf. 1:6f.)? Cf. also the paraphrase in *Ant. Bibl.* 32:2, "In me adnuntiabuntur generationes."

⁴⁹Dion. Hal. *Ant. Rom.* 7.37. Cf. J. M. Creed, "Paresis in Dionysius of Halicarnassus and in St. Paul," *JTS* 41 (1940) 28–30, and literature referred to in n. 43 above.

⁵⁰*Dia tēn paresin* could also be taken to indicate the *causa finalis*, "So that the prosecution . . . could be dropped." In the translation, *dia pisteōs* has been left out as a Pauline comment. How far parts of v. 26 belonged to tradition may here remain an open question.

⁵¹Texts given by Spiegel, *Last Trial* 90–92; cf. n. 33 above. Cf. already Jub. 18:12, "And the prince Mastema was put to shame." According to *Ant. Bibl.* 32:1, 4, the mouths of envious angels were shut.

⁵²The notion of the covenant is imported into the text of the fragment by Käsemann, *Exegetische Versuche* (see n. 43 above). Cf. P. Stuhlmacher, *Gottes Gerechtigkeit bei Paulus* (Göttingen, 1965) 89. Apart from exegetical details, however, my results concur with Käsemann's.

⁵³Cf. *eis to einai auton dikaion* (Rom. 3:26; cf. Isa. 45:21, Neh. 9:8); H. Ljungman, *Pistis* (Lund, 1964) 37, 106, etc.

⁵⁴Vermes, *Scripture and Tradition* 221f., has seen that the Akedah motif was not introduced by Paul but has not attempted to distinguish between Paul's interpretation and the inherited materials with which he worked.

⁵⁵This would also apply to passages like Rom. 4:25; 5:5-10; 1 Cor. 5:7; Eph. 1:7; and Col. 1:13f. The question whether or not they contain any allusion may therefore be left open.

⁵⁶Rom. 3:27 (cf. 2:17ff.); 4:1-5.

⁵⁷Rom. 4:4.

⁵⁸Cf. especially Rom. 4:17—Abraham believed in God, "who gives life to the dead." In Jewish tradition the second of the Eighteen Benedictions ("who makes the dead alive") was connected with the Akedah (Spiegel, *Last Trial* 28–37). Cf. already Heb. 11:19 and 4 Macc. 7:19; 13:17; 15:3; 16:25.

⁵⁹Rom. 3:22; cf. vv. 29-30; 10:12; and also Gal. 2:14b and the possible addition of *pantōn* in Rom. 8:32.

⁶⁰Rom. 1:16; 3:2; 9:4f.

⁶¹Rom. 11:28.

⁶²Rom. 15:8f. The phrase *hyper alētheias theou* is virtually synonymous with *eis endeixin tēs dikaiosynēs autou*, as shown by 3:3-7.

⁶³Cf., e.g., J. Munck, *Paul and the Salvation of Mankind* (Richmond, 1959) 255–81; J. Jeremias, *Jesus' Promise to the Nations* (London, 1958) 55–73.

⁶⁴Rom. 8:32; John 3:16. The phrase "God sent forth his Son" might be a variation of this; cf. especially Gal. 4:3f. Influence from wisdom terminology is assumed by E. Schweizer, "Zum religionsgeschichtlichen Hintergrund der 'Sendungsformel' Gal 4:4f., Rom 8:3f., Joh 3:16f., 1 Joh 4:9," *ZNW* 57 (1966) 199–210; *TDNT* 8 (1972) 376f.

⁶⁵Cf. also "My beloved Son" (Mark 1:11, etc.). Cf., e.g., Vermes, *Scripture and Tradition* 221–25. Due to the possibility of various connotations and biblical allusions, it is hard to know the extent to which the New Testament use of terms like *monogenēs*, *huios agapētos*, and *amnos* was originally derived from Genesis 22. There is only scant

evidence for the theory of Vermes (202f.) that Isaiah 53 was related to the Akedah in pre-Christian Judaism.

[66]The fact that early traditions associate the Akedah with Passover, rather than with New Year, should be mentioned here. Cf. Spiegel, Vermes, and Le Deaut.

[67]Spiegel, *Last Trial* 81–86, 103f., 113, etc. thinks that ancient pagan beliefs, suppressed in Judaism, continued and returned in Christianity from Paul onward.

[68]Ibid. xvi.

8

The Neglected Factor
in New Testament Theology

THE TERM "New Testament theology" refers here not to the theology contained in the New Testament writings but rather to the discipline that has this theology as its subject matter. In its broad and generally accepted sense, the word "theology" means the doctrinal formulation of religious beliefs. Accordingly, the discipline "New Testament theology" deals with the general content of the New Testament writings, not only with their doctrine of God. *Theo*-logy in the strict sense of the word is what I have called the neglected factor.

PRELIMINARY REMARKS: INDIRECT DISCOURSE

New Testament theology, as practiced in the contemporary scholarly community, does not speak about God but about the way in which the New Testament authors talk about God; its discourse about God is indirect. Nevertheless, the discipline concentrates on what the New Testament has to say, has its natural setting in a theological curriculum, and should be distinguished from a history of early Christian religion and thought. The discipline is therefore faced with the question of whether or not it is a hybrid, carrying with it the risk that future Christian ministers will be trained to talk about God only in indirect discourse.

This apparently unavoidable bracketing of direct discourse about God does have some advantages. First, it creates possibilities for intersubjective argumentation and verification within the community of scholars, regardless of church affiliation. Second, if understood as a critical study of the vocabulary, syntax, form, and function of theological discourse in the New Testament, the discipline avoids the false pretention that scientific discourse can communicate a more adequate knowledge of God than the common language of Christian faith. Third, within the framework of the whole theological enterprise, examination of the theology (or theologies) contained in the New Testament has a critical function over against later forms of discourse about God, whether they are dependent upon philosophical theism, are determined by catholic or sectarian traditions, or represent more emotional types of piety. Finally, one may also hope that the discipline will play an active role in suggesting possible ways to talk about God and "things divine" today.

"GOD" IN CURRENT NEW TESTAMENT THEOLOGY

For more than a generation, the majority of New Testament scholars have not only eliminated direct references to God from their works but have also neglected detailed and comprehensive investigation of statements about God. Whereas a number of major works and monographs deal with the Christology (or ecclesiology, eschatology, etc.) of the New Testament, it is hard to find any comprehensive or penetrating study of the theme "God in the New Testament." Likewise, a survey of indexes to periodical literature shows that relatively few articles in journals and Festschriften have been devoted to the theme.

The neglect of the doctrine of God can also be illustrated by statements of influential New Testament scholars and by textbooks on New Testament theology. In a remark about Paul, Rudolf Bultmann has stated a fundamental principle of his own: "Every assertion about God is simultaneously an assertion about man and vice versa. For this reason and in this sense Paul's theology is, at the same time, anthropology."[1] In practice, Bultmann has concentrated upon the first part of this statement, representing New Testament theology as anthropology, while paying little attention to the "vice versa." Oscar Cullmann has stated that "early Christian theology is in reality almost exclusively Christology."[2] It is not clear whether or not it has ever occurred to him that this statement might also be formulated the other way around. Even George Eldon Ladd, who represents the evangelical tradition and considers New Testament theology "primarily a descriptive discipline," has little to say about God in his recent textbook, apparently without being aware of any problem.

When considering treatments of New Testament Christology, we note that most pay astonishingly little attention to the relationship between faith in Christ and faith in God, to the transfer of divine names, attributes, and predicates to Jesus, or to the emergence of "trinitarian" formulations. The provocative thesis of McGiffert, that Jesus was "the God of the early Christians," seems to have been forgotten. What is more, neither studies of the concept of God in the Old Testament nor efforts of systematic theologians to reformulate the traditional doctrine of God have made any great and lasting impact upon New Testament theology.

The neglect has not, however, been complete. Some textbooks on New Testament theology have, with various modifications, retained the outline of traditional systematic theology and have dealt with the *locus de Deo* in an opening section (e.g., F. C. Grant, A. Richardson, K. H. Schelkle). This procedure, however, tends to isolate statements about God's "essence and attributes" from their context within the New Testament. Most reconstructions of the teaching of Jesus pay considerable attention to his concept of God as Father and related themes (e.g., Joachim Jeremias); but if the task of New Testament theology is to describe and interpret what is said in the canonical writings, reconstruction of the teaching of the historical Jesus falls outside this discipline (cf. Bultmann). That the theme calls for fresh efforts has in recent years been a growing awareness among scholars who otherwise represent different trends or schools. Important contributions include several articles by Gerhard Delling, a book by W. Thuesing, and a recent Claremont dissertation by Antoinette Wire.

REASONS FOR THE NEGLECT

The neglect of *theo*-logy in New Testament theology has been conditioned by the history of the discipline and of Christian theology in general. Here it is only possible to make tentative suggestions about contributing causes.

A pronounced Christocentricity has roots in the nineteenth century, for example, within the school of Ritschl. The reaction against metaphysical theology can be traced even further back, at least to Schleiermacher and Kant, possibly to Melanchthon and Luther. "Demythologizing" and "existential interpretation" have reinforced this tendency. It has been a common assumption that the most important elements in the New Testament are those that are specifically Christian. Attempts have been made to prove that there is a specifically Christian concept of God, characterized by the motif of God's love for sinners (Karl Holl, Gustav Aulén, Anders Nygren), but this attempt has at best been only partially successful. The concept of revelation, understood as the self-disclosure of God, has provided the dominant model for much post-Enlightenment and even earlier theology but has failed to provide an appropriate framework for treatment of the discourse about God in the New Testament.

One can also detect some reasons for the neglect within the New Testament itself, for it contains few, if any, thematic formulations about God comparable to, for instance, the First Mandate of Hermas: "First of all believe that God is One, who created all things, and prepared and made all things to be out of that which is not, and encompasses everything although He is not Himself encompassed by anything." By and large, the concept of God contained in the Old Testament Scriptures, as interpreted in contemporary Judaism, is taken for granted.

It is possible to detect traces of philosophical concepts (e.g., Acts 17:24-29) and points of contact with apocalyptic or mystical theosophy (e.g., Revelation 4); but these elements are less prominent than in various branches of contemporary Judaism. The New Testament authors never deal explicitly with the anthropomorphic and anthropopathic language of the Old Testament, which caused a problem for both Hellenistic and Rabbinic Judaism, and later for patristic writers as well.[3] New Testament statements that verbalize some aspect of the concept "God" are neither doxological or possess a special function within an argument (e.g., Rom. 1:18ff., 9:14ff., or even John 4:24; 1 John 1:5; 4:8).

The great majority of references to God occur in contexts that deal with some other theme. They serve as warrants and backing for promises, appeals, and threats, or for statements about Jesus, the Jews, the church, salvation, moral conduct, prayer, and so forth. There is no uniform New Testament doctrine of God, but rather considerable diversity; one need only contrast the letters of Paul and the Book of Revelation, or the Lucan and the Johannine writings. This variety, however, ought to have been cause for investigation, not for neglect.

Some Proposals

The elementary but all too neglected task must involve a careful, analytic description of words and phrases and of their use within sentences and larger units of speech (e.g., narratives, kerygmatic, creedal and hymnic texts, maxims, doctrinal and parenetic topoi). As the New Testament is a complex and multidimensional entity, the most appropriate form for dealing with its theology (both in the wider and the narrower sense of the term) is not a comprehensive textbook but a monograph that concentrates upon one topic in such a way that it contributes toward a better understanding of an aspect of the whole. New Testament theology should take account both of the historical setting of the writings and of "trajectories" of thought. Yet the discipline differs from the history of early Christian thought in more or less the same way as an introduction to the New Testament differs from a history of early Christian literature. If the tasks are not distinguished, the result is likely to be either unwarranted preference for the canonical writings over against other sources, or subordination of the witness of the New Testament writings to reconstructed lines of development, or both.

One option for the comprehensive survey would be to represent the form and function of theological language within the context of the New Testament writings, arranged according to their literary genre, whereby common traditions might be treated in introductory chapters. Gerhard von Rad's *Theology of the Old Testament* would provide a model for this approach. The consequence of such an approach would be a breakdown of the accepted distinction between New Testament Theology and introduction to the New Testament—possibly a desirable result. A systematic treatment of major themes of New Testament Theology is a second option, though such a formal presentation runs the risk of becoming a collection of proof texts and comments or a series of loosely connected essays, unless one chooses a vantage point that allows for a comprehensive perspective from which the whole of the New Testament can be examined. Bultmann's concentration on the "kerygma" and "existential self-understanding" is the outstanding example of how this may be done. The question then arises as to how far other sets of questions might prove less lopsided and more fruitful.

The central task of early Christian theology was to come to terms with the crucifixion of Jesus. The conviction that the crucified "King of the Jews" was right and had been vindicated by God, who raised him from the dead, forms the basis of the theology of the New Testament in all its varieties. The statements of this conviction cannot all be subsumed under the heading "kerygma." The early Christians waited for the public vindication of Jesus in the near future. In the meantime they experienced charismatic gifts, miracles, inspired preaching, common life and worship, boldness in persecution, and so forth as manifestations of the Holy Spirit, whose coming attested to the exaltation of Jesus. The Easter faith did not render Jesus' preaching about God and his kingdom obsolete; rather, it caused the sayings of Jesus to be remembered and reshaped as words of the Lord (Paul) or of "the living Jesus" (Gospel of Thomas). The evangelists integrated parts of the sayings tradition into the story of the crucified and risen Christ, each in his own way. The chief method for doing theology was to interpret the crucifixion of Jesus and related events and experiences by means of the inherited Sacred Scriptures, and to reinterpret the Scriptures in light of these events and experiences. The matrix of early Christian theology is Sacred Scripture, as read and interpreted in a first-century Hellenistic environment—not solely apocalyptic (contrary to Ernst Käsemann).[4]

The various theologies contained in the New Testament all share a common core and common themes. Only on this account is it possible to compare them with one another and to identify tension and dissonance. Any representation of New Testament theology has to take due account both of the unity and of the variety, whether the order of presentation is thematic or treats the individual writings.

SOME COMMENTS ON THE DOCTRINE OF GOD

Articulated beliefs about God in contemporary Judaism informed the way early Christians understood the crucifixion of Jesus and related events and experiences. At the same time, faith in the crucified Messiah resulted in a new articulation of language used to speak about God. The presence of these two elements is not a matter of historical origins alone. Traditional (i.e., Jewish), more or less generally accepted, and specifically Christian statements about God are combined and interpenetrate one another in all the New Testament writings, even if the manner of combination varies a good deal.

It is misleading to contrast the universalism of Christian faith in God the Father with Jewish particularism. Already ancient Israelite faith in God brought together universal and specific components (contrast wisdom literature with representations of God as the national God of Israel and the personal God of Abraham, etc.). A mediation was achieved by means of the doctrine of election (e.g., Deuteronomy, 2 Isaiah) and—in classical Judaism—through the concept of the Torah as a cosmic principle, identified with "Wisdom," and even exhibiting similarities to the Greek *logos* or *nous*. The combination of general and specific components, then, is common to Jewish and Christian teaching about God; the difference lies in the location of the particular elements. New Testament faith in God is shaped by the "name" of Jesus Christ in a way that has made other peculiar features (the temple, the law, circumcision, etc.) lose their significance, insofar as they are not understood as promises and prefigurations pointing to him.

The interpenetration of general, traditional, and specifically Christian components in New Testament discourse about God can be illustrated by several themes that are common in the New Testament, even if spelled out in a variety of ways.

1. *God is one.* Greek philosophers, Jews, and Christians concurred in this statement, but not without differences. Greek monotheism was compatible with religious pluralism: "One God and many gods"; "being one, he has many names." Jewish monotheism was universalistic but exclusive: "I am he, and there is no god beside me" (Deut. 32:39; cf. Isa. 44:6, etc.). New Testament authors integrate, in several ways, exclusive loyalty to Jesus Christ with universal monotheism: "For us there is one God, the Father . . . , and one Lord, Jesus Christ" (1 Cor. 8:6; cf. Matt. 23:8-10; Eph. 4:5-6; 1 Tim. 2:5). The concepts of Christ as the Son and image of God, the mediator of creation, and the Word incarnate represent not only developments of Christology but also affirmations of the oneness of God.

2. *The Creator is the giver of life.* The correlate of this statement is that life is a gift, to be received with gratitude and trust. Both the predication of God as the "one who makes the dead alive" and the specifically Christian identification of God as "the God who raised Jesus from the dead" and who continues to give true life through the gospel and the Spirit reaffirm the more general concept of God as the giver of all life.

3. *God is the sovereign ruler.* The New Testament contains a number of general statements about the limitations of human existence and the corresponding sovereignty of God. But God's omnipotence is more specifically asserted with reference to Jesus and

his exaltation, whereby God proved that he is the God who puts down the mighty and exalts the humble, who is able to do what he has said, and who eventually shall overcome all opposition. Thus Paul can see power in weakness as the signature of God's work among human beings.

4. *God is the righteous judge.* This theme has two aspects: God is impartial and renders to each according to what he or she has done; and God will set things right. Both convictions have roots in general "wisdom," were taken up in eschatology, and remain axiomatic for the New Testament authors. The forensic terminology can be applied to God's vindication of the crucified Christ (e.g., 1 Tim. 3:16), as well as to the redemption available through him (thus especially Paul, John, Revelation). Specific events, including the mission to the Gentiles, are seen as evidence that God is impartial and that "there is no distinction" (cf. Rom. 3:22, 29f.; 10:12; Acts 10:34). The correlation of specific and general assertions about God is illustrated by apparently contradictory statements about his judgment (e.g., Rom. 3:28; 5:9f. versus 14:10-12; John 3:18-21 versus 5:28f.).

5. *God is merciful.* The emphasis on God's love and mercy is generally considered to be characteristic of the New Testament, and rightly so. Yet even statements about God's love can be of a general nature (e.g., Matt. 5:44f.) and use language derived from the Old Testament and Jewish prayers (e.g., Eph. 2:4).

All of these themes could be elaborated in detail and in a way that takes account of differences among the various writings. Other themes might be added as well. These examples are intended only to illustrate the combination and interpenetration of general, traditional (i.e., Jewish), and specifically Christian components in discourse about God in the New Testament. They also show that New Testament *Theology* cannot be properly treated in isolation from Christology, pneumatology, anthropology, and soteriology—and vice versa.

CONCLUDING COMMENTS

The New Testament writers pay remarkably little attention to the problem of theodicy or to other problems inherent in any theology that asserts that God is simultaneously omnipotent, just, and loving. There are several reasons for this: The general concept of God is more or less taken for granted; the writers do not deal with dogmatic theory but address some vital issue, if they do not present their "theology" in narrative form; they expect that God will in the near future publicly vindicate both himself and his faithful servants. Yet the more profound reason why New Testament authors do not seem concerned about problems and inconsistencies in their "doctrine of God" may be that all general and traditional attributes of God are predicated of "the Father of Jesus Christ," that is, the Son of Man, who was abandoned and subjected to violence, injustice, and hatred—and who is one with his Father.

The New Testament writings provide specific data for Christian discourse about God and contain a number of paradigms that in various ways exemplify how these data may be—or should be—integrated with the language used about God in the Old Testament and in Jewish tradition, and with assertions about God that express a general human sense of gratitude for the gift of life, or of confidence and anxiety, responsibility or failure. The New Testament does not, however, provide any one model for a systematic doctrine *de Deo.*

If the New Testament is considered the norm, most modern and ancient models for the doctrine about God seem to be unsatisfactory in one respect or another.

1. Concentration on the most specifically Christian motifs fails to take due account of the whole New Testament evidence. This may result in the isolation of Christian faith from human experience and reflection, and of Christianity from Judaism. The extreme consequence of this concentration is illustrated by Marcion's radical distinction between the God who sent Jesus from the God who created the world.

2. The opposite emphasis on a general concept of God tends to make the history of Jesus—or the "Christ myth"—a mere paradigm of God's universal manner of dealing with humankind. The result may be that Christianity becomes a sectarian variety of universal, pluralistic, civil, or revolutionary religion.

3. Models that distinguish between God's work in creation and his work in redemption account better for the complexity of the Bible (New and Old Testaments). But the usual categories (e.g., "nature and grace," "general and special revelation," "natural and revealed theology," "law and gospel") tend to erect two-level structures and compartmentalize assertions about God that are held together in the New Testament.

4. The attempt to deduce general theological, anthropological, and ethical statements from specific (i.e., christological) assertions

by means of *analogia fidei* integrates the various components in a much more speculative way than do the biblical writings themselves. Christology is then overburdened. As an unintended consequence of this model, Christian discourse about God may be used to support general programs of action in such a way that it eventually loses its specificity.

The theme "God" has been neglected in New Testament theology, but not in Old Testament theology or in philosophical and dogmatic theology. On the basis of my limited familiarity with recent works in these fields, I must question how far and how well any of these works deals with the interrelation of general components, Judeo-Christian heritage, and specific assertions of faith in Jesus Christ and his God and Father. I would venture to say that attention to this neglected factor in New Testament Theology will have important implications for the systematician as well.

Notes

[1]Rudolf Bultmann, *Theology of the New Testament* I (trans. K. Grobel; New York: Scribner's, 1951–55) 191.

[2]Oscar Cullmann, *The Christology of the New Testament* (trans. S. C. Guthrie and C. A. M. Hall; Philadelphia: Westminster, 1959, 1963) 2–3.

[3]See Alan F. Segal, *Two Powers in Heaven* (Leiden: Brill, 1977).

[4]This represents an important qualification of Käsemann's position that "apocalyptic was the mother of all Christian theology" (cf. "The Beginnings of Christian Theology," in *New Testament Questions of Today* [Philadelphia: Fortress, 1969] 102).

Bibliography

Aulén, Gustaf. *The Drama and the Symbols*. Trans. S. Linton. Philadelphia: Fortress, 1970.

Bultmann, Rudolf. *Theology of the New Testament*. 2 vols. Trans. Kendrick Grobel. New York: Scribner's, 1951–55.

Cullmann, Oscar. *The Christology of the New Testament*. Trans. S. C. Guthrie and C. A. M. Hall. Philadelphia: Westminster, 1959, 1963.

Delling, G. *Studien zum Neuen Testament und zum hellenistischen Judentum: Gesammelte Aufsätze, 1950–68*. Ed. F. Hahn, T. Holtz, and N. Walter. Göttingen: Vandenhoeck & Ruprecht, 1970.

Grant, F. C. *An Introduction to New Testament Thought*. New York: Abingdon–Cokesbury, 1950.

Holl, Karl. *The Distinctive Elements in Christianity*. Trans. N. V. Hope. Edinburgh: T. & T. Clark, 1937.

Käsemann, Ernst. *New Testament Questions of Today*. Philadelphia: Fortress, 1969.

Ladd, G. F. *A Theology of the New Testament*. Grand Rapids: Eerdmans, 1974.

McGiffert, A. C. *The God of the Early Christians*. Edinburgh: T. & T. Clark, 1924.

Nygren, Anders. *Agape and Eros*. Trans. P. S. Watson. Philadelphia: Westminster, 1953.

Rad, Gerhard von. *Old Testament Theology*. 2 vols. Trans. D. M. G. Stalker. New York: Harper & Row, 1962–65.

Richardson, A. *An Introduction to the Theology of the New Testament*. London: SCM, 1958.

Schelkle, K. H. *Theology of the New Testament*. Trans. W. A. Jurgens. Collegeville, Minn.: Liturgical Press, 1971.

Segal, Alan F. *Two Powers in Heaven*. Leiden: Brill, 1977.

Thuesing, W., and Karl Rahner. *A New Christology*. Trans. D. Smith and V. Green. New York: Seabury, 1980.

Wire, Antoinette. "Pauline Theology as an Understanding of God: The Explicit and the Implicit." Ph.D. diss., School of Theology at Claremont, 1974.

9

Trinitarian
Baptismal Creeds and
New Testament Christology

IT IS COMMON KNOWLEDGE that the New Testament writings contain no explicit doctrine of the Holy Trinity, except for the secondary addition in 1 John 5:7, the famous *Comma Johanneum*: "There are three who witness in heaven, the Father, the Word, and the Holy Spirit, and these three are one." It is equally well known that the New Testament contains some formulations that can be called trinitarian, if the word is understood in a broad sense, that is, formulations that mention God, Jesus Christ, and the Holy Spirit in syntactic coordination or parallelism (e.g., Matt. 28:19; 2 Cor. 13:13; 1 Cor. 12:4-6; 1 Pet. 1:2). There is no problem describing the data. The question is how the data are to be interpreted.

On the one hand, one can observe that in addition to the triadic formulations there are a number of passages that refer to God, to Christ, and to the Spirit within the same context and as parts of a cluster of ideas, even if there is no formal parallelism, so that one cannot speak of a trinitarian formula. One can then go on to argue that such free variations reflect an underlying trinitarian pattern. For example, the conservative Norwegian scholar Olaf Moe attempts to prove that even Paul presupposes a trinitarian baptismal commission and a trinitarian baptismal confession.

On the other hand, one can point out that the New Testament also contains triadic formulations that do not mention the three persons of the Trinity but instead speak, for example, of God, Christ, and the holy angels (1 Tim. 5:21; cf. 1 Thess. 3:13; Luke 9:26), or of the name of God, the name of the city of God, and the name of Jesus himself (Rev. 3:12). One can further observe that even the form of those triads, which may be called trinitarian, is very flexible, lacking any fixed order or titles: Father, Son, and Holy Spirit (Matt. 28:19); Spirit, Lord, God (1 Cor. 12:4-6); the Lord Jesus Christ, God, the Holy Spirit (2 Cor. 13:14); he who is and who was and who is to come, the seven spirits before his throne, and Jesus Christ, the faithful witness (Rev. 1:4-5). In view of this great flexibility, it may be argued that the New Testament texts do not presuppose any fixed formula or rudimentary doctrine of the Trinity but simply reveal stylistic preference for triadic formulations.

It is thus possible to assign either maximal or minimal importance to the "trinitarian" formulas within the New Testament, or to find some middle road between the extremes. The more important question, however, pertains to the relationship between the New Testament data and later trinitarian dogma. This has been a controversial topic for centuries. At one time it was common to take the dogma for granted and to read the New Testament in light of these dogmatic categories. At least a vestige of this approach can still be detected in the works of some conservative scholars. For Catholic theologians it has been possible to view the formulation of dogma as the result of an ongoing revelation, or at least as a more adequate appropriation of the revelation than that contained in Scripture. The underlying assumption is that the dogma states in precise ontological terms the revealed truth that the more popular New Testament writings suggest in more poetic, metaphoric language.

By contrast, the predominant liberal trend in Protestant scholarship has from the outset sought to liberate the New Testament, early Christian religion, and the historical Jesus from the straitjacket of dogma. Adolf von Harnack's monumental *History of Dogma* is still the classic, but by no means the most radical, manifestation of this trend. Most present-day New Testament scholars are likely to hold some intermediate position between Harnack's characterization of dogma as the work of the Hellenistic spirit on the gospel and the view that the dogma is a precise formulation of the revealed mystery of the Holy Trinity. It would be difficult to outline the various positions. The strange fact is that during the last half century New Testament scholars have, by and large, left it to historians of Christian doctrine and theologians to discuss the relationship between the dogma and the New Testament data that were discussed in the later trinitarian and christological controversies.

I am aware of only one recent book on the topic, *The Trinity in the New Testament* (A. W. Wainwright, 1962), and can mention only one article by a New Testament scholar, inspired by Karl Barth's trinitarian doctrine in his *Church Dogmatics* (K. L. Schmidt, *RHPR* 1938). Heated theological controversies in New Testament studies have revolved around other matters, including New Testament Christology and the historical Jesus, kerygma and Heilsgeschichte, eschatology and early Catholicism, demythologizing and existential interpretation, and the like. Conservative scholars have to a considerable extent directed their energy toward proving that Jesus had a "messianic self-consciousness" (a concept that was taken over from the liberal tradition). Critical scholars, on the other hand, no longer feel the same need as their nineteenth-century predecessors to liberate the gospel message or the living religion of early Christianity and Jesus himself from the alleged sterility of a rigid dogmatic orthodoxy. Polemics against trinitarian dogma are no longer a part of their agenda.

It is my contention that this neglect is, in the long run, an unhealthy state of affairs. The result of such a situation is often a dichotomy between biblical and systematic theology. What is more serious is the gap between biblical scholarship (which is being popularized) and the practice of the majority of churches, which not only accept the Ancient Creeds but also continue to use trinitarian doxologies and the Nicene Creed in their worship services. In theological education it is, I fear, often left to the individual student to come to terms with the dichotomy between the results of biblical studies and the doctrinal and liturgical tradition of the denominational churches.

There is, however, also another, more historical reason why the topic "trinitarian creeds and New Testament Christology" ought to be put back on the agenda. It is anachronistic to speak about the New Testament rather than about early Christian literature, religion, and history unless one is aware that to deal with the New Testament writings is to deal with a collection of writings that were canonized (i.e., put on the list of books that were to be read publicly in worship and to be regarded as normative for Christian faith and practice). What we call the New Testament is by definition the second part of the Christian collection of sacred writings of the Old and the New covenants, the second part of the Bible. Only if we keep this in mind is it legitimate and meaningful to speak about introduction to the New Testament or New Testament theology as discrete disciplines, distinguishable from the history of early Christian literature and the history of early Christian religion and thought.

167

If this is so, we have to keep in mind that the period in which the Christian Bible received its shape was also the period in which the Christian faith was summarized in formulations of what was considered to be the core of the apostolic preaching and, thus, to represent "the rule of faith" and truth. The baptismal confession was considered a pledge of allegiance to this apostolic faith, attested by the apostolic writings and summarized in the rule of faith. A contemporary work on New Testament theology can accept the presuppositions or the opinions of an Irenaeus or some other church father or of the emerging orthodoxy only with a critical eye. Neither would it seem possible to ignore the statements of faith and the convictions attending the formation of the New Testament and at the same time claim to be dealing with New Testament theology or Christology. One should at least ask to what degree a common core exists amid all the diversity of New Testament theologies, and also to what degree this common core might be formulated into something like "the rule of faith." It is fairly common to speak about the gospel, the kerygma, or Christology as being at the center of the New Testament. But we should at least be open to the possibility that ancient creeds or formulations of the rule of faith might serve at least as well in pointing to what the diverse New Testament writings are all about.

This lengthy introduction has raised larger and more complex questions than I can possibly handle in one lecture. I must concede that even in the course of a whole term I would not have been able to answer all the questions to my own or anyone else's satisfaction. In the remainder of this lecture, I will sketch two different approaches to the questions that I have argued ought to be put back on the agenda of New Testament studies. I shall first deal with the form and use of trinitarian—or tripartite—creeds without entering into a discussion of Nicene and later orthodoxy. This sketch will consist principally of a survey of data. The latter part of the lecture will deal with some aspects of New Testament Christology. Sketching an approach that I have worked out in lecture courses at Yale, I will discuss the difficulty of dealing properly with faith in Jesus Christ without relating it to faith in God and the role of the Holy Spirit in early Christian belief and experience.

This means that I shall deal only with two select aspects of this complex issue. I shall not, for example, discuss the importance that Greek philosophy, or ontology, no doubt had for the formulation of Nicene and later trinitarian orthodoxy. Nor shall I deal with the role that interpretation of the Old Testament, Jewish exegetical traditions, and possibly other divine triads may have played. Studies by Carl Andresen, George Kretschmar, Cardinal Daniélou, and others have shown that Harnack and his contemporaries overestimated the degree to which emerging dogma was shaped by a philosophical interpretation of Christian doctrine as contained in the New Testament writings and confessed in the early creeds. But when this is granted, it remains true that baptismal creeds provided a framework into which the definitions of Nicene and post-Nicene orthodoxy were inserted. Moreover, the creeds inform us about the faith confessed by ordinary men and women and not just about the teachings of the theologians. For the purpose of this lecture I set aside the history of doctrine and concentrate upon the form and function of baptismal confessions and related summaries of Christian faith.

The foundations for historical study of the creeds (or symbols) were laid in the nineteenth century. One of the great pioneers was Carl Paul Caspari, a German Jew who was converted to Christianity and later became professor of Old Testament in Christiania, as Oslo was called in his time. It was, however, not through his work as an Old Testament and Arabic scholar but through his contributions to the study of the creeds and related aspects of ancient church history that Caspari laid a foundation upon which later generations of scholars have built. How that happened is another story that I cannot relate here; in any case, Caspari remains, beside Sigmund Mowinckel, the most outstanding scholar ever connected with the University of Oslo. The work of Caspari and other pioneers was summarized in Ferdinand Kattenbusch's monumental two-volume work on the Apostles' Creed.

The work of Caspari, Kattenbusch, and their contemporaries included minute investigations of specific creeds and creedlike formulations. Their overarching goal, however, was to find the most original form of the baptismal symbol, a goal they believed they had reached, or at least in part. The form of our Apostles' Creed was demonstrated to be secondary. The earliest known creed was called the Old Roman Symbol, or *Romanum*, which on the whole has the same structure as the familiar text but differs from it in a number of details. The clause "Creator of heaven and earth" is, for example, not part of the first article, nor is "descended to hell" found in the second, or "the communion of saints" in the third article. This Old Roman Symbol was considered to be the archetype for all Western creeds and, possibly, for the Eastern creeds as well. It was traced back to the second or even to the late first century of the Christian era. Some scholars even tried to reconstruct still earlier forms, some of them on the assumption that a tripartite creed already existed in the apostolic age.

In the twentieth century the study of the creeds has taken a new direction analogous to the shift from source criticism to form criticism in New Testament studies. But whereas the revolution in New Testament studies was inaugurated by programmatic works by Martin Dibelius and others, the fresh approach to the study of the creeds came much more gradually. Eduard Norden, one of the ancestors of "Formgeschichte," had included some comments on the Apostles' Creed in his study of the history of forms of religious speech. But in Hans Lietzmann's *Symbolstudien*, published in the 1920s and early 1930s, one can still observe a gradual shift from the search for the original creed to a study of form and function—almost from one article to the next. Yet Lietzmann never followed the new approach very consistently. The fundamental shift since the days of Caspari and Kattenbusch is more visible in what is now the standard work in the field, J. N. D. Kelly's *Early Christian Creeds*. But Kelly's goal is still to write about the classical creeds and their prehistory rather than to write about the form and use of baptismal confessions and summaries of faith in the early Christian centuries.

The shift from a search for the original to a form-critical approach meant that early trinitarian creeds had to be studied in the context of the history of liturgy as much or even more than in connection with the history of doctrine. In fact, the investigation that more than any other inaugurated a new epoch was an article by Dom Puniet on baptism, published in the *Dictionnaire d'archéologie chrétienne et de la liturgie* and almost buried among the incredible riches of materials collected in this encyclopedia. Puniet demonstrated that the writings of Tertullian and Cyprian, as well as other evidence, presupposed a rite in which the threefold baptismal immersion was accompanied by three questions of faith: "Do you believe in God the Father . . . in Jesus Christ . . . and in the Holy Spirit?" whereby the candidate for baptism each time responded, "I believe." Puniet's discovery received spectacular confirmation when it was revealed that what had been known as the Egyptian Church Order and some Latin Verona fragments were in fact versions of Hippolytus's *Apostolic Tradition*. This work, written shortly after A.D. 200, contains an interrogatory creed whose general structure is very similar to the declaratory creed that had been assumed to be the Old Roman Symbol. The precise wording, however, is not identical. As the wording of Hippolytus occasionally coincides with that of later Western, but not Roman, symbols, these appear to be sisters rather than direct descendants of the declaratory Roman creed. The interrogatory creed of Hippolytus must now be considered the earliest Roman symbol. In the beginning of the third century, this creed was assumed to represent apostolic tradition, but there is no reason to believe that the exact wording was fixed at that time.

What is more important, it has become clear that declaratory creeds beginning with "I believe in . . . ," the form that is familiar to us, were not customary before the end of the third century, when the rites of *traditio* and *reditio symboli* became parts of an extended preparation of catechumens for baptism. The practice of keeping the wording of the symbol secret from noninitiates did not develop until after these rites had become common. Thus, there is no reason to assume that writers such as Irenaeus and Tertullian alluded to a symbol whose wording they never quoted because of an alleged arcane discipline, and the attempts to prove that they knew the Old Roman Symbol have broken down. Moreover, it is no longer possible to think of the rule of faith as a more theological interpretation of the baptismal symbol, as for example, Harnack did. It is more appropriate to think of the baptismal symbol as a response to the apostolic preaching, which—in the view of Irenaeus and others—was attested in the writings of the apostles and summarized in formulations of the rule of faith.

The general result of all of this is that there was no "original" creed. Fixed forms of creeds with a stereotyped wording are the end product of a long process. A certain flexibility remained even after the use of declaratory creeds had become customary. This is the case in the West but even more so in the East, where local creeds that contained the key phrases of Nicene orthodoxy (*homoousios*) could long be regarded as statements of the faith of the Nicene fathers. The wording of baptismal interrogations was open to even more variation, depending on location and occasion. Some late examples of baptismal interrogations illustrate the same flexibility. In some cases the established form of the declaratory creed is also used in the interrogation; in other cases brief baptismal questions summarize a fuller declaratory creed whose wording had been disclosed and recited at an earlier stage of the ritual of initiation. Several versions of baptismal questions reflect the variability of the early centuries, even though they can be attested to only at a later date. A form-critical study must take all of the material into account rather than attempt to reconstruct the earliest forms.

The great majority of interrogatory as well as declaratory creeds have a basic trinitarian structure. The same structure, and often a similar phraseology, recurs in many summaries of the rule of faith and in private, official, or synodal declarations of faith. Thus, similar forms can be used for various purposes, without any strict correlation of form and *Sitz im Leben*. I will try, as briefly as possible, to sketch both the consistency and the flexibility of the forms.

The core element of baptismal confessions is the three names—God the Father, Jesus Christ (or Christ Jesus), and the Holy Spirit. With very few exceptions, these names, and not the Matthean terms "the Father, the Son, and the Holy Spirit," are used. The order, however, remains constant—in contrast to the trinitarian formulas within the New Testament, which mention either God or Christ or the Holy Spirit in the first place. Even the opening clause remains remarkably constant. The great majority of creeds begin with a declaration of faith in "God, the Father, the Almighty" (Pantocrator) or "One God, the Father, the Almighty." This is all the more remarkable because the collocation "God, Father, Pantocrator" is not biblical phraseology. Christians could recognize that they shared a common faith and a common symbol.

Some baptismal, mainly interrogatory, creeds contain only the core elements (the three names). Such very brief forms, however, are attested only at a fairly late date. The data do not favor the assumption that the most basic form is also the earliest and that everything else represents later additions. We must rather assume that, as time went on, more and more elements became relatively constant, while the early period left more room for improvised additions to the established core.

The trinitarian core was expanded in two principal ways. First, each of the three articles could be expanded by means of appositional words, phrases, and clauses that identified the three persons by stating who and what each was and the actions and events associated with each name (with the person as known and proclaimed). Second, other items of faith were added to the basic trinitarian confession.

The first form of expansion, which may be termed the explication of the names, implied the addition of attributes or appositions: in the first article, "Father" and "Almighty," and, less frequently, "One," "the Father of Jesus Christ," "unborn," "immortal, invisible." In the second article the most common appositions are "the Son of God," "the only one" (*monogenēs*, only begotten), "our Lord," or "one Lord" at the beginning, and later "the Word" (Logos) or phrases like "the firstborn of all creation." Several creeds, principally but not exclusively of Eastern provenience, contain similar appositions in the third article: "the Spirit of truth" or phrases like "the Paraclete."

What was implied in the names could also be made explicit by means of verbal statements, mostly in the form of participial constructions or relative clauses. Most declaratory creeds contain fairly extensive summaries of the story of the Christ: in the Roman form, from his conception; in most Eastern creeds, from his eternal existence to his second coming. Most interrogatory creeds have shorter forms. Thus, a baptismal question, of Roman origin and widely used in the Western part of Christendom, reads simply, "who was born and suffered" (*natum et passum*). Other examples may be found in Irenaeus, who speaks of baptism "in the name of God the Father and in the name of Jesus Christ, the Son of God, who was incarnate and died and rose again, and in the Holy Spirit of God" (*Epid.* 3). In a similar reference, Justin writes, "and in the name of Jesus Christ, who was crucified under Pontius Pilate" (*Apol.* 1.61.13).

Several creeds contain similar verbal clauses in the third article, the most common of which is "who spoke through the prophets" (thus already Justin). Some Eastern creeds even summarize the "story" of the Holy Spirit: the Spirit spoke through the prophets, came down upon the Jordan, was given to the apostles and later to all believers.

The first article seldom, if ever, contains any verbal clauses, but it is important in this connection to observe that the syntactic distinction between nominal attributes and verbal constructions (participles and relative clauses) does not coincide with the semantic distinction between predicates of being and predicates of action. To confess God as Creator (or Maker) of heaven and earth, in spite of the use of a noun, identifies God in terms of his action. The second question in the ancient Milanese rite had the form: "Do you believe in our Lord Jesus Christ and his cross?" It contains no verb, but the question nevertheless refers to what happened to Christ. By contrast, the clause "born by the Father before all ages," common in Eastern creeds, speaks of the eternal being of Christ and not about any event, in spite of the participial construction. In the third article, the identification of the Holy Spirit as the Paraclete denotes the comforting and guiding action of the Spirit, while the participle *to zōopoioun* (which gives life) points to the essential nature of the Spirit as much as to any specific action. The clause that states that the Spirit "proceeds from the Father (and the Son [*filioque*])" may originally have referred to the coming of the Spirit but was later applied to the eternal origin and nature of the third person of the Trinity.

To summarize: Each of the three articles or interrogations of faith is, to a highly varying degree, developed by means of appositional words, phrases, or clauses that identify each of the three names in terms of being or actions and, in the second article, of the story of Christ.

The way each of the three names or persons is identified is open to variation from one creed to another and from one article of a creed to the others. Both brief and more extended creeds normally spell out the central second article at greater length, including key elements of a christological kerygma. The early Roman symbols identified God only as Father and Almighty and added no apposition to the Holy Spirit. The later addition of "Creator of heaven and earth" provided the first and second but not the third article with what I have called "predicates of action." In the major Eastern creeds the three articles are more similar in composition; all of them explicate the names and identify the persons by statements about actions and events and about who and what they are. The same creeds also include statements about Christ's eternal being and incarnation. Even apart from the Nicene addition they are more "dogmatic" than the Western type of baptismal confessions and more similar to doctrinal summaries of the faith.

In some baptismal symbols and professions or other summaries of faith, the addition of explicatory and identifying words, phrases, and clauses is the only compositional principle for expansion of the basic trinitarian core. But as the third article of the Apostles' Creed and the Constantinopolitan form of Nicenum attest, there are also traces of a different compositional principle.

Though Hippolytus provides uncertain evidence, the third question is likely to have included reference to the holy church and the resurrection of the flesh (body). The somewhat younger declaratory Roman creed has "the Holy Spirit, the holy church, the forgiveness of sins, the resurrection of the flesh." These concluding parts of the symbol neither assume the form of appositions nor identify the Holy Spirit. Only with some difficulty can one apply these items to the specific work of the Holy Spirit and thereby obtain some analogy to the form of the first and second articles. Are not the creation of the church, the forgiveness of sins, and the future resurrection the work of God the Father and of Jesus Christ as well as the work of the Holy Spirit?

In the Western creeds (probably already from Hippolytus onward), confessions about the church, the resurrection, and the like

174

are evident in the third article. There are, however, clear indications that these items were initially appended to the threefold name rather than subsumed under faith in the Holy Spirit. In the second-century apocryphon *Epistula Apostolorum* 5, we are told that the five loaves of the multiplication miracle symbolize "faith in the Father, the Ruler of the entire world, and in Jesus Christ, our Saviour, and in the Holy Spirit, the Paraclete, and in the Holy Church, and in the forgiveness of sins." Several brief Egyptian creeds should be construed in a similar way, as having four or five parts (rather than three times three, as Lietzmann once assumed, arguing that these brief creeds had been expanded within the Roman creed and interpreted by the insertion of the clauses "who was born by the Holy Spirit and the virgin Mary" and "who was crucified under Pontius Pilate"). The original independence of the items appended to the three names is clear when they appear as part of a separate fourth question, as in Carthage at the time of Cyprian, who has transmitted the wording: "Do you believe in the forgiveness of sins and life eternal through the holy church?" (*Epist.* 69.7 and, with reversed order, in 70.2). In Eastern declaratory creeds the ecclesiological-soteriological component of the creed can still be set off from the faith in the three persons. Finally, Rufinus and other interpreters related the church, forgiveness, and resurrection to baptism in the threefold name, even though they also commented upon creeds that formally included these items as parts of the third article.

Over against this highly diversified background we can now see that the Roman creed, both in its interrogatory and declaratory form, had a specific form of composition that was characterized by (1) the incorporation of a relatively extended christological summary in the second article, while the statements about God and about the Holy Spirit remained very brief; (2) the integration of the church (and forgiveness) and resurrection into the third article. This compositional pattern was clearly influential, especially in the Latin-speaking areas of Christendom, but also in the Greek-speaking regions. This Roman influence must, however, be dated considerably later than formerly assumed. Other compositional patterns continued to exist for a long period; these included, for example, short interrogatory creeds or more extended forms with an explication of each of the three names and no additions (see appendixes).

There is yet another form that deserves mention, a pattern in which a trinitarian statement is followed by a christological summary. Irenaeus used this form to state the content of the Christian faith. Later the pattern was frequently used in private and official professions of faith and in synodal creeds, mainly during the trinitarian and christological centuries after the council of Nicea. There are, however, at least two examples of baptismal interrogations that follow the same pattern: first the Trinity, then Christology. Since one of these examples is in Latin and the other Armenian, it would not be implausible to suppose they represent more than singular exceptions. We know that trinitarian formulas and christological summaries existed in relative independence of one another. They could be combined in two ways, either by adding a christological summary after a trinitarian formula or by incorporating the summary into the second part of a trinitarian creed. There is, however, no reason to suppose that the pattern "Trinity plus Christology" is the earlier form. It is itself likely a modification of a "binitarian" pattern for statements of faith in praise of God the Father and the Lord Jesus Christ. We might also use the ancient terms and say that the pattern is first the "theology" and then the "economy" (of salvation). If the theology was spelled out in trinitarian terms, a two-part summary results in which a statement of trinitarian faith is followed by statements about the person and work of Jesus Christ. It is quite natural that this pattern is much more common in doctrinal formulations than in baptismal confessions.

In the New Testament writings this binitarian pattern occurs much more frequently than trinitarian formulas, and writers like Irenaeus and Tertullian often state the rule of faith in a binitarian form, whereby the sending of the Holy Spirit may be included as part of the work of Christ. There is, however, only sparse and uncertain evidence that two-part questions or confessions were used at baptism. Baptism in two names is, to my knowledge, only attested in the sect of the Elchasaites. It is quite unlikely that a dyadic or binitarian form was a transitional stage between confession of faith in Jesus and a trinitarian confession at baptism. This is, I think, related to the fact that the rite of baptism initially involved a single, and later a threefold, immersion in water.

The ceremony of a threefold immersion accompanied by a triadic interrogatory creed is attested by Hippolytus, Cyprian, and Tertullian, and probably presupposed already by Irenaeus and Justin. Even Clement and Origen presuppose a baptismal interrogation, either preceding or accompanying the immersion. The practice, in other words, can be traced back at least to the mid-second century (Justin). The Didache attests that a threefold baptismal immersion or effusion of water had become customary already before that time. We cannot assume, however, that the act was accompanied by a threefold interrogation and confession. The other practice, which later became universal, whereby the person who administered the act said, "In the name of the Father—and of the Son—and of the Holy Spirit," would seem to have been early Syriac and may already be presupposed in the Didache. It is also likely that from the beginning the ritual included an invocation, with praise of God and prayer (as in a Jewish berakah), and that fairly early on it included an epiclesis of the three names.

The great commission in Matthew 28 does prescribe baptism "in the name (*eis to onoma*) of the Father and of the Son and of the Holy Spirit," but this does not mean that it prescribes a specific liturgical form or formula. In this context, the construction *eis to onoma* is probably to be understood as a Semitism. It speaks about intentionality of the act: those who become disciples should be baptized with reference to, for the sake of, or simply with the Father, the Son, and the Holy Spirit in mind. Even so, the names must somehow have been uttered or invoked, but the formulation does not tell us how this was done, nor is it clear that Matthew presupposes the rite of a threefold immersion. It is fairly clear that the original practice was to baptize "in the name of Jesus," in the form of a single immersion.

We do not really know when the practice of a threefold immersion or effusion of water accompanied by a trinitarian confession or invocation emerged. It is quite possible that the threefold repetition of the act at one point simply served to make the rite more efficacious, as is the case with many rites and practices. Trinitarian formulas certainly existed prior to and independent of the threefold baptismal rite and the practice of a threefold interrogation. Trinitarian formulas within the New Testament vary a great deal with respect to form and function. Several, for example, are used in greetings or blessings (2 Cor. 13:14; cf. Rev. 1:4-6; 1 Pet. 1:2; Jude 20-21). Apparently, the threefold repetition of the baptismal rite and the trinitarian formulas were associated with each other, and the great commission in Matthew 28 reinforced the association, resulting in the practice of tripartite baptismal interrogations and, later, declaratory trinitarian creeds.

At this point it may be less than obvious that this survey of complicated questions about the form, function, and, to some extent, the origin of trinitarian creeds has much to do with the second part of my presentation on New Testament Christology. This question can be addressed only briefly.

1. The study of baptismal confessions, summaries of faith, and related texts from the second and later centuries is of great importance for the study of kerygmatic summaries, hymns, confessions, and other christological formulas in the New Testament. The abundance of material from the later centuries allows for pursuit of form-critical studies in a methodical and controlled manner. By way of contrast, more limited New Testament material has left room for numerous unverifiable conjectures, often based upon the assumption that one can reconstruct a specific text by eliminating alleged secondary glosses added by Paul or some other author. The post–New Testament data prove that pattern and phraseology are remarkably constant but that it is hardly ever possible to find any two texts that are exactly alike. Moreover, the same patterns recur in interrogatory and declaratory creeds, in formulations of the rule of faith, in professions of faith intended to prove orthodoxy, in conciliar documents, and the like. On the other hand, various forms may be used both in baptismal confessions and in the other types of texts, so that there is no single correlation between form and function. Moreover, there is no evidence that the most basic and simple formulations are necessarily also the earliest. It is time for students of New Testament Christology to take serious account of such insights.

2. It is, moreover, important to observe that the earliest trinitarian confessions assumed the form of affirmative answers to questions of faith. The baptismal symbols affirm faith in God the Father, in Jesus Christ, and in the Holy Spirit, in whose name(s) the baptism is performed. Since baptism is especially related to the work of Christ, especially to his death and resurrection, it is quite natural that the second article is usually spelled out in greater detail than the first and the third. The additional items, which became integrated into the third article, all deal with the benefits of baptism in the threefold name: incorporation into the holy church, assertion of forgiveness of sins, promise of resurrection or eternal life. It is misleading to consider the baptismal confessions general summaries of Christian doctrine, an approach that may easily reveal that some important aspects are missing.

The New Testament writings contain some trinitarian formulas but no doctrine of the Holy Trinity and no clear evidence for trinitarian confessions. But there are fairly clear indications that those who were baptized confessed their faith and did so in the form of an answer to a question. The controversial term *eperōtēma* in 1 Peter 3:21 probably does designate the practice of interrogation with an affirmative answer. If so, baptism would not be characterized as an appeal to God, but rather as a commitment or a pledge to God of a good conscience (intention), through the resurrection of Jesus Christ. In any case, it is clear in Romans 10:8ff. that it is the same word of Christ that is proclaimed by the apostle and that is near, upon the lips and in the heart of a person who confesses "Jesus is Lord" and believes that God raised him from the dead.

There is, in general, a close correlation between missionary proclamation and baptismal confession. If this is kept in mind, the difference between christological and trinitarian confession and between baptism "in the name of Jesus" and baptism in the three-fold name loses much of its relevance. Whether the person who joined the church confessed "Jesus is the Christ, the Son of God" or acclaimed Jesus as Kyrios or used some less formal words, the confession expressed an acceptance of a "yes and amen" to the message proclaimed. The missionary proclamation centered on the crucified and risen Christ but also implied a call to turn from idols to serve the true and living God, the Creator who gave life to the whole universe and who had vindicated Jesus, the crucified Messiah, by raising him from the dead. The Holy Spirit had, through the Holy Scriptures, spoken beforehand about the coming of Christ, and now the Spirit had been poured out and was promised to those who believed and were baptized. This is, of course, a very rough sketch that may not cover all types of missionary preaching; but on the whole, we may safely assume that even if the explicit confession of converts spoke explicitly only about faith in Jesus, this confession implied a positive response to preaching that included talk about God and the Holy Spirit as well as a christological kerygma.

3. With few exceptions both interrogatory and declaratory creeds place the confession of faith in Jesus Christ within a trinitarian framework. I find this more relevant to the New Testament data than do most modern studies, which tend to treat New Testament Christology in isolation—whether they deal with the kerygma, or with the names and titles of Christ, or with confessional and other stereotyped christological formulas. Until quite recently, a study of the ways in which the New Testament authors talk about God has been neglected, and New Testament scholars have, by and large, left it to their colleagues in historical and systematic theology to discuss the relationship of New Testament data to trinitarian faith and dogma. My thesis is that New Testament Christology can be treated properly only if it is related to faith in God,

as present in the Jewish Scriptures and in contemporary Judaism, which also had assimilated elements of Greek philosophical monotheism. At the same time, what is said about Christ cannot be isolated from early Christian experience of the Holy Spirit, the Spirit of God and of Christ. Jesus is represented as the Christ of God, the Son and agent of God, the righteous sufferer who was vindicated by God; language used to speak about God is transferred to Jesus as well.

Generalized talk about revelation will not do. There are statements to the effect that Jesus is the one who has made God known, but we read at least as often that it is God who reveals Jesus—to the disciples, after the resurrection, and finally, at the second coming. What is said about God is not derived from Christology, so that the second article ought to have been the first; but neither does the New Testament contain any general theistic doctrine of God that is then supplemented by Christology. We hear much more that God demonstrated his sovereign power by raising Jesus and thus proved himself to be the God who makes the dead alive. In a similar way, God's dealings with Jews and Gentiles demonstrates that he really is the impartial judge he was believed to be. The death of Jesus for us proves that God is merciful and is the loving Father. The folly of the cross is a manifestation of his inscrutable wisdom. There is constant two-way traffic: given concepts of God are used to interpret what happened to Jesus and what occurred within the Christian church and its mission, and faith in God is in turn shaped by faith in Jesus and related events.

In a somewhat similar fashion, the Holy Spirit is interconnected with God and with faith in Jesus Christ. It is hardly conceivable that the Easter events would have led to the conviction that Christ had been vindicated and a new age had dawned if there had not been a related conviction that the Holy Spirit had been poured out and was experienced in charismatic phenomena, in the communal life, in the mission to Jews and Gentiles, and as an assistant in trials and a power in weakness. The Spirit is the Spirit of God, who inspired the prophets and who sent Jesus; it is also the Spirit of the risen Christ, to a degree that makes the formulations "Christ in you" and "the Spirit in you" interchangeable. The confession "Jesus is Lord" is evidence that a person has received the Holy Spirit, and the confession of Jesus as the Christ is a criterion by means of which the Spirit of God can be distinguished from the spirit of falsehood. To spell this out in detail and with scholarly care would require a series of lectures on New Testament Christology, with due attention to the differences between individual authors and writings. In generalized terms I may say that, according to the New Testament, God the Father, Jesus Christ, and (less clearly) the Holy Spirit each have a discrete identity, and yet none of the three can be described adequately unless the interrelationship among them is taken into account.

4. The trinitarian dogma, as it was later formulated, may seem to imply the logical paradox that three are one and one is three. Theologians have tried to find analogies that, at least in part, might render the mystery less incomprehensible. Neither the early trinitarian creeds nor the New Testament contains any doctrine of the Trinity in this strict sense. If the form of the trinitarian creeds is filled with biblical content, we are faced with a mystery and a paradox of a different order, namely, that whether we are dealing with the Creator and Ruler of all things—to whom we owe thanks for the gift of life and to whom we are to give account for what we have done with our lives—or with Jesus, a Jew who once was crucified under Pontius Pilate, or with communal and individual experiences of love, joy, peace, charismatic utterance, and religious experience in the present, all have to do with one and the same God. It is easy to go astray by separating the three articles from one another and by misconstruing the one or the other. What is called for, if we are to hold them together, is not the acceptance of a logical contradiction or a system of theological orthodoxy but something much deeper—what I might call a form of life that corresponds to the baptismal confession of faith in God the Father, in Jesus Christ, his Son, our Lord, and in the Holy Spirit.

Addendum: Types of Early Baptismal Creeds

1. The trinitarian core (without expansions)

Interrogations
Do you believe in God the Father Almighty?
Do you believe in Jesus Christ?
Do you believe in the Holy Spirit?
(Crowe missale [ed. Warner]; Whitaker, p. 215)

Declarative
I believe in the Father and the Son and the Spirit of Holiness.

> We believe in the name of the Father and of the Son and of
> the Spirit of Holiness.
> (Syriac History of John the Son of Zebedee, ed. Wright, *Apoc-*
> *ryphal Acts*; Whitaker, pp. 22–23)

2. Core, with brief expansion of the second question

Interrogations at Milan, fourth century
> Do you believe in God the Father Almighty? . . .
> Do you believe in our Lord Jesus Christ and his
> cross? . . .
> Do you believe also in the Holy Spirit? . . .
> (Ambrose, *De sacramentis*, 2.7; cf. *De mysteriis*)

3. Explication of all three names

Allusion (brief interrogations?)
> All those . . . who believe that our instruction and message
> are true, and promise that they are able to live according to
> them, are admonished to pray . . . and are reborn. . . . For
> they receive a lustral washing in the water
>> in the name of the Father and Lord (*despotēs*) of the universe,
>> and of our Savior Jesus Christ,
>> and of the Holy Spirit.
> Over the person who has . . . repented of his sins
>> the name of the Father and Lord God of the universe is
>> named. . . .
> Moreover, it is
>> in the name of Jesus Christ
>>> who was crucified under Pontius Pilate, and
>> in the name of the Holy Spirit,
>>> who through the prophets announced beforehand the
>> things relating to Jesus,
>> that the person who is enlightened is washed.
> (Justin, *Apol.* 1.61; see Kelly, *Creeds*, pp. 42–44, 70–73)

4. Additions to the triadic core

Possible allusions
> [The five loaves of Mark 6:30 par. signify faith]
> in the Father, the ruler of the universe (*Pantokratōr*?)
> and in Jesus Christ our Savior,
> and in the Holy Spirit, the Paraclete,
> and in the Holy Church,

and in the forgiveness of sins.
(*Epist. Apostolorum* 5; Denzinger §1)

Short Egyptian creeds
I believe in God the Father the *Pantokratōr*,
and in his only (begotten) Son, our Lord Jesus Christ,
and in the Holy Spirit,
and in the resurrection of the flesh,
in [*en te*] holy catholic church.
(Papyrus Der-Palyzeh; Denzinger §2)

I believe in one God the Father, the ruler of all (*Pantokratōr*),
and in one Son, the Lord Jesus Christ,
and in the Holy Spirit,
and the resurrection of the flesh,
and one holy catholic church.
(Ethiopic rite, Denzinger §5; for variants cf. Hahn, pp. 140–41; Whitaker, p. 94)

5. Four questions of faith

Allusions (?)
Do you believe in God the Father?
And do you believe in Jesus Christ his Son,
   who was born of the Holy Spirit and the Virgin Mary?
And do you believe in the Holy Spirit?
Do you believe in the holy church, the forgiveness of sins,
   the resurrection of the flesh?
(Maximus of Turin, *Tractatus de baptismo* [*MPL* 75: 775–80])

6. Trinitarian/christological pattern

Do you believe in the all-holy Trinity, in the Father, Son, and
   Holy Spirit?
Do you believe in the birth of Christ?
Do you believe in the baptism of Christ? . . . in the crucifixion?
   . . . in the burial? . . . the resurrection? . . . the ascension of
   Christ?
In his sitting at the right hand of God?
In the coming again of Christ to judge the living and the dead?
(Ms. P [13th c.] in *Rituale Armenorum*, ed. Conybeare and Ma-
   clean; Whitaker, p. 67)

7. Roman and other Western creeds: Appositional clauses in the second article; ecclesiological and soteriological items integrated in the third article

Interrogations	*Declarative*
Dost thou believe in God the Father almighty?	I believe in God the Father almighty;
Dost thou believe in Christ Jesus, the Son of God,	and in Christ Jesus his only Son, our Lord,
Who was born by the Holy Spirit from the Virgin Mary,	Who was born from the Holy Spirit and the Virgin Mary,
Who was crucified under Pontius Pilate, and died,	Who under Pontius Pilate was crucified, and buried,
and rose again on the third day living from the dead,	on the third day rose again from the dead,
and ascended into the heavens,	ascended to heaven,
and sat down on the right hand of the Father,	sits on the right hand of the Father,
and will come to judge the living and the dead?	whence he will come to judge the living and the dead;
Dost thou believe in the Holy Spirit in the holy Church?	and in the Holy Spirit, the holy Church, the remission of sins, the resurrection of the flesh.

(Kelly, *Creeds*, p. 114)

8. Main Eastern type: Appositional clauses added to all three names; soteriological/ecclesiological items added

Niceno–Constantinopolitan Creed
(Kelly, *Creeds*, pp. 297f.)

9. Appositional clauses in the first two articles: later Western type
North Africa
(Denzinger, §§21–22 [cf. §16, Aquileia; §17, Moesia/Dacia])
Gallia, later Roma
(Denzinger, §§27,30)
Uncertain Eastern examples: Antioch (Denzinger §50); Eusebius
(Denzinger §40); Nicaea 325

Select Bibliography

Andresen, Carl. *Die Kirchen der alten Christenheit*. Stuttgart: W. Kohlhammer, 1971.

Badcock, F. J. *The History of the Creeds*. London, 1930. 2d ed., 1938.

Campenhausen, H. von. "Das Bekenntnis im Urchristentum." *ZNW* 63:210–53.

Caspari, Carl Paul. *Alte und neue Quellen zur Geschichte des Taufsymbols und der Glaubensregel*. Brussels: Culture et Civilisation, 1964.

Daniélou, J. *The Origin of Latin Christianity*. Trans. D. Smith and J. A. Baker. Philadelphia: Westminster, 1977.

———. *The Theology of Jewish Christianity*. 1964.

Denzinger, J. D. *Enchiridion Symbolorum*. Barcelona: Herder, 1976. 1st ed., 1957.

Ghellinck, J. de. *Patristique et moyen âge*. Vol. 1. Brussels and Paris, 1946. 2d ed., 1949.

Hahn, August. *Bibliothek der Symbole und Glaubensregeln der alten Kirche*. Breslau: F. Morgenstern, 1877.

Hamilton, J. N. D. "Creeds and Baptismal Rites in the First Four Centuries." *JTS* 44 (1943) 1–11.

Harnack, Adolf von. *History of Dogma*. 7 vols. London: Williams & Norgaate, 1896–1912.

Heurtley, C. A. *Harmonia symbolica*. Oxford: University Press, 1854 or 1858.

Kattenbusch, Ferdinand. *Das apostolische Symbol*. 2 vols. Hildesheim: Olms, 1962.

Kelly, J. N. D. *Early Christian Creeds*. New York: D. M. Day, 1961.

Kretschmar, Georg. "Die Geschichte des Taufgottesdienstes." In *Leiturgia* 3, ed. F. K. Müller, Kassel, 1970, 1–348.

———. "Die Grundstruktur der Taufe." *Jahrbuch für Liturgik und Hymnologie* 22 (1978) 1–12.

———. *Studien zur frühchristlichen Trinitätstheologie*. Tübingen: Mohr, 1956.

Lietzmann, Hans. *Symbole der alten Kirche*. 4th ed. Kleine Texte, vols. 17–18. Berlin: DeGruyter, 1935.

———. *Symbolstudien 1–14*. Darmstadt: Wissenschaftliche Buchgesellschaft, 1966.

Lindroth, H. *Den apostoliska trosbekännelsen*. Stockholm, 1933.

Moe, Olaf. "Hat Paulus den trinitarischen Taufbefehl Matth. 28, 19 und ein trinitarisches Taufbekenntnis gekannt?" In *Reinhold–Seeberg–Festschrift* I, Leipzig, 1929, 179–96.

Norden, Eduard. *Agnostos Theos*. Leipzig, 1933.

Puniet, P. de. "Baptême." In *Dictionnaire d'archéologie chrétienne et de liturgie* II 1. Paris, 1910.

Samme. "The History of the Baptismal Formula." *JTS* 16 (1965).

Scheidt, H. *Die Taufwasserweihegebete*. Münster, 1935.

Schmidt, K. L. In *RHPR* (1938).

Seeberg, A. *Der Katechismus der Urchristenheit*. Munich: Kaiser, 1966.
Severinsen, P. *Daabens Ord*. Odense, 1924.
Wainright, A. W. *The Trinity in the New Testament*. London: SPCK, 1962.
Whitaker, Edward Charles, ed. *Documents of the Baptismal Liturgy*. London: SPCK, 1970.

Appendix A

Rudolf Bultmann's
Theology of the New Testament

THE APPEARANCE of Bultmann's *Theology of the New Testament* is a major event in the history of biblical scholarship, for two reasons.[1] First, Bultmann is the first to publish a comprehensive treatment of New Testament theology in more than a generation. His work is distinguished as much by unity of conception as by mastery of materials. Until now, no New Testament theology by a scholar of our generation has been equal to the standard works of the liberal and conservative schools. F. Büchsel wrote a textbook useful for the beginner. E. Stauffer is as arbitrary as he is provocative. F. C. Grant has published a fine introduction to New Testament thought. The late Maurice Goguel's two volumes on the rise of Christianity and of the church synthesize the results of decades of comprehensive and penetrating study. But only Bultmann has presented a New Testament theology of broad scope in our generation.[2]

Second, it is equally important that this theology of the New Testament is the work of Rudolf Bultmann; it is the culmination of his lifelong work as an interpreter of the New Testament. One might say that all his work since World War I has pointed toward such a comprehensive summary. This book is the equal of his two classic works, the *History of the Synoptic Tradition* and his commentary on the Fourth Gospel (*The Gospel of John*, ET 1971). This should be a sufficient indication of the book's importance.

ITS PLACE IN THE HISTORY OF BIBLICAL SCHOLARSHIP

At the outset, it may be useful to clarify the work's place in the history of biblical studies (cf. Epilogue, II, 237–51). It synthesizes many diverse trends in New Testament scholarship. First of all, it is continuous with previous work in biblical criticism and history-of-religions research (II, 250). This may be observed at every point. The structure as well as many details reveal Bultmann's background in the history-of-religions school. He builds upon the research of men such as W. Wrede, W. Heitmüller, and W. Bousset—and frequently retains even their disputed conclusions. But Bultmann has also assimilated the research of the last generation. The book's word studies, models of conciseness and precision, illustrate that Bultmann's *Theology* was written during the period of publication of Kittel's *Theological Dictionary*.[3] In contrast, the form-critical method has not affected the work to the degree one might have expected.[4] He has little regard for "typology," eagerly pursued by many scholars today. He remains critical and judicious.

Yet for Bultmann critical and historical research is only preliminary. The reconstruction of early Christian history stands "in the service of the interpretation of the New Testament writings under the presupposition that they have something to say to the present" (II, 251). By setting this course, Bultmann distinguishes himself not only from the history-of-religions school but also from a scholar such as Goguel. Goguel was a historian who investigated the phenomena of early Christianity in order to understand how religious experience led to the creation of a new religious object and functioned historically through the development of theology and of social structures.

Bultmann's work (unlike, for example, H. Weinel's)[5] is properly titled *Theology of the New Testament*. In his biblical theological approach he shows his kinship with the great theological renewal of the years following World War I, associated with names such as Karl Barth and Gogarten.[6] However, this new orientation has not necessitated for Bultmann a break with comparative religion; he, unlike many others, has succeeded in integrating theology and historical research. His work with the texts requires that faith be viewed in relation to its object, namely, as faith in the kerygma. Faith cannot be conceived as a nontheoretical attitude (e.g., as cultic piety or as mysticism). Faith in the kerygma always implies a specific understanding that becomes theologically explicit in historical situations.

The nature of New Testament theology demands that it be presented not as dogmatic system but rather in its historical development. It follows directly from the theology of the New Testament itself that no universally valid Christian dogmatic is possible. Each generation must face the theological task anew in the specificity of its historical situation. To replace a traditional dogmatic system with a system of Heilsgeschichte is not particularly helpful; Stauffer is reproached because he turns theology into a religious philosophy of history (II, 248). The center of the New Testament for Bultmann is not the "Christian understanding of time and history"[7] but the message of the pardoning of sinners through God's act in Jesus Christ. Accordingly, the theological statements of the New Testament are the explication of the understanding founded in faith and given in specific historical situations; in this insight Bultmann follows A. Schlatter: the act of thinking and the act of living should not be separated (II, 237).

But even the addition of this reference to Schlatter is not a sufficient description of Bultmann's place in the history of biblical scholarship. Schlatter's concern was careful description, and he was guided by the belief that unbiased observation would disclose not only the life of the historical Jesus but also the significance of the "history of Christ." Bultmann, in contrast, pursues the kerygma that is grasped only in faith and the theological understanding that follows from it. Therefore, he must move from mere observation to putting questions to the texts: How do they understand the kerygma? What understanding of God, humankind, and the world does the kerygma provide? This constant questioning of the texts is not merely a hermeneutical means by which to establish what the Scriptures themselves say; the texts are also questioned as to how far the theology implicitly and explicitly present in them is a proper expression of the self-understanding of faith. Out of the distinction between, and interrelation of, kerygma and theology arises the task of content criticism (II, 238f.). This understanding of the task springs neither from history-of-religions research nor from the influence of Barth or Schlatter.

As precedent for his content criticism Bultmann appeals to Luther and his criticism of the Epistle of James and of Revelation (II, 239). Bultmann's theology of the New Testament stands in the Reformation tradition, specifically the Lutheran understanding of Scripture.[8] Bultmann finds that content criticism is not only an abstract possibility but an actual necessity. He is led to this conclusion by his observation that traces of the "Development toward the Ancient Church" (par. 51–61) are already present within the New Testament. I take his point to be that the "Catholicism" of the early church cannot be criticized on the basis of the New Testament without criticizing parts of the content of the New Testament itself; this cannot, in fact, be easily contradicted. Catholicism can hardly be opposed with imitative biblicism. It appears today, therefore, that not only a liberal Catholicism of Anglican character, as is represented by F. C. Grant, but even Roman Catholicism is often more open to historical investigation of the New Testament than is a biblicizing Protestantism.

For Bultmann, as for Luther, the kerygma, or gospel, is the point of orientation and the center of all theology. His preference for Paul and John is genuinely Lutheran. Bultmann obtains the criteria for his content criticism from them. In no recent biblical theology is the Pauline doctrine of justification made so pivotal and presented so impressively. It is no accident that Bultmann's New Testament theology ends with the ecclesiastical institution of penance, where Luther's reformation began. With his content criticism he sets *Christum contra Scripturam*.[9]

The question might be posed whether content criticism should not be a task of systematic theology rather than of New Testament scholarship. Does Bultmann not cross the boundary between biblical theology and systematic theology? In fact there is no sharp line for him. Biblical theology leads him to the point of which criticism stops and preaching begins, while Goguel's presentation presses on to the threshold of philosophy of religion. The boundary, however, is not crossed, at least not intentionally. Bultmann's interpretation sets forth the understanding of human existence implied in the theological statements of the New Testament. This is to him a scholarly task. This interpretation of New Testament theological statements in the categories of existentialism should not be confused with existential knowledge of God.[10] It is evident, however, that one cannot understand Bultmann's theology of the New Testament without considering his hermeneutical principles; these in turn presuppose a specific philosophical analysis of human existence.

Therefore, Bultmann's presentation belongs to the category of philosophically determined interpretations of the New Testament. It employs quite consciously a terminology stemming from a specific philosophical tradition. That must be taken into account, especially by one who, like the reviewer, considers himself an outsider in relation to German philosophy. Although in his work on the problem of hermeneutics Bultmann begins with Wilhelm Dilthey and Count Yorck von Wartenburg,[11] he leaves no doubt that fundamentally he draws especially upon the existential philosophy of the early Martin Heidegger. Insight into the "historicity of existence" has decisively clarified the problem of understanding historical documents and appears to Bultmann to be the appropriate "preunderstanding" for the interpretation of the New Testament.

These philosophical presuppositions explain the terminology—often quite difficult for the non-German to understand—with which Bultmann interprets the New Testament. They also explain the somewhat "schoolmasterish" tone in which he questions the New Testament writings concerning their understanding of existence and criticizes their mythological view. He knows how to state not only what the New Testament writings say but also what they express "in reality" (e.g., I, 259). He knows the real intention of Paul (I, 301) and can even further develop his thought (I, 253). His intention in this is neither to make dogmatic judgments nor to employ a particular theological method; existential interpretation means, rather, that the writings of the New Testament are to be questioned as to how they understand human existence in history. In the same way, all classical historical phenomena are to be questioned and interpreted in terms of their understanding of existence. Bultmann himself has impressively done this in his *Primitive Christianity*, in relation to the Old Testament and Judaism, Hellenic culture and Hellenism.[12]

Bultmann brings three questions to the New Testament: (1) Does the New Testament present a unique understanding of existence? (2) What are the specifics of this understanding? (3) Is this understanding of existence a possibility for contemporary man? Bultmann finds that a new self-understanding in faith is made possible through the kerygma and is developed by Paul and John. Therefore content criticism is a legitimate scientific enterprise, for it deals with the question whether this specifically Christian self-understanding is retained or abandoned in the other New Testament writings.

Bultmann asks what the writings of the New Testament have to say to the present through what they said in their specific historical situations. Thus, not only the kerygma but also the believing self-understanding made possible by it is to some extent extricated from the concrete historical limitation imposed by the New Testament. For as Bultmann views the theology of the New Testament, the facts of both the history of Jesus and of early Christianity, like "mythological" cosmology, eschatology, and Christology, are meaningful only insofar as they can illuminate the understanding of existence. The connection of the "act of thinking" with the "act of living," taken concretely by Schlatter, is traced to prior understanding of the historicity of existence. The theology of the New Testament is presented not as historically given but as existentially significant. One can therefore say: the New Testament is dehistoricized; and one will have to ask whether this dehistoricizing of the New Testament is no more characteristic of the theology of Bultmann than the famous demythologizing, which is, of course, but another side of the same concern.

In this respect Bultmann approximates the Enlightenment, which in the interpretation of the New Testament laid aside "everything local and temporal, everything individual and particular" (II, 243). Certainly he does not seek to extract timeless, universal truths; he seeks to determine the new possibility of understanding human existence by distilling it out of concrete history. Thus he stands nearer to F. C. Baur, for whom Hegelian philosophy rendered a service similar to that which Heidegger renders for Bultmann. A parallel phenomenon, again from different philosophical presuppositions, is the Swedish Lundensian theology represented by A. Nygren in his *Agape and Eros*, in which the writings of the New Testament and the history of doctrine are examined for the basic motif lying behind the concrete statements.

We all depend upon philosophical traditions to some extent. Certainly, important advances in New Testament historical research often have been associated with philosophical reflection. One cannot deny that existential philosophy—itself influenced by Christian tradition—can render worthwhile services in the interpretation of the New Testament. Bultmann is not forced by his philosophical presuppositions to lose sight of the kerygma and thereby to eliminate it, as did Baur and the theology of the Enlightenment. In relation to Nygren, Bultmann has an advantage, since it is easier for him to clarify how the gospel frees us from the law. Moreover, the connection with Heidegger has helped him to break through and to correct the earlier dominant understanding of New Testament anthropology that was determined by the idealistic tradition. Yet, by embracing existential philosophy, he sets forth the theological statements of the New Testament only in a peculiarly anthropological metamorphosis. The question arises whether or not Bultmann absolutizes his philosophical preunderstanding in such a way that he decides in advance what the New Testament writings may or may not really say.

The lineage of Bultmann's theology can be traced in quite diverse directions. One cannot, however, speak of eclecticism. Bultmann's theology is a syncretistic phenomenon only in the same sense as is the Johannine, in which—at least if we are to believe Bultmann—very distinct traditions are worked into a consistent unity. The inner consistency of this presentation is impressive; it is almost uncanny. It seems to rest on a kind of preestablished harmony of critical biblical study, Reformation faith, and modern existential philosophy. A defect at one point might easily make the whole impressive structure totter.

It is not easy to enter into genuine dialogue with the work. That a circular method is present is easily verified. The hermeneutical propriety of the existential approach is demonstrated by New Testament theology, which is in turn existentially interpreted. However, that need not be a vicious circle; it could also be a legitimate hermeneutical circle. For the decisive test of any hermeneutical method lies in its appropriateness in relation to the text to be interpreted. This test presupposes an exegesis of the text, while the exegesis already assumes a hermeneutical method. Bultmann works out the interrelation with such consistency, however, that the result appears to be a closed system, bewildering at least one observer.

What has been said about the place of the work within the history of research enables us to make a preliminary evaluation of the book's worth. The principal achievement of Bultmann's *Theology of the New Testament* is that it both differentiates and correlates kerygma and theology; the theological statements are understood as an explication of faith in the face of specific historical challenges. Thus, the separation of the "act of thinking" from the "act of living" is avoided. Two misunderstandings of the New Testament are thereby overcome: orthodox and rationalistic intellectualism, and the anti-intellectualism of the liberals and of the history-of-religions school. In this regard, one can only hope that subsequent work will not fall short of this achievement.

The main problems of Bultmann's work arise from the existentialistic interpretation of the theology of the New Testament in terms of a new self-understanding and the consequent dehistoricization of the New Testament. Discussion with Bultmann has to focus here.[13] This review can only make a beginning by substantiating and elucidating these two theses.

THE OUTLINE OF THE BOOK

The outline of the work is clear. In the center stands the theology of Paul (I, 185–352); it serves as the point of historical orientation, and greatest stress falls on it. The centrality of Paul may be seen by what Bultmann relegates to "Presuppositions and Motifs of New

Testament Theology": "The Message of Jesus" (I, 3–32), "The Kerygma of the Earliest Church" (I, 33–62), and "The Kerygma of the Hellenistic Church aside from Paul" (I, 63–183). "The Theology of the Gospel of John and the Johannine Epistles" stands independently beside Paul (II, 3–92). A fourth and final section deals with "The Development toward the Ancient Church": "The Rise of Church Order and Its Earliest Development" (II, 95–118), "The Development of Doctrine" (II, 119–54), "Christology and Soteriology" (II, 155–202), and "The Problem of Christian Living" (II, 203–36).

A glance at the table of contents shows that in one respect Bultmann's work carries out the program advanced by W. Wrede.[14] Moreover, one is reminded of W. Bousset's *Kyrios Christos*. What Bousset had presented in monograph form, Bultmann carries through for the whole of New Testament theology. By choosing one option, Bultmann has succeeded in presenting both the unity and the diversity of the New Testament. He thus masters this persistent problem of New Testament theology. The unity lies in the determinative importance of the kerygma for theology throughout the New Testament. Furthermore, all New Testament writings presuppose not only Jesus and the earliest church but also the development of Christianity in Hellenistic communities. The post-Pauline writings all belong in some way to the development toward the ancient church and are in various ways affected by the same questions. Above all, between John and Paul, Bultmann finds an essential affinity (II, 6f.).

The outline of the work itself reveals a preference for Pauline and Johannine theology. In a certain sense only in the Pauline and Johannine writings can one speak of a comprehensive and consistent theological perspective. This was already observed by Wrede, but Bultmann has gone further: the close relation of believing self-understanding to the kerygma is explicit only in Pauline and Johannine theology. Bultmann's arrangement tends to neglect unduly the theology of the other New Testament writings. It is striking that the theological perspectives implicit in Matthew, Mark, and Luke-Acts are only indicated but not really analyzed.

Bultmann begins his book by asserting that "the message of Jesus is a presupposition for the theology of the New Testament rather than a part of that theology itself." There are no good reasons to object at this point. The history-of-religions school had already recognized that New Testament Christianity could neither be identified with the religion of Jesus nor be derived directly from it.[15]

194

The kerygma of Jesus Christ, the Crucified and Risen One, is the foundation of the whole theology of the New Testament, including that of the Gospels. The preaching of Jesus isolated from this kerygma and critically reconstructed is only a presupposition. Yet the words and work of Jesus do belong to the theology of the New Testament insofar as (and in the forms in which) they were handed on by the church, interpreted, and presented in the Gospels. To be sure, the substance and the consequences of the Christian faith could be developed with little attention to any details of Jesus' life, as was done by Paul. But what characterizes the New Testament is the inclusion of Gospels as well as epistles. Certainly the Gospels, too, may be approached with questions concerning the understanding of existence that they imply. But this understanding is expressed only in an indirect way. The direct unfolding of the kerygma takes the form of stories about what Jesus said and did as recollected and interpreted by Christian faith. This interpretation of Jesus' history should be closely analyzed in a theology of the New Testament.[16] Bultmann does not feel obliged to do so because he sees the theology of the New Testament to be statements concerning believing existence; but in view of the sources, this is quite one-sided. Bultmann abstracts the eschatological kerygma from the history of Jesus presented and interpreted in the Gospels and dehistoricizes it in ultra-Pauline fashion. This is clear even in the outline of the work.

Bultmann does recognize that the message of Jesus, precisely because it is *his* message, is not only historically antecedent to but also a necessary presupposition for New Testament theology. For this reason he deals with it in his work. In an analogous way, perhaps, the Old Testament, as the Holy Scripture presupposed by the New Testament writers, ought to have been discussed. That is not necessary for Bultmann because he finds no necessary connection between the kerygma and the Old Testament, nor does he see the kerygma within a comprehensive perspective of salvation history (for which he appeals to John; cf., e.g., II, 122). In general, although significant nonbiblical parallel material is presupposed, it is cited only occasionally. In this respect the book *Primitive Christianity in Its Contemporary Setting* is a valuable supplement to the larger work. But here as well Bultmann deals less with historical details than with the essential characteristics of Judaism, Greek culture, and early Christianity. These are somewhat systematized but sharply, suggestively, and clearly worked out.

Thus the main questions that are to be raised with respect to the organization of Bultmann's book are at the same time questions about his interpretation of the New Testament. It may be said parenthetically that Bultmann's ordering of the material, like any other order, leaves some difficulties unresolved. It turns out to be impossible to distinguish clearly between the "Hellenistic Church aside from Paul" and "The Development toward the Ancient Church." For example, the material treated in paragraph 11, "The Church's Relation to Judaism and the Problem of the Old Testament," properly belongs to the post-Pauline period.

THE HISTORY OF PRIMITIVE CHRISTIANITY

Bultmann brings a precise description of the history of primitive Christianity into the service of existential interpretation. The picture drawn by Bultmann has also made original contributions to historical reconstruction. His work is not simply a synthesis of prior achievements. In questions of introduction he is critical; he differs from H. J. Holtzmann very little. However, unlike Goguel, for example, he has freed himself from Baur's image of early Christian history and builds on the work of the German history-of-religions school. The stress on pre-Pauline Hellenistic Christianity is notable; so is the judgment that the Johannine writings are not dependent on Paul (II, 3ff.). For Bultmann's sketch of early Christianity it is important that he, like many others, emphasizes the significance of eschatology for the whole of primitive Christianity. This eschatological context is important for his understanding both of the kerygma and of the church. At such points one notes how much has happened in New Testament research from Bousset to Bultmann. Even if Bultmann emphasizes the changes in the understanding of existence from Jesus to the ancient church, the historical continuity that connects them is more easily seen in his work than in Bousset's. The decisive problems were largely present, though latent, in the church from the beginning (e.g., I, 118 and 12).

The message of Jesus is delineated in essentially the same way as in Bultmann's *Jesus and the Word*.[17] His presentation is impressive, even to one who might disagree on many points.[18] In the *Theology*, the question of Jesus' messianic self-consciousness is handled in some detail. With Wrede, it is still answered negatively. The methodological problems of any quest for the historical Jesus become particularly evident at this point. Detailed criticism and overall judgment of tradition are joined together. These extremely complicated questions cannot, however, be discussed here.

For a comprehensive evaluation of Bultmann's biblical theology, though, it is important to see that the negative result on this point actually supports his existential interpretation. The conclusion that Jesus did not claim to be the Messiah precludes the possibility that Jesus' messiahship can be established historically. Only in the decision of faith is Jesus to be apprehended as the revealer and Savior. For Bultmann, historical criticism's inability to draw a picture of Jesus' personality serves to deny faith any historical security. As the preacher and as the one preached, Jesus' person signifies the demand for decision. According to Bultmann, no verifiable data mitigate the *skandalon* of the Word. This explains why Jesus' messianic self-consciousness, as well as his whole history, is regarded as theologically irrelevant. To the evangelists, however, Jesus' history is not an indifferent matter, though they also know the offense; the hidden glory of this history is visible only to faith. My question to Bultmann is this: Does he not avoid the offense given with the concrete history of Jesus and thereby also lose sight of the glory, visible to faith, in this history? The kerygma isolated from Jesus' history is in danger of becoming a paradox without content.

His description of the earliest church is also dependent on the method he employs. Anyone who attempts to describe the Jerusalem church must proceed by inference. But there is a wide gulf between what *must* go back to the primitive community and what may possibly derive from it. As with the quest for the historical Jesus, it would be appropriate to clarify the maximal as well as the minimal limits in order to approach the historical facts from both sides.[19] Like Bousset, Bultmann tends to utilize only the material that can be critically established with near certitude. Bultmann makes no use of the history of later Jewish Christianity, which provides relevant though difficult opportunities for comparison.[20]

It is worth nothing that Bultmann stresses that the earliest church understood itself as the eschatological community and that tendencies toward the development of ecclesiastical forms, traditions, succession, and so forth already existed. The view that the dominant title for Jesus was "Son of Man" (I, 49) seems questionable to me; it is found almost solely in sayings attributed to Jesus. The use of the name "Christ" in the Pauline epistles presupposes that the title "Messiah" stood at the center of the oldest kerygma.[21] This is confirmed by the passion narratives, for they also focus on Jesus as King of the Jews. The scriptural proof for the messiahship and suffering of Jesus must have been developed in the earliest church. The traditional testimonies in the New Testament, therefore, should have been used more extensively in the description of its kerygma.[22]

With Bousset, Bultmann denies that Jesus could have been culticly venerated by the earliest Palestinian church (I, 50). Nevertheless, he leaves more room for the possibility that Jesus was thought already to exercise his kingly authority from heaven. He refers, among other texts, to Matthew 11:22f.; 16:17-19; 18:20. Furthermore, he assumes, at this point with less skepticism than Goguel, that the earliest church was conscious of possessing the Spirit (I, 41). He does not deny that the name of Jesus was invoked, at least in exorcism. It is only a small step to assert that exclamations of homage and supplication as well were directed to the exalted Messiah, Jesus. The contention that the *maranatha* exclamations could originally have been addressed to God (I, 51f.) seems to me a mere expedient. It is true that the use of *kyrios* in acclamations has no direct counterpart in Semitic usage. Yet the very framing of the question—whether the *kyrios* cult existed on Palestinian soil or not—is hardly suited to clarify the attitude of the earliest church to its exalted Messiah.[23]

The contributions made in the section "The Kerygma of the Hellenistic Church aside from Paul" go far beyond Bousset. Such a comprehensive picture of Christianity before and alongside Paul has not been previously drawn. Bultmann isolates traditional material primarily by lexical and form-critical analysis of the Pauline and non-Pauline writings. The endeavor is extremely suggestive and fruitful. Much remains hypothetical, but it could hardly be otherwise. It might be interesting to compare Bultmann's attempt with those of British and American scholars, independent of Bultmann and largely unknown to him.

The use of the term "kerygma" in the heading fits only part of the content of the section and can promote a common misuse of the word. What makes Hellenistic Christianity relevant for Bultmann is the kerygma at its core. To this extent, his use of the word "kerygma" in the chapter heading is justified. Yet the result is a certain one-sidedness. Preaching to Christian congregations is not to be characterized as kerygma; it should have been possible to give a fuller picture through analyses of forms, patterns, and ideas. Further, more could have been said concerning the use of christological formulas in confession, prayer, thanksgiving, and exhortation. That the kerygma evokes not only believing understanding but also confession and thanksgiving, praise of God and Christ, is insufficiently treated in the book as a whole (yet cf. II, 155).

In his treatment of the sacraments, Bultmann seems too dependent on Heitmüller's important but dated work. The naming

198

of Jesus' name as an independent sacrament concurrent with baptism (I, 137) can be derived neither from Paul nor from Luke nor from liturgical history. That baptism was performed in the name of Jesus expresses rather the relation of water baptism to the kerygma. This relation is not established by the interpretation given in Romans 6 but is its presupposition.

Seen from outside, early Hellenistic Christianity is a "syncretistic phenomenon" for Bultmann.[24] He emphasizes gnostic influence even more strongly than does Bousset. Bultmann correctly makes a sharper distinction than Reitzenstein does between mystery religions and Gnosticism. Because he sees a new understanding of existence emerging in pre-Christian and in Christian Gnosticism,[25] Bultmann assigns Gnosticism much greater historical significance than do historians of religion such as M. P. Nilsson or A. D. Nock, who work more empirically, using archaeological evidence. It remains, however, an open question whether or not one may speak of a homogeneous gnostic movement, of a religion's taking form in individual groups and congregations (I, 167). Bultmann's reference to the Qumran manuscripts as sources of a pre-Christian gnosticizing Judaism (II, 13) only makes this question more urgent.[26] The whole complex of problems will have to be worked through anew on the basis of the Qumran and Nag Hammadi documents.[27]

THE DEVELOPMENT TOWARD THE ANCIENT CHURCH

As an outline of historical development, Bultmann's fourth section, "The Development toward the Ancient Church," is closely connected with the first. Here, too, Bultmann makes important contributions. He stresses that ministry constitutes the ancient church; ecclesiastical order acquires divine sanction. Picking up the discussion between A. Harnack and R. Sohm, Bultmann perceptively observes that "Harnack focuses upon the Ecclesia as historical phenomenon; Sohm understands it from the point of view of its own understanding of itself" (II, 96). Bultmann brings to light the problems underlying a history of the ancient church; this can contribute substantially to their clarification. For example, his distinction between a regulative and a constitutive significance of church law is valuable.

It is questionable whether or not the apostles are properly to be termed charismatic leaders (II, 103f.). As Bultmann himself stresses, an apostle is one who has been commissioned. Apostles are to be designated as charismatics only in the specifically Pauline sense whereby even everyday community activities are considered charismatic (1 Cor. 12:28). The distinction between the original meaning of "apostle" (messenger of Christ in the end time) and its later assessment (initiator of a stream of tradition) could possibly have been sharpened.

The paragraphs on "Paradosis and Historical Tradition" and "The Problem of Right Teaching" (54 and 55) are extremely suggestive. The incisive formulations compel thorough reflection. In a certain sense, the whole of Bultmann's work revolves around the problem of revelation and history. The problem stems from the special character of paradosis, that it speaks of an event, at once eschatological and historical (II, 121ff.). Both Matthew and Mark express the paradox, though in different ways. But in Luke–Acts, Bultmann finds that the paradox has been resolved in the interest of a theology of history. This criticism of the Lucan writings makes clear the way in which Bultmann "dehistoricizes" the New Testament.

Luke, unlike Paul, is interested in a "life of Jesus"; eschatological awareness fades away and is replaced by a consciousness of standing within a continuing history of salvation. However, Bultmann goes too far when he claims that Luke understands Christianity as "a new religion" and as "an entity of world history" (II, 116f.). The chronological synchronisms imply little more than that Jesus lived at a definite point of time in world history. Acts is not simply an account of the establishment and early history of the Christian community; its intention is rather to report the growth of the Word. The active Word, not a chronological interconnection of cause and effect, provides the continuity of history. Therefore, the speeches do not have the same significance as those of the ancient historians. Moreover, Acts is not so isolated in the New Testament as Bultmann thinks. The Pauline epistles attest that the church that understood itself as an eschatological community was not uninterested in reports concerning the Jerusalem church or in the expansion of Christianity, and so forth (cf., e.g., 1 Thess. 2:14; 1:6ff.; Rom. 1:8; Gal. 1:23). Stories about Jesus have such an organic place in preaching that one should not regard historical tradition and preaching as antithetical.

Certainly, the first volume of Luke–Acts is not, strictly speaking, a Gospel. It is a narrative about the event whose saving significance the apostolic kerygma proclaims. The second volume is an account of the apostolic preaching that brought this kerygma to the Gentiles. The note of eschatological fulfillment is clearly sounded in both parts of the work (Luke 4:16ff. and Acts 2:16ff. are programmatic for each volume). Luke, like Matthew and Mark, knows that human eyes are opened to the saving significance of Jesus' history by the appearances of the risen Christ (Luke 24:33ff.). However, the mere existence of Luke's two-volume work indicates that he does not perceive as paradox the historicity of the saving event. This is the heart of Bultmann's objection to Luke. But did primitive Christianity identify the eschatological events with the end of history, as Bultmann assumes? The eschaton implies the end of the present course of time, but at least for a more naive view, that does not mean the end of all temporality and of history.[28] From this perspective a historical event may well have eschatological significance. The problem was located elsewhere; without the revelation of the risen Christ and the testimony of the Spirit, it was impossible to see eschatological significance in *Jesus'* history. If I understand correctly, Bultmann judges Luke–Acts by the standards of a secular scientific historiography and a dehistoricized eschatology, both of which are foreign to the author, instead of understanding Luke's work from his own much more "naive" outlook. Bultmann has censored Luke without giving him a fair chance to speak. But we must grant that this is a logical consequence of his total approach.[29]

The discussion of the various theological perspectives found within late canonical and early postcanonical writings focuses on "Christology and Soteriology" (par. 58). The inclusion of the Apostolic Fathers enables us to see more clearly the tendencies of developing tradition. He approaches the texts with this question: how is the relation of present to future salvation understood? Closely connected is the question of the relation of indicative to imperative, which stands in the foreground in the section entitled "The Problem of Christian Living" (par. 59–61). Characteristic of the developing church is the general tendency toward the disappearance of the understanding that existence is totally renewed in faith. Thus even the meaning of the eschatological "interim" is lost. The radical fallenness of man enslaved by sin is no longer seen, and the meaning of baptism is limited to forgiveness of past sins. Legalism creeps in and cannot be overcome by the sacramental emphasis. The imperative is understood moralistically; this is noticeable in many concrete demands. As the discipline of penance is institutionalized, the church becomes an institution of salvation.

Great differences exist among the individual writings. What is striking is Bultmann's positive evaluation of Ignatius, who in his own way expressed the *totaliter-aliter* of the new existence and understood faith to involve the whole being and the whole doing of the believer (*existentiell*). Bultmann stresses that there is a strong Pauline influence within Colossians, Ephesians, and the Pastorals; even Barnabas comes off rather well. In general, however, the writings are quite sharply criticized on the basis of existentially interpreted Pauline and Johannine theology.

But to what degree is it legitimate to judge these writings by standards extracted from Paul and John? Bultmann writes: "Both in terminology and in substance it is the influence of the synagogue that is here at work pushing aside the theology of Paul (and of John)" (II, 215). But may one speak of a "pushing aside"? Writings such as Hebrews and Barnabas, James and the Didache, 1 Clement and Hermas are affected only in a very superficial way, if at all, by specifically Pauline or Johannine theology. These writings draw on traditions that stem from early Christian circles distinct from those of Paul and John. Bultmann seems not to have freed himself radically enough from the old tradition of purely documentary research. The writings are so quickly examined and judged in terms of Paul and John that insufficient attention is paid to what they themselves have to say.

This is especially clear in the case of Hebrews, in which the fundamental conception is entirely different from that of Paul. Paul awaits a new creation through the eschatological act of God and sees it already realized in Christ. In contrast, for the author of Hebrews the world to come was created "from the foundation of the world" (4:3); it exists already in heaven. Accordingly, eschatological salvation is viewed not in terms of a new creation but in terms of entering a new heavenly-eschatological world. The event is described in cultic categories; salvation is not being pronounced righteous but being granted free access to God in worship. With this wholly different orientation it makes little sense to state that the Pauline antitheses *pistis—erga* and *charis—erga* are absent, or that there is no mention of dying and rising with Christ, or that there are only traditional statements about the Spirit (II, 168).

This premature comparison with Paul carries with it the consequence that even Hebrews' "understanding of existence" is prejudiced. Bultmann sees that the believer is proleptically placed into heavenly existence through baptism and is thereby freed from the world (II, 167–68). But he relates Hebrews' rejection of a second repentance much too closely to its affirmation by Hermas. In Hebrews, the impossibility of a new conversion is a necessary consequence of the singular finality of the forgiveness of sins in the death of Christ and is asserted parenthetically, not as a canon of church discipline. The life of the believer stands primarily under the promise rather than under the demand of God. For Christians who already share in eschatological existence and who live on earth as strangers, the present is an interim in more than the chronological sense. Because Christ has made entrance into the sanctuary possible for them, they should "draw near with a true heart" (10:19ff.). This summons touches their whole manner of life. Thus the imperative is really grounded in the indicative, even though the relation is not dialectical or paradoxical in the same way as it is in Paul.

Details may be debated. The fundamental question, illustrated by our discussion of Hebrews, is this: Does Bultmann prematurely apply a standard extracted from Paul and John to other early Christian writings? But to assess the whole work, we must judge whether or not Bultmann has correctly interpreted Pauline and Johannine theology.

THE INTERPRETATION OF PAULINE THEOLOGY

The division "The Theology of Paul" moves beyond mere description to profound interpretation. It is a great achievement. It represents the center of the work in more than an external way. The correlation of kerygma and believing understanding and the resulting conception of what constitutes New Testament theology are derived primarily from Paul. That is why Paul provides Bultmann with his principal standard for evaluating other New Testament writings.

Yet it is necessary to make it clear from the beginning that even Paul's theology is not simply empirically described. Bultmann's principal concern is to interpret the basic theological position that is the foundation for Paul's specific statements (I, 190). The essence of Paul's theology is more or less distilled from these specific formulations within their historical setting. The abstraction of this theological position is achieved in two ways: (1) Bultmann largely ignores the specific historical challenges in response to which Paul developed his theology, even the basic fact that Paul became the founder of Christian theology precisely as an apostle to the Gentiles; (2) Bultmann looks for what is characteristic of Pauline theology, further divesting it of historical concreteness. He thinks he must criticize Paul's statements by Paul's intention.

Bultmann presents Pauline theology as anthropology, arranging the material under two headings: (1) man prior to the revelation of faith; (2) man under faith. Existentialist leanings are obvious. Yet the arrangement is appropriate to the material. It corresponds to the outline of Romans as well as to the preaching pattern ("once you were . . . but now you are . . .") identified by Bultmann (I, 105f.). Naturally these patterns presuppose the kerygma, which Bultmann set forth in the section on the Hellenistic community. It is an obvious advantage for Bultmann that he has dealt with traditional materials in Paul's letters prior to studying the letters themselves. Bultmann has thereby freed himself from treating such traditions as an integral part of Paul's theology; he can vigorously and impressively pursue the main line of specifically Pauline thought. But this method of Bultmann's is questionable in that it enables him to reduce the meaning of common Christian tradition for the theology of Paul to the mere *that* of the kerygma. In this way, Bultmann's arrangement involves from the outset a critical stance toward the theology present in the epistles. It is true that Paul does not begin Romans with an extended statement of the "salvation-occurrence" (I, 301). The reason is simply that he presupposes the Roman congregation to be informed; thus the brief reference in 1:2-4 is an adequate reminder.

The section "Man prior to the Revelation of Faith" begins with a treatment of Paul's anthropological concepts. This treatment yields a formal analysis of the ontological structure of human existence (I, 191–227). At this point Bultmann's existentialist leanings are especially clear. There are some good reasons for this arrangement. Paul's theological statements do indeed have presuppositions that are not expressed because they were self-evident to him. Analysis of his anthropological concepts contributes to the clarification of such presuppositions. What is objectionable is Bultmann's limitation to anthropological ideas, so that something like an existentialist analysis of the structures of existence emerges. Bultmann himself knows not only that "Paul's theology is at the same time anthropology" (I, 191) but also that any statement about man speaks "about man as he is qualified by the divine deed and demand and by his attitude toward them" (I, 191). The divine existence of God is a presupposition just as self-evident for Paul as the human existence of man. The God who addresses man in the kerygma is not an unknown God for Paul but the Creator, already known from

204

the Old Testament, who directs history and who is himself its goal. Bultmann does mention this (I, 228f.), but with extraordinary brevity.

It is impossible in a review to do justice to the richness of Bultmann's presentation. Following the paragraphs on "Flesh, Sin, and the World," a section on the *dikaiosynē theou* opens the chapter of "Man under Faith." It is noteworthy—not just because of the contrast to Bousset and Wrede—that the doctrine of justification is strongly emphasized. In a purely descriptive presentation such a concentration would be one-sided. Bultmann's presentation is not affected, however, by such an objection, for Paul's essential concern is expressed nowhere so clearly as in the doctrine of justification. It is basic to Bultmann's understanding that *dikaiosynē* is here a forensic-eschatological term. It is not a human virtue but signifies humanity's relation to God. This is worked out very clearly.

Bultmann's criticism of W. Mundle clarifies the fundamental significance of the doctrine of justification: the works of the law represent human achievements in general.[30] Paul sets forth his doctrine of justification in his debate with Jews and Judaizers. Yet the polemic against works righteousness has a parallel in the polemic against the Greeks; they seek a wisdom of their own in order to have something about which to boast. In this Bultmann is quite right. Mundle's interpretation is correct only insofar as a Christian legalism not appealing to the Mosaic law was not an actual, conscious problem for the apostle. Since this was the case with Paul, it is understandable that legalism was not seen as a problem in the post-Pauline period. Again Bultmann detaches the fundamental meaning of Paul's theology from its historical situation. This is also clear in his whole treatment of the law (I, 259–69).

In Paul, the law confronts humans as the Mosaic law. According to Bultmann's interpretation, this is significant only insofar as it shows that the law is understood by Paul not as an ideal moral law but as a command of God demanding obedience in the concrete situation. What Paul had to say concerning the place of the law in pre-Christian epochs silently falls victim to critical interpretation. It is even more remarkable that Bultmann, for whom the argument of Romans 1–8 is so basic, has almost nothing to say concerning Romans 9–11. Does not a descriptive exegetical approach suggest that chapters 9–11 are central to Paul's principal concern in writing to the Roman Christians? According to Bultmann, however, the mystery of the history of salvation in these chapters is derived from

"speculative fantasy" (II, 132) and is theologically irrelevant. Bultmann convincingly locates the center of Paul's theology in the doctrine of the justification of sinners through the grace of God, and
he explicates all Paul's thought from this perspective. But Bultmann
slights the historical data when he isolates the doctrine of justification from the framework of salvation history and from futuristic
eschatology.

The question of the relation between the history of salvation
and believing self-understanding becomes acute in "Christ's Death
and Resurrection as Salvation-Occurrence" (par. 33). This section
illustrates Bultmann's claim that the task of demythologizing is
raised by the New Testament itself.[31] The problem arises because
Paul understands the grace of God not as an attribute of God but
rather as an act of God. It is the event in which God bestows the
gift of grace, radically transforming the human situation. But at the
same time, this act of grace, this salvation-occurrence, embraces
the death and resurrection of Jesus.

Bultmann first of all traces the use of the various terms by
which Paul expresses the saving significance of the cross. He finds
them problematical because they can all lead to the view that believing submission to the grace of God is dependent on a previous
acceptance of the reported data of salvation. According to the true
intention of Paul, however, "the decision-question whether a man
is willing to give up his old understanding of himself and henceforth
understand himself only from the grace of God and the question
whether he will acknowledge Jesus Christ as the Son of God and
Lord should turn out to be one and the same question" (I, 300–
301). To see that for Paul the Crucified One was the preexistent
Son of God and that the resurrection of Jesus was taken to be an
established fact makes the problem even more pressing.

Bultmann finds the answer in Paul's idea that the salvation-
occurrence continues to take place in the preaching of the Word:
"The salvation-occurrence is nowhere present except in the proclaiming, accosting, demanding, and promising word of preaching"
(I, 302). The references to the incarnation of the Preexistent One
are mythological expressions of the fact that "there exists a divinely
authorized proclamation of the prevenient grace and love of God"
(I, 305). Similarly, the resurrection—rather, the Resurrected One—
is said to be "present in the proclaiming Word" (I, 305). It is quite
clear to Bultmann himself that his exclusive concentration on this
point is not a complete portrait of Paul but a critical interpretation.
The question is whether and to what extent his interpretation actually does justice to the intention of the apostle.

Bultmann's concern is that the character of faith as genuine decision and the inner unity of the concept of faith be preserved at all costs. The kerygma must be understood as address, and that is not possible, according to Bultmann, if it is understood as an account of demonstrable (or nondemonstrable) data, or as a communication of objective knowledge. Whether the data that are held to be true by objectivizing thought are considered historical or mythological really makes no difference. "Demythologizing" and "dehistoricizing" are two aspects of the same protest against objectivizing language. Bultmann rejects such language as inadequate to the theological enterprise. Paul himself has given no account of the difference between objectivizing and existential thought; this is a task for the scholarly interpreter. Thus, his interpretation must be a critical one.

Bultmann's contention that one encounters the salvation-event in the kerygma and is summoned to decision reflects Paul's thought accurately; so does his contention that the preaching of the salvation-event is itself part of the salvation-event (cf. 2 Cor. 5:18—6:2). Bultmann is also faithful to Paul when he maintains that knowledge of the salvation-event is distorted if it is thought to pertain to objective data and propositions to which one can subscribe without surrendering one's unbelieving self-understanding. Historical and dogmatic insight, faith that works miracles, gifts of grace, charitable acts, and heroic self-giving—these will all be corrupted if they become the occasion for unloving self-assertion (1 Cor. 1–4, 8, 13). The saving significance of Christ's death is recognized only when his death is understood to take place for us, that is "for my brother" as well as "for me." In this way, the death of Christ leads to a new self-understanding. Accordingly, the kerygma is understood properly only when it is understood as address.

The decisive question at this point is whether or not the kerygma, if it is to be understood as personal address, can at the same time communicate information. Bultmann tends to see an exclusive antithesis; that, however, is not Pauline. Rather, the apostle thinks that the kerygma is a summons to faith precisely because it reports an event that happened prior to any human decision made in response to preaching. The prior event as the eschatological act of God is nevertheless absolutely decisive for human existence. Only because it is preached can human beings know the saving significance of this event, and only by sacrificing their former self-understanding can they believe truly; otherwise they would show that their faith is not genuine. But that does not mean that the event becomes salvation-occurrence only because it is preached.

God is not visible apart from faith, but it does not follow, as Bultmann himself has emphasized elsewhere, that apart from faith God does not exist.[32] In the same way, the saving act of God in Christ is visible only to faith; but this is not to say that only preaching and faith make the Christ-event the saving act of God. It is God's saving act apart from our faith and before our preaching. This is what Paul expresses when he depicts the death of Christ as expiatory sacrifice, substitution, cosmic event, and so forth. It is also expressed when, in opposition to the Gnostics at Corinth, he adduces evidence for the historicity of the resurrection.

The essential and unrelinquishable *extra nos* of righteousness and salvation in the theology of Paul seems to me to demand that the salvation-event be viewed as a once-for-all event of the past, not simply as a here-and-now occurrence present through preaching. If we are to speak of an event that has a dimension beyond human self-understanding, we can hardly avoid using categories of objectivizing thought. Since the Christ-event is proclaimed not as a this-worldly fact but as an eschatological act of God, how could Paul have spoken other than "mythologically"—even if the language of existentialism had been available?

Pauline theology is detached from faith as an existential attitude and falls prey to objectivizing thought when Paul's images of the cross's saving meaning are systematized into a scholastic theory of atonement, or when the evidence for the resurrection of Jesus is rationalized into a pseudoscientific proof. Precisely in their more naive and fragmentary form, Paul's "mythological" statements seem to me an appropriate reference to the *extra nos* of salvation. They express his true intention and ought not to be interpreted away by the critic.

Naturally, the use of categories of objectivizing thought can always lead to misunderstanding. Rational assent can be confused with genuine faith. Theological wisdom can become a ground for boasting (*kauchēma*). Paul struggles against such deviations. But one cannot escape this danger by understanding the kerygma exclusively as address and by interpreting the theological statements existentially. Existentialist understanding can be confused with true faith just as easily as can dogmatic orthodoxy.

To emphasize that the decisive salvation-occurrence has already happened in Christ apart from us and prior to preaching is not to make surrender to God's grace dependent on previous acceptance of the data of salvation. It is true that the surrender of faith occurs when one is confronted by the gospel as a promising and demanding address; the salvation-event is represented through baptism and is made concrete through the ministry of the preacher and the existence of the community. But the "objective" presupposition for preaching and sacraments is that the salvation-event has already happened prior to preaching and independent of the community. More than anyone else, the preacher must recognize the givenness of God's grace in Christ that is to be proclaimed. This must also be made clear in the theological explication of believing understanding, even if all knowledge remains imperfect.

Bultmann is no doubt aware of the *extra nos*, as his interpretation of the doctrine of justification shows. His rejection of tendencies toward historicizing and mythologizing is a matter of passionate religious concern: the kerygma must be rescued from objectivizing thought that puts it at our disposal, thus safeguarding the *extra nos*. Nevertheless, the *extra nos* is endangered if the kerygma is reduced to the bare *that* of the cross. This becomes clear in Bultmann's analysis of the concept of faith (I, 314–30). Just as Bultmann characterized the kerygma as personal address, so here he characterizes faith as decision. The emphasis on decision is so strong that it is not made sufficiently clear that faith saves not because it is an act of obedience and results in a new self-understanding but because it is faith in Jesus Christ.

Finally, I must raise the question whether or not Jesus Christ remains a person in Bultmann's existential interpretation. Is there not a danger that the eschatological event designated by the name "Jesus Christ" evaporates to a mere occurrence? Bultmann's fear of a romantic category of personality, on the one hand, and of mythological conceptualization, on the other, results in a lack of clarity at this point. For Paul, the personhood of Jesus Christ is beyond any doubt—indeed, the Crucified One is identical with the Exalted and Coming One. Certainly, knowledge of the historical Jesus as well as revelations of the exalted Lord could be misused for human self-glorification (2 Cor. 5:16; 12:1ff.); Jesus Christ cannot be placed at one's disposal precisely because he himself is personally the exalted Lord. From one side it is correct that Paul's Christology is simultaneously soteriology. But the "mythological" statements have a dimension beyond soteriological significance. They refer to the person of Jesus Christ himself, apart from us and also apart from preaching and church.

Pauline ethics and eschatology are treated under the general heading "Freedom" (par. 38–40). Again, this would hardly be appropriate in a descriptive reproduction, but it makes good sense in Bultmann's interpretation of characteristic Pauline thought. Here the relation between the indicative and the imperative is clarified: "Freedom is the reason for demand, and the demand actualizes the freedom" (I, 336). Then the present reality of the future life is set forth. In comparison, Paul's specifically eschatological teachings are only fleetingly touched upon, since Bultmann regards them as unessential. As in earlier paragraphs, many things deserve attention, and a few questions could be asked. It is not possible to go into details however.

In conclusion: I agree to a great extent with Bultmann's interpretation of Paul's theology and gratefully acknowledge how much I have learned from him both in years past and now in studying his *Theology of the New Testament*. In general Bultmann has worked out the characteristic features of Paul's theology very well. In my opinion, however, he underestimates the degree to which the beliefs Paul shared with the early church remained important for him. Bultmann rightly appreciates Paul's characteristic deepening interpretation and critical corrective; but he exhibits an ultra-Pauline one-sidedness in that he isolates Paul's characteristic thought and places it at the center of New Testament theology.

The Interpretation of Johannine Theology

The analysis of John's theology independently supports the conclusions gained from the interpretation of Paul. The spiritual atmosphere of John is Oriental Christianity; he delineates the figure of Jesus in images from the gnostic redeemer myth. John differs from Paul by making salvation itself rather than the way to salvation the central issue (II, 75). Accordingly, the organization of the material must differ, even if John's theology is also interpreted existentially and to that extent anthropologically.

Bultmann begins with "Johannine dualism." Such dualistic images as light and darkness, life and death, and so on derive from gnostic thought but take on a new meaning because of John's belief in creation. They signify the double possibility of human existence: either from God or from man himself (II, 20f.). The dualism becomes a dualism of decision: In the decision between faith and unfaith, a person's being definitively constitutes itself, and from then on the *whence* of being becomes clear (II, 25). Because the world remains creation, "man's life is pervaded by the quest for reality (*alētheia*), the quest for life" (II, 26.). However, because people imagine they can give themselves their own answer and seek to create security, truth is perverted into a lie, creation into the "world." This is particularly clear in the example of Jewish religion (II, 26–32).

The sending of the Son signifies the *krisis* of the world; life appeared in the world of death for salvation and judgment. In the person of Jesus "the transcendent divine reality became audible, visible, and tangible in the realm of the earthly world" (II, 33). His coming (and his departure) is the eschatological event. However, in opposition to Gnosticism, it is emphasized that the revealer is the specific historical man Jesus of Nazareth. That is the offense of John 1:14.

Bultmann raises the question how the coming of Jesus can more precisely be understood as divine revelation in the world. To answer this question, Bultmann follows a method of progressive reduction, excluding one element after another (II, 40ff.). Jesus is not the revealer as a mystagogue communicating teachings, formulas, and rites. Neither is he the revealer as a personality in which the divine is visible. Many passages in the Gospels portray Jesus as divine man (*theios anēr*), but neither his supernatural knowledge nor his miracles make his ministry revelatory.

Christ's incarnation is the decisive salvation-occurrence. But death and resurrection play no role as "salvation-data" in the traditional sense; nor are the sacraments important. His words are identical with his work, but they mediate no tangible content at all except that they, as words of *Jesus*, are words of life, God's words. The entire revelation he brings is concentrated in the great "I am" sayings. The result of this progressive reduction is simply that Jesus, as the revealer of God, reveals nothing except that he is the revealer (II, 66).

Yet this bare fact—*that* he is the revealer—is not devoid of content because the revelation "is represented as the shattering and negating of all human self-assertion and all human norms and evaluations. And, precisely by virtue of being such a negation, the Revelation is the affirmation and fulfillment of human longing for life, for true reality" (II, 67f.). The way in which this is to be understood positively is worked out in the chapter entitled "Faith" (II, 70–92). As hearing, seeing, and knowing, faith and faith alone is the way to salvation for John as well. Faith is the overcoming of the offense, deciding against the world for God. This decision of faith understands itself as a gift and has its assurance precisely in that faith in Jesus does not seek guarantees but simply hears and obeys.

In the world the believer is withdrawn from worldly existence; faith is a transition to eschatological existence. The glory proper to faith consists in its gift of knowledge (John 17:3) and in the accompanying freedom, love, joy, and so forth. The discussion of the relation of the indicative to the imperative is especially important. Unlike Paul, John deals with the problem in view of the actual repeated sinning of the believer (especially in 1 John, but also in John 15). As in Paul, the relation of the indicative to the imperative is thereby understood to be dialectical. Purity from sin is a purity *extra nos*, and the imperative reminds believers of what they already are, thanks to the prevenient love of God encountered in the revealer (II, 80).

Apart from this last point, I have sought to develop only the train of thought without referring to the many specific and fruitful insights. For Bultmann's interpretation of John is so self-consistent that its overall structure must be the starting point for any evaluation. In contrast to his interpretation of Paul's theology, Bultmann's analysis of John's theology is not an overtly critical interpretation. Bultmann seems rather to assume that John himself had already anticipated the necessary criticism of popular beliefs. Yet even in John, Bultmann's existential approach turns out to be a critical interpretation in the sense that he must move beyond what John actually said.

Bultmann's approach is critical first of all because he does not base his interpretation on the canonical form of the Gospel of John, but rather on the gospel that he himself critically reconstructed in his commentary on John. There, however, the interpretation of John's theology was itself a factor contributing to the literary reconstruction. Thus, references to the sacraments, futuristic eschatology, and to some extent the framework of biblical history are eliminated. We cannot discuss here the extent to which this is justified.

In the second place, Bultmann's approach is critical because he disregards the literary form of John's work: it is a Gospel, or better, a testimony (*martyria*; cf. John 21:24). The narrative form is important to Bultmann only as an expression of the *that* of the historicity of Jesus. This interpretation is alleged to be appropriate on the grounds that John himself has dealt very freely with the traditions of Jesus' life (II, 127). From the perspective of the critical study of history, this is undoubtedly an accurate observation. But this historical perspective was completely foreign to the fourth evangelist. Precisely for that reason it is hard to agree that he was critically aware of his free use of tradition. Can we doubt that he accepted the facticity of what he related, even of crude miracle? In any case, his readers in antiquity understood what he wrote in that way, except for Gnostics and allegorists. In other words, if I were unable to understand what Bultmann does with John as critical interpretation, I would be forced to see it as an unwarranted modernization.

The same could be said with regard to demythologizing. It is certainly true that the statements concerning the preexistence of Jesus characterize the absolute and decisive significance of his words (II, 62). But to draw the conclusion from this that the mythological statements have lost their mythological sense is again modern and critical; so is the contention that Jesus is not seriously (!) presented as "a preexistent divine being" (II, 62).

That Jesus revealed nothing except that he is the revealer I can regard only as a result of critical interpretation, even though I fully recognize the intellectual power and the logical rigor with which Bultmann has carried through his progressive reduction. But may one approach John with such logical criteria? It is true that in the last analysis it is the person of Jesus that matters, and that not only the miracles but also the "salvation-data" are meaningful only because of their relation to him. But does it follow that they are insignificant and superfluous? Especially with regard to the Easter story, I find this rather dubious. The possibility of misunderstanding (II, 45) in no way proves that for the evangelist nothing extraordinary could be visible in the history of Jesus except for his audacious claim that God is encountered in him (II, 49).

A thoroughgoing discussion of Bultmann's interpretation of John would involve a detailed examination of his commentary. Scholarship will long be occupied with it, and I will often return with profit not only to the commentary but also to the appropriate paragraphs of his *Theology of the New Testament*. However, I cannot avoid the conclusion that in Bultmann's existential interpretation John's theology, too, is demythologized and dehistoricized. Of course this is not to claim, still less to prove, that the existential interpretation is not legitimate. It is only to state my judgment that it cannot be legitimized through John's theology as it is present in the New Testament. Thus we return again to the hermeneutical starting point.

Concluding Remarks

Existential interpretation involves modernization. We all modernize whenever we preach or do theology. But one must give account for what one does; this Bultmann does consistently and methodically. Within New Testament scholarship, however, it is hazardous to modernize. Would it not be better to present as best we can New Testament thought in its full historical and mythological realism? This task is necessary and does not preclude a personal involvement with the message of the New Testament. But precisely for the sake of this involvement there can be no thoroughgoing separation between exegetical and theological endeavors to understand the New Testament, despite the need to distinguish them. Bultmann's existential interpretation has arisen from painstaking attention to the material. It is fruitful for understanding the New Testament, as his *Theology of the New Testament* proves. Yet I believe that there is no single method that provides a normative model.

Surely, the writings of the New Testament and what they have to say to the present are best served when neither *one* presentation of their theology nor *one* hermeneutical method is alone made valid and normative. Therefore, I cannot view Bultmann's book as *the* theology of the New Testament for our generation. But the work is more than a rich storehouse of exegetical observations, the mere accumulation of which merits admiration. The work qualifies as a classic in the history of New Testament studies. It provides an abundance of valuable insights. The impressive synthesis as well as the many details demand a critical involvement that cannot fail to provoke independent study of the New Testament writings. Whoever uses it in this way will receive greater profit from this book than from a dozen others.

Notes

[1]R. Bultmann, *Theology of the New Testament* (trans. K. Grobel; New York: Scribner's, 1951–55; German original, 1948–53).

[2]Büchsel, *Theologie des Neuen Testaments* (Gütersloh: Bertelsmann, 1935); E. Stauffer, *New Testament Theology* (trans. J. Marsh; London: SCM, 1955); F. C. Grant, *An Introduction to the New Testament Thought* (Nashville: Abingdon, 1950); M. Goguel, *The Birth of Christianity* (trans. H. C. Snape; New York: Macmillan, 1954; French original, 1946) and *The Primitive Church* (trans. H. C. Snape; New York: Macmillan, 1964; orig. pub., 1948). The impressive scope of Bultmann's *Theology* stands out even in light of works published after his.

[3]G. Kittle and G. Friedrich, eds., *Theological Dictionary of the New Testament* (trans. G. Bromiley; Grand Rapids: Eerdmans, 1964–74).

[4]In this regard, comparison with Gerhard von Rad's *Old Testament Theology* (trans. D. Stalker; New York: Harper & Row, 1965) is illuminating.

[5]H. Weinel, *Biblische Theologie des Neuen Testaments* (4th ed.; Tübingen: Mohr, 1928).

[6]One of the real differences between Barth and Bultmann has been from the outset their theological point of departure; for Barth, it is the situation of the preacher, for Bultmann, the situation of the hearer of the Word.

[7]Thus O. Cullman, *Christ and Time* (trans. F. V. Filson; Philadelphia: Westminster, 1950) 26.

[8]Cf. Karl Barth, "Rudolf Bultmann—an Attempt to Understand Him," in *Kerygma and Myth* II (ed. H. W. Bartsch; trans. R. H. Fuller; London: SPCK, 1962) 83–132. Barth comes to the conclusion that Bultmann is primarily to be understood as standing in a Lutheran tradition. I find it remarkable that Bultmann does in fact implicitly accept this as a basis for discussion. This I infer from what I take to be his reply, the countercriticism of Barth in "Adam and Christ according to Romans 5," in *Current Issues in New Testament Interpretation* (ed. W. Klassen and G. F. Snyder; New York: Harper, 1962) 143–65.

[9]Cf. Gerhard Gloege, *Mythologie und Luthertum* (Berlin: Lutherisches Verlagshaus, 1952) 43.

[10]For Bultmann's distinction between "existential" and "existentiell," cf. his *Jesus Christ and Mythology* (New York: Scribner's, 1958) 66, as explicated on p. 74.

[11]R. Bultmann, *Essays Philosophical and Theological* (trans. J. C. G. Greig; London: SCM, 1955) 234ff.

[12]Cf. also Bultmann's Gifford Lectures, *History and Eschatology* (Edinburgh: Edinburgh University Press, 1957).

[13]It is unfortunate that the discussion of Bultmann's theology has often dealt more with his essay "New Testament and Mythology" (*Kerygma and Myth* I, 1–44) than with his major works.

[14]The booklet published by Wrede in 1897 has finally been translated. Cf. Robert Morgan, "The Task and Methods of 'New Testament Theology,' " in *The Nature of New Testament Theology* (SBT 2/25; London: SCM, 1973) 68–116.

[15]In his book *Primitive Christianity in Its Contemporary Setting* (trans. R. H. Fuller; New York: World, 1956), Bultmann deals with the preaching of Jesus in the section on Judaism. Bultmann has subsequently defended his position in "The Primitive Christian Kerygma and the Historical Jesus," which is included in *The Historical Jesus and the Kerygmatic Christ* (trans. and ed. C. E. Braaten and R. A. Harrisville; New York: Abingdon, 1964) 15–42.

[16]Cf. M. Dibelius, *Gospel Criticism and Christology* (London: Ivor Nicholson & Watson, 1935).

[17]R. Bultmann, *Jesus and the Word* (trans. L. P. Smith and E. H. Lantero; New York: Scribners's, 1934; German original, 1925).

[18]It is typical that Ernst Percy in his *Die Botschaft Jesu* (Lund: Gleerup, 1953) organized much of his work as a discussion with Bultmann.

[19]Cf. my remarks on the problem of method in "The Problem of the Historical Jesus," chap. 5 above.

[20]Cf. H. J. Schoeps, *Theologie und Geschichte der Judenchristentums* (Tübingen: Mohr, 1949), and Bultmann's critical review in *Gnomon* 26 (1954) 187–89.

[21]Cf. my essay "The Messiahship of Jesus in Paul," chap. 1 above.

[22]Cf. C. H. Dodd, *According to the Scriptures* (London: Nisbet, 1953); B. Lindars, *New Testament Apologetic* (Philadelphia: Westminster, 1961).

[23]W. Bousset, *Kyrios Christos* (trans. J. Steely; Nashville: Abingdon, 1970; German original, 1913).

[24]It is regrettable that the essay of Lyder Brun ("Urmenighetens Kristustro," in *Norsk teologi til reformasjonsjubilæet* [NovTSup 18, 1917] 80–128), owing to language and circumstances of time, has been overlooked in the German debate regarding Bousset's views.

[25]Bultmann, *Primitive Christianity* 175. Cf. H. Gunkel, *Zum religionsgeschichtlichen Verständnis des Neuen Testaments* (Göttingen: Vandenhoeck & Ruprecht, 1903).

[26]Cf. Hans Jonas, *The Gnostic Religion* (Boston: Beacon, 1958).

[27]Cf. also Bultmann's preface to the third German edition.

[28]Bultmann writes that when the expectation of the early church is one day fulfilled, this fulfillment will never become a past, a source of confidence on which one gratefully looks back, as Israel looked back on the crossing of the Red Sea. It will be God's last deed, by which he puts an end to history (I, 36). The rabbis, in contrast, discuss only whether in the days of the Messiah men will mention in prayer only the messianic redemption or will still remember the exodus from Egypt (*m. Ber.* 1:5; cf. *b. Ber.* 12b–13a). I suspect that early Palestinian Christians thought as the rabbis rather than as Bultmann.

[29]Bultmann's view does find support in the works of H. Conzelmann, *The Theology of St. Luke* (trans. G. Buswell; New York: Harper & Row, 1961), and of E. Haenchen, *The Acts of the Apostles* (trans. B. Noble et al.; Philadelphia: Westminster, 1971), but these authors have not spoken the last word.

[30]I, 238f. Cf. W. Mundle, *Der Glaubensbegriff des Paulus* (Leipzig: M. Heinsius, 1932) 99ff.

[31]Cf. Bultmann, *Kerygma and Myth* I, 10f.

[32]Cf. Bultmann, *Jesus Christ and Mythology* 70f.

216

Appendix B

Julius Wellhausen on the New Testament

DURING the last part of his career, Julius Wellhausen devoted his major scholarly efforts to the study of the New Testament. His works in this field caused great interest and heated controversies, not only because they were written by the recognized master of Old Testament studies, but also because they represented a fresh and provocative approach to the sources and the historical problems. Wellhausen's work on the New Testament never had the same impact as his classical studies on Israelite history and literature. Only in conjunction with the works of, for example, W. Wrede, A. Schweitzer, and the pioneers of the history-of-religions school did Wellhausen's contributions mark a period of transition from nineteenth- to twentieth-century New Testament scholarship. Wellhausen, however, had a profile of his own and cannot simply be considered one among several representatives of radical criticism. His studies have retained an interest of their own, even apart from their importance as part of the lifework of a scholarly giant. In recent decades there has been a renewed interest in the pioneering work of German scholars at the turn of the century. But, if I am not mistaken, only scant attention has been paid to Wellhausen.

In order to relate Wellhausen's work on the New Testament to his entire scholarly production, biography, and personal religious attitude, one would have to study a variety of sources, including his extensive correspondence. The present essay is based solely upon a reading of works that he himself submitted for publication.[1] I have not attempted a comprehensive, well-balanced presentation but have highlighted points that have been of special interest to me. I hope these points will reveal the similarity between Wellhausen's approach in the *Prolegomena* and his approach to the sources for the history of Jesus and the origins of Christianity.[2] Even so, I shall not come close to the sovereignty of Wellhausen, who preferred to deal only with those questions on which he had something new and important to say.

PRELIMINARY SURVEY AND CHARACTERIZATION

All of Wellhausen's major works on the New Testament appeared during a remarkably short span of time: the commentary—if commentary is the right word—on Mark in 1903, those on Matthew and Luke in 1904, and the introduction to the first three Gospels in 1905.[3] Critical analyses, or notes, on the Fourth Gospel, the Book of Revelation, and Acts followed in 1907, and a book on the Gospel of John in 1908.[4] A revised edition of the introduction appeared in 1911, and a more comprehensive analysis of Acts not until 1914, although most of the work on this project seems to have been completed earlier.[5]

Wellhausen did, probably from the outset, assume that the religious history of Israel aimed at Jesus as its fulfiller (O. Eissfeldt). The work of his teacher in Göttingen, Heinrich Ewald, celebrated by Wellhausen in an eloquent testimonial,[6] had embraced both Testaments. At an early stage of his career, Wellhausen had himself written on the Pharisees and Sadducees.[7] His major work on Israelite and Jewish history included a chapter on Jesus, entitled "Das Evangelium," which in later editions became the concluding chapter of the book.[8] Having completed this great historical synthesis, Wellhausen turned to more penetrating investigation of problems related to the New Testament, beginning with the Semitic background of the Greek language in the Gospels.[9]

The intensity with which Wellhausen worked on the problems during the first decade of the twentieth century and the immediately preceding years is apparent in the way in which he modified or even changed his position on several problems (e.g., the Aramaic substratum of the Gospels, the "Son of Man," and the messiahship of Jesus). The second edition of the *Einleitung* was expanded by a number of appendixes (see secs. 11–20, pp. 107–76). The chapter on the language of the Gospels (7–32) was completely rewritten, and there were also important changes in those portions that on the whole were left as they were. Wellhausen tended to state his opinions apodictically, but both the shifting points of view and apparent self-contradictions indicate that many of his proposed solutions were of an experimental nature. He wanted to provoke, to call attention to neglected areas of study, to point to inconsistencies in the texts that called for explanation, to raise radical historical questions, and to do all of this with the utmost vigor, so that it would not be possible to sweep the problems under the rug again. Once the problems were clearly recognized, the solutions might be modified both by Wellhausen himself and by others.

It is not a matter of chance that most of what Wellhausen wrote on the New Testament took the form of notes and comments on the sources. The results of his Gospel studies were summarized in two forms: a fresh translation of the three first Gospels (except Matthew 1–2 and Luke 1–2), and the discussion of textual, linguistic, literary, and historical problems in the *Einleitung*. He started with examination of the sources, making fresh observations and raising questions of his own, rather than taking over the problems from others and repeating what had already been repeated. His remarks about scholars to the right and to the left were often ironic or even sarcastic, sometimes nasty and sometimes absolutely devastating. In the second edition of his *Einleitung*, Wellhausen omitted many such asides (the point did not have to be repeated once it had been made), but he added some new ones, for example, about A. Deissmann, who compared the literary level of the sayings collection with that of papyri written by illiterate people.[10] The second edition, however, pays more serious attention to the history of research and current debate than did the first.[11]

Wellhausen did not care to reproduce the sorts of things that might be found in standard commentaries. He only adduced a small number of parallels in order to give reasons for his understanding of vocabulary or syntax. In general, he commented on a passage only if he had something of his own to contribute. Without aiming at any systematic order, he offered scattered remarks about text-critical, linguistic, literary, or historical questions. Apart from the full translation, the form of his exposition of the first three Gospels did not differ substantially from his critical analysis of Acts, whereas his studies on the Fourth Gospel dealt principally with the original source and later expansions. This peculiar type of commentary was of little value to a beginning student or to a pastor but fascinating, instructive, and provocative to the initiated reader.[12] The cool, critical attitude of an outside observer did not exclude occasional expressions of unabashed subjectivity, criticism of inept redactors, praise for beautiful and moving stories, and even reluctance to add comments to the translation of the Gethsemane pericope.

Aramaic Background and Text of the Gospels

Wellhausen was one of the pioneers of the study of the Aramaic background of the Gospels. He began with the assumption that at least the original form of Mark and the sayings common to Matthew and Luke had been written in Aramaic, but gradually modified his claims.[13] He became increasingly skeptical about alleged mistranslations and translation variants, though he retained some examples that he found convincing.[14] In the end, he drew attention chiefly to syntactic constructions that were common in Aramaic but unusual, if not impossible, in Greek.[15]

The question of which Aramaic dialect came closest to the Aramaic spoken in Palestine at the time of Jesus occasioned a somewhat heated debate between G. Dalman and Wellhausen. Dalman objected that Wellhausen was not really familiar with rabbinic Aramaic, while the latter objected that the Aramaic spoken at the time of Jesus must have differed from the Aramaic of Palestinian Targumim and rabbinic texts, and that exact retroversion of sayings of Jesus was impossible.[16] On this point he seems to have been correct, but recent discoveries have provided so many new texts that the debate between the two pioneers has become obsolete.

Wellhausen's interest in textual criticism was related to the study of the Aramaic background of the Gospels. The manner in which he proceeded on this question characterizes his work as a whole. He rarely consulted critical editions but worked with editions of the most famous manuscripts—Vaticanus, Sinaiticus, and Cantabrigiensis (D)—comparing them with the earliest Syriac witness (Sinaitic) and, to some extent, Old Latin evidence. He found especially interesting the Semitisms of the D, most of which he considered to be original. Wellhausen was not, however, a one-sided advocate of the Western text; he practiced text-critical eclecticism on the basis of the manuscripts he had consulted, in general favoring variants that deviated from literary Greek or those that could be supported exegetically.[17] This form of reasoned criticism on the basis of primary evidence still has some value, at least as a reminder for an exegete not to rely too comfortably upon any standard edition.

Source Analysis

It is practical to make a terminological distinction between *source criticism* and *source analysis*. Source criticism is a historical discipline whose aim is to discern the value of a text as a source of historical information either about the persons and events it describes or about its historical context. Source analysis has the sense of *Quellenscheidung*; it seeks to distinguish between various discrete sources or between various layers—original or secondary—in a literary text. In the tradition of the great German historians of the nineteenth century, Wellhausen used source analysis as one, but by no means the only, tool of source criticism.

Wellhausen accepted the two-source theory as the basic solution to the synoptic problem. He assumed that the Gospel of Mark had been expanded and altered at some points but refused to use synoptic comparison as a tool for reconstruction of the original form.[18] The copies used by Matthew and Luke were, on the whole, identical with the text of Mark transmitted in the manuscripts. In most cases it was impossible to tell whether the secondary elements in Mark had been added in oral or written transmission. Wellhausen assumed that variants in Matthew's and Luke's renderings of sayings of Jesus presupposed that a written collection of sayings ("Q") had already existed in Aramaic, but he never attempted any detailed reconstruction of the source and grew increasingly skeptical about the possibility of any such attempt. Matthew and Luke had access to different recensions of the Greek Q, which had itself been subjected to several corrections, some of which were based upon the Aramaic original.[19] On the whole, internal source analysis of the writings is of little importance for Wellhausen's criticism of the first three Gospels.

By contrast, the questions of sources, alterations, and additions are at the center of Wellhausen's investigations of the Fourth Gospel. He began with data that suggest the present form of the Gospel is a second, expanded, and revised edition. Chapters 15–17 have been inserted between 14:31 and 18:1, the sequence in chapters 5–7 has been rearranged, 8:44 must originally have referred to Cain as the murderer, and there are several other interpolations.[20] In his comprehensive analysis of the Gospel, Wellhausen revised his position, assuming that a gradual expansion had occurred both before and after the major revision of the original writing (the *Grundschrift*). He detected not only seams and discrepancies but also a number of doublets, additions and additions to additions, variations of similar themes, and even conflicting points of view. According to Wellhausen's reconstruction, the original draft contained only one Galilean and one Judean period, John 7:3-4 marking the transition. It was mainly narrative but included some discourse material, including the coming of the Paraclete but not the presence of the risen Lord. The later layers include the pilgrimages of Jesus to festivals in Jerusalem, the most typical Johannine sayings, and materials from the earlier Gospels. Some accretions were early, others late (e.g., 5:43, a reference to Bar Kochba), but exact reconstruction of various layers would be a hopeless enterprise.

The details of Wellhausen's analysis have proved to be of less permanent value than his general insight that the present shape of the Fourth Gospel presupposes a long and complicated prehistory that includes written drafts. Since most of the additions were made in the circle in which the *Urschrift* originated, the Gospel was to be considered a historical unity, in spite of its various layers. The Gospel presupposes the break between Judaism and Christianity; the Jews are seen as representatives of the hostile world. The universalism, however, is the result of developments within a circle of originally Christian Jews, as is the Christianization and alteration of the history and teaching of Jesus. The Fourth Gospel is inner-Christian, esoteric; even discourses addressed to the Jews are intended for a Christian audience. Preceding forms of Christian faith are corrected, but there is no good reason to assume an influence of non-Jewish (e.g., Greek) ideas. Neither the idea of the Logos nor other concepts demonstrate any real affinity to Philo, and Johannine "gnosis" differs from genuinely gnostic ideas about redemption of the individual soul.[21] Many of these suggestions have been elaborated and widely accepted in recent years, but modern scholars have hardly been aware of the degree to which Wellhausen had anticipated some of their insights.

It is, by contrast, difficult to find much continuity between Wellhausen's analysis of the Apocalypse of John and present-day research. It was published at a time when source analysis of apocalyptic and other writings was flourishing and is mainly of interest as an illustration of Wellhausen's special methodology. He was skeptical about overly subtle literary analysis and always tried to find a correlation between sources and historical situations. In this case, he found the key to be that Christian hatred against Rome did not begin before Domitian, if even then.[22] For that reason, fragments that bore traces of an earlier origin and yet were anti-Roman had to be of Jewish origin (e.g., Rev. 11:1-2 and parts of chaps. 12, 13, and 17). The author who incorporated these fragments had also reworked earlier Christian texts, including the letters in chapters 2–3, and there were some secondary additions.

In the critical analysis of Acts, Wellhausen's main concern was to detect which historical information the book might contain. He did not find very much. The speeches were literary compositions; many of the reports were distorted; the descriptions of the tumult in Ephesus and the sea voyage of Paul (Acts 19 and 27) were taken over from non-Christian sources. The author made use of several cycles of traditions, including an itinerary of Paul in Acts 16ff., but Wellhausen made no attempt to separate discrete sources—a remarkable fact. On the basis of Galatians 1:23, Wellhausen assumed that Paul had indeed persecuted the churches in Judea. He further conjectured that Paul had been converted before the death of Stephen, with whose circle Paul had no special connections.[23] In accordance with the chronology of Eduard Schwartz, Wellhausen assumed that Paul's second journey to Jerusalem (Gal. 2:1-10) had occurred before the persecution of Herod Agrippa (44 C.E.).[24] The report in Acts 12 contained valuable historical information, even though it glossed over the fact that not only James but also John the son of Zebedee was martyred at that time.[25]

HISTORICAL CRITICISM OF THE GOSPELS

It would be one-sided though not wholly inappropriate to regard Wellhausen's New Testament studies as a kind of prolegomena to a history of Jesus and early Christianity that Wellhausen never wrote, and to my knowledge never intended to write. Even his philological and source-analytical investigations reveal that he was primarily a historian of great stature. A close correlation and mutual interdependence of history and source criticism are characteristic of his New Testament studies as well as of his *Prolegomena* to the history of Israel.

Wellhausen worked on the principle that the earliest source is the most reliable, and tried to demonstrate that this principle does in fact apply to the Gospels. Not only Matthew and Luke were secondary, but even Q was dependent upon the earliest Gospel, Mark. Wellhausen did not a priori deny the possibility that the later sources may contain early and even genuine traditions, but he found only very few examples in which it could be established that this was indeed the case.[26] His skepticism at this point was based largely upon the assumption that Mark wanted to write down the whole of the tradition.[27]

For Wellhausen, the exile and the restoration in Judea marked a sharp distinction between the ancient religion of Israel and Judaism, the religion under the law, codified in the Priestly Codex and the Pentateuch. In a somewhat similar way, the crucifixion of Jesus marked the watershed between Judaism and Christianity. Christianity is faith in the gospel, that is, in the message about Jesus as the crucified and risen Christ. Jesus, however, was a Jew and not a Christian.[28] The Christian concept of the crucified Messiah is not simply an alteration of the Jewish concept; it runs contrary to it and has only the name in common. The leap from one concept to the other is only to be understood as something that happened after the fact.[29] This insight is the result of Wellhausen's critical investigation of the sources, but it is also a presupposition for his evaluation of their historical reliability.

Mark wrote his Gospel in order to show that Jesus was the Christ.[30] During his public ministry in Galilee (Mark 1:16—6:13), Jesus did not proclaim himself as the Messiah, but for Mark his miracles were primarily evidence of his messianic power and authority. In the section that precedes the passion (Mark 8:27—10:52), the Christian gospel comes into the foreground in the form of esoteric, proleptic instruction of the disciples about the suffering and the resurrection of the Son of Man and, more indirectly, in the call to follow him on the road to martyrdom. In general, Mark has only collected disconnected stories and sayings that have been arranged in terms of three periods: Jesus in Capernaum, Jesus on the way, and Jesus in Jerusalem.[31] Only scattered pieces provide historical information about Jesus; the judgment that the Gospel as a whole lacks the marks of history extends even to the passion.[32]

In the later Gospels the story of Jesus has been thoroughly Christianized.[33] Not only John but also Matthew and Luke have projected the themes of Christ and the church back into the history of Jesus, each in his own way.

Matthew is a Christian rabbi who represents Jesus both as the present Messiah, who is already laying the foundation for the kingdom of heaven on earth, and as another Moses, who gives laws and instructions to the church. The animosity toward the official representatives of the law is part of the competition between two communities, both of which were striving for the same goal: fulfillment of the law in righteousness.[34]

Luke aspired to be a historian but did not succeed. He exercised criticism in omitting some Marcan pericopes (e.g., the repetitions in Mark 6:34—8:26), but included many secondary variants, elaborations, and embellishments, such as the scene in Luke 4:16-30, in which Jesus introduces himself publicly as the Anointed One.[35]

Luke is not familiar with Palestinian geography; he is more open-minded, universalistic, and individualistic, more literary and sentimental than Matthew. In general, Luke represents a later stage of development, but the differences between Luke and Matthew should not be exaggerated. Both of them combine heterogeneous materials, and neither is a theologian. Luke can, for example, express the most vivid expectation of the parousia, but at the same time he internalizes the gospel.[36]

The anonymous author whose work is at the basis of the Fourth Gospel was, according to Wellhausen, a creative personality who handled the tradition with great freedom. The Johannine chronology is correct to the extent that Jesus was crucified before Passover and that his ministry in Jerusalem had lasted over some period of time (cf. the section "Source Analysis" above), but otherwise the Christian gospel has not only penetrated the tradition but overpowered it. Thus, the Fourth Gospel stands apart and does not represent a stage in the development of the common tradition. John presupposes Paul but goes further in emancipating Christianity from its basis in Judaism. He does not, however, reintegrate the historical person into a Pauline type of Christology; rather, "the historical Jesus is completely and right from the beginning absorbed by the heavenly."[37] It is not necessary to give further details, but it should be mentioned that Johannine Christianity, as Wellhausen understood it, is church oriented, not individualistic.

Wellhausen's studies in the Gospels led him to the conclusion that, in the course of transmission, the discourse materials had been developed and enlarged to a much greater degree than the stories about Jesus.[38] Most of his contemporaries reacted against his radical criticism of the logia tradition, as have later scholars, but one must try to understand his reasons.

Wellhausen could point to the creation of new sayings of Jesus in apocryphal gospels and agrapha and also to the Johannine discourses in the same connection. There are also examples, especially in Matthew, of oblique reports that have been turned into direct discourse. Moreover, the special character of, for example, the parables in Matthew and the paradigmatic stories in Luke indicate that the materials peculiar to the later evangelists do not belong to the ancient tradition.[39] Aramaisms pervade the whole gospel tradition and constitute no criterion for authentic sayings of Jesus.

The most controversial aspect of Wellhausen's radical criticism was his devaluation of the materials common to Matthew and Luke (Q) as a source for the teachings of Jesus.[40] Wellhausen had argued that Mark had the primary and Q the secondary version of sayings of Jesus when the two sources overlapped—a theory that presupposed that the Greek Mark was a translation of an Aramaic Gospel.[41] In his controversy with Harnack, Wellhausen did not insist upon this point. In any case, Q presupposed familiarity with the Marcan tradition, including the Galilean miracles and the passion of Jesus.[42] Wellhausen further argued that the isolated apothegmata in Mark represented the ancient tradition, whereas the more coherent discourse compositions in Q belonged to a later stage.[43] Still more important, the teaching in Q is more esoteric, addressed to the disciples and, in fact, aimed at the church, for whom Jesus was already the present Messiah.[44]

Both Wellhausen himself and his critics observed the analogy between his gospel criticism and his chronology for the sources in the Pentateuch. The ancient sources (JE) were predominantly narrative; the discourses and laws in Deuteronomy and the Priestly Codex were later and had been incorporated into the narrative framework by a redactor. In a similar way, Matthew and Luke had incorporated the logia into the narrative of Mark.

In his work with the New as well as with the Old Testament, Wellhausen remained a source critic who held to the earliest written form of a text without attempting to reconstruct its hypothetical prehistory in oral tradition. In some respects he anticipated the later form critics; the Marcan framework is redactional, not historical; the ancient tradition consisted of isolated, small units, handed down, shaped, and expanded in popular tradition.[45] Wellhausen could himself make bold historical conjectures in order to recover the historical events, but he was very skeptical about attempts to save a historical kernel of sayings that in their preserved form presuppose a post-Easter situation like, for example, the passion predictions in Mark. Thus, he was very critical of A. Jülicher's attempt to reconstruct authentic "pure parables"; in Wellhausen's opinion, the elimination of "allegorical features" often spoiled the point of the tales.[46]

With great consistency, Wellhausen refused to attribute to Jesus simply whatever was original, true, or valuable: "The truth attests only itself and not its author."[47] Wellhausen could be merciless when he found examples of redactional ineptitude, but I know of no scholar who has been more generous in his praise of the beauty and splendor of inauthentic sayings and unhistorical tales.[48]

Wellhausen's criticism left only a minimal amount of material as reliable sources for the teaching of Jesus: mainly some scattered, occasional, and polemical sayings, mostly to be found in Mark 1:16—4:12 and 11:15—13:2. Most of the parables were eliminated, as was the Sermon on the Mount, together with the rest of Q and the materials peculiar to Matthew or Luke, not to mention John. What remains is no more than inadequate fragments, barely sufficient to give an impression of the teachings of Jesus.[49]

Having reached this conclusion, Wellhausen somewhat surprisingly reintroduced the secondary materials, not as a direct source for the teaching of Jesus, but as evidence for the impact that his person made upon the church, which came into being after his death, upon its ethics and way of life, as well as upon its theology: "Without this after-effect in the life of the Christian community we too (i.e., like Paul) would have been unable to visualize the religious personality of Jesus. It appears, however, only in the shape of a reflection, broken through the medium of Christian faith."[50] "The spirit of Jesus lived on in the earliest church, which not only created the gospel about Jesus but also further developed his ethics."[51] Such statements are not pious mollifications of Wellhausen's radical criticism. They explain how it was possible for him to think that the Jerusalem church was capable of producing some of the most impressive sayings of Jesus, at the same time as they explain why he himself did not write a history of Jesus but prepared a fresh translation of the Gospels with critical notes, comments, and introduction.

FRAGMENTS OF THE HISTORY OF JESUS

At the time of Wellhausen's most important contribution to New Testament studies, the leading scholars in the field were no longer attempting to write a comprehensive "life of Jesus"; they were satisfied to write about "problems of the life of Jesus."[52] It is an exaggeration to say that Wellhausen himself "sought to furnish proof that the Gospels cannot be used as sources for the history of Jesus, but offer only testimony to the messianic faith of early Christianity."[53] The scattered fragments of historical information that he found might well, with the help of historical conjectures and imagination, have been synthesized into a sketchy but coherent picture. What we do find are a number of scattered, fragmentary, and often tentative remarks about the history of Jesus. What Wellhausen achieved by this procedure was to cut through the filigree work of conventional historical and pseudohistorical criticism in order to concentrate on the key issues: the crucifixion of Jesus, the emergence of the Christian faith, and the question whether and in what sense Jesus considered himself to be the Messiah.

Wellhausen found it quite unreasonable to doubt that Jesus was indeed crucified as "King of the Jews." He accepted the historicity of the inscription of the charge and of the mockery by the soldiers.[54] More important, however, the resurgence of the conviction that Jesus was the Messiah and the transformation of the Jewish concept into the Christian faith in the crucified and resurrected Christ would be incomprehensible unless Jesus had in fact been executed as a Messiah.[55]

Wellhausen doubted that a Jewish court could have condemned Jesus because he confessed to be the Messiah and considered Mark 14:61-62 a secondary addition to the trial scene. Jesus was, rather, found guilty of blasphemy because he had spoken against the temple. While this provided the legal basis for the sentence passed, it would not suffice as an accusation before the Romans; to Pilate the high priests did therefore denounce Jesus as a messianic pretender.[56]

To Wellhausen, as to others, the most important problem in the life of Jesus was whether and in what sense Jesus considered himself to be the Messiah. The fragments that Wellhausen considered authentic sources for the teaching of Jesus aggravated rather than solved this problem.

In his *Israelitische und jüdische Geschichte* Wellhausen had, in the fashion of nineteenth-century liberalism, depicted Jesus as the teacher who planted the seed of the kingdom of God and made it the goal of moral endeavor.[57] His historical source criticism compelled him to abandon this view. The notion of the presence of the kingdom was a correlate of the faith in Jesus as the present Messiah, who had proclaimed the coming of the kingdom of God and thereby anticipated the Christian gospel.[58] Like most of the materials in Matthew and Luke, even the parables in Mark 4:26-32 are secondary creations. Wellhausen did not deny that Jesus occasionally used the term "the kingdom of God" in its futurist sense, eliminating the political connotations of the Jewish concept, but he denied that the kingdom was the main topic of Jesus' teaching. In his call to repentance, Jesus, like John the Baptist and the prophets before him, stressed the threatening doom more than the promise.[59]

Jesus did not proclaim a new faith but taught his hearers to do the will of God. The teachings preserved by Mark, the primary source, are mostly polemical but include also some occasional utterances, made according to the needs of a general public misguided by its leaders.[60] Rejecting the traditions of the scribes and the Pharisees, Jesus did not rebel against the law, but neither did he feel constrained by it; he evaluated its statutes according to their inner worth, whether they promoted or inhibited the life of human beings. One might say that for Wellhausen the double commandment, to love God and one's neighbor, is the summary of the teachings of Jesus as well as of the law.[61]

Wellhausen understood the teaching of Jesus within the context of, and in contrast to, the Judaism of Jesus' time. He did not overcome the inherited tendency to depict Pharisaism as the dark foil for Jesus, but he realized that Jesus' free attitude toward the law together with his polemic against the scribes and, especially, his prediction of the destruction of the temple might appear to undermine the foundations of the Jewish religion and the Jewish commonwealth.[62]

Neither the public teaching of Jesus nor the hostility of Jewish leaders provided sufficient explanation for the fact that the teacher from Nazareth was crucified as King of the Jews. In dealing with the key question of the messiahship of Jesus, Wellhausen wavered and modified his position over the years.

During his ministry in Galilee, Jesus spoke and acted with authority, but not with messianic authority. In authentic sayings of Jesus, the term "Son of Man" is not a messianic self-designation but is used in the general sense of a human being.[63] Having abandoned the view that Jesus secretly planted the kingdom of God on earth, Wellhausen found the parable of the sower to contain the clearest expression of the self-consciousness of Jesus: He was a teacher who scattered his seed at random and reflected on the uncertain success of his words.[64]

In his first sketch, Wellhausen had found a striking formulation for the attitude of Jesus to the hope of the Jews: "Only in this sense can he have called himself the Messiah: they should not expect anybody else: He was not the one whom they wanted but he was the true Messiah whom they ought to want."[65] This, however, did not provide a satisfactory answer to the historical question.

As the crucifixion of Jesus as a messianic pretender had to have some basis, Wellhausen saw no reason to doubt that already in Galilee Peter confessed Jesus to be the (Jewish) Messiah. On the Mount of Olives a crowd of Galileans hailed Jesus, in the expectation that he would restore the kingdom of David, and the cleansing of the temple may have enhanced their hope.[66] It is difficult, however, to recognize how Jesus himself reacted.[67]

Wellhausen dismissed the popular theories of a crisis in Galilee that caused Jesus to withdraw in a state of depression or to go up to Jerusalem with militant heroism to challenge the enemy in his den. According to Mark, Jesus was rather at the peak of his popularity when he left Galilee, most likely in order to escape Herod.[68] In the first edition of the *Einleitung*, Wellhausen added that Jesus intended a religious regeneration of his nation; in order to win individuals, he would not have had to go to Jerusalem. As the regenerator, and as the one who was to fulfill the hopes of Israel, Jesus could accept the name of the Jewish restorer—as an act of accommodation.[69]

As one might expect, Wellhausen was not in the long run satisfied with the rationalist concept of accommodation. More than earlier, he was in 1911 inclined to think that in Jerusalem Jesus no longer acted merely as a teacher but also acted as an agitator, who at least gave the impression that he claimed the authority of a messianic ruler for himself. He did not, certainly, plan an insurrection against the Romans, but he wanted to free his nation from the yoke of hierocracy and nomocracy. "To a certain degree Reimarus may possibly be right."[70] This enigmatic statement is left without further comment. I take this to imply that, in the end, Wellhausen found that the historian could perceive reasons for the charge that Jesus pretended to be the Messiah but that the sources did not permit an answer to the question of whether or not Jesus thought of himself as the Messiah.

In accordance with his historical source criticism, Wellhausen found all predictions of the passion and resurrection of the Son of Man to be secondary, as were sayings about the parousia of Jesus. Jesus is likely to have expected the end of the world to be near and even to have anticipated his own death. At least in his comments on Mark 14:22-25, Wellhausen even assumed that during the last supper Jesus established a covenantal fellowship with his disciples, whereby the idea of communion by sacrifice was added to that of table fellowship.[71] If any, the saying of Jesus in Mark 14:25 must be authentic, as Jesus here speaks of a reunion in the kingdom of God where he will be one of the guests, without claiming any special role for himself.[72]

Wellhausen perceived a similarity between Jesus and the Old Testament prophets from Amos onward, to a degree that may have conditioned his general view from the outset. He did, however, also see important differences. The prophets preceded the written law; Jesus presupposed both the codification of the law and the minutiae of its interpretation in scribal tradition. He was a sage, not a prophet. The prophets made monotheism the foundation of social morality; in a different historical setting, Jesus was more individualistic and internalized the ethos of practical monotheism, by his own way of life as much as by his teaching.[73] At one time, Wellhausen had drawn a direct line from Jesus to faith in God held by free individuals in an invisible community of the Spirit.[74] With the years, his approach became more consistently historical: the teaching and the person of Jesus, as well as his crucifixion, were presuppositions for the origin of Christianity and for the church that was the outcome of his life, although he neither founded nor foresaw it.

Opposed to Pharisaic Judaism and contrasted with the church, Jesus appears as a lonely figure, perhaps more so than Wellhausen intended. He was accompanied by disciples who thought of him as the Jewish Messiah. However, we learn mainly that Jesus did not select the group of twelve, that he did not send out apostles, and that he did not call them to follow him in service and suffering. Jesus is not likely to have given them any private instruction about the kingdom of God, or about his own fate, or about how to pray and to organize a common life.[75] Yet, Wellhausen asserted, the conversation with Jesus in everyday life made a lasting impression upon the disciples, in whom he continued to live after his death, in their hearts more than in their memories.[76] This affirmation does not follow from the premises of radical source criticism; it appears to be a postulate conditioned by Wellhausen's conviction that a paradigmatic life and an individual type make greater impact upon religious history than concepts and rules.[77] This conviction would even seem to be a presupposition for Wellhausen's treatment of the sources, as it explains why he treats secondary gospel traditions as indirect evidence for the impact made by the personality of Jesus more than as sources for the history of the early church.

BEGINNINGS OF CHRISTIANITY

Wellhausen never drew a coherent sketch of early Christian history, but it is possible to assess his views by collecting a number of scattered remarks. The Easter appearances convinced the disciples that the crucified Jesus had been vindicated and was now the heavenly Messiah. The story of the empty tomb is secondary, even though the Gospel of Mark from the beginning ended with 16:8.[78]

In his last publications Wellhausen stressed more than before that Christianity was born out of enthusiasm, in a moment of ecstatic vision.[79] If the term "myth" is to be applied, Christianity was not at a later stage contaminated by myth but was from the beginning founded upon the myth of the resurrection. What happened was not a gradual idealization but a sudden metamorphosis of the crucified Messiah.[80]

As the basis of Christian faith, the resurrection of Jesus also became the warrant for the hope of future redemption. Thus, the Jewish concept of the Messiah was applied to Jesus, with the difference that Jesus at his parousia would vindicate his own, the Christians, and punish their enemies, the Jews.[81] After some hesitation, however, Wellhausen increasingly emphasized that the expectation of the parousia was secondary. According to the circumstances, it might be actualized or recede into the background, whereas faith in the elevation of Jesus as the heavenly Messiah constituted Christianity from the beginning and remained its foundation.[82] Wellhausen even modified his own view of the "Son of Man" sayings: the passion and resurrection predictions of Mark represented an earlier stage of development than the sayings about the coming of the Son of Man.[83]

It deserves to be mentioned that Wellhausen clearly, although only in passing, considered Peter to have played the most important role in the origins of the Christian gospel of the crucified and risen Christ. His experience of an apparition of the risen Christ was contagious, and later both Paul and the Fourth Gospel built upon the foundation laid by Peter.[84] This, however, does not imply that Peter in any way stands behind the Gospel of Mark.[85] For those who had known Jesus, the message that he who was crucified had been elevated as the heavenly Christ was sufficient. The traditions that were collected and written down in the Gospels are, by and large, not memories of the apostles but products of the community in Jerusalem, for whom Jesus was founder, head, and teacher of the church.[86]

The analogy with Paul is one reason—possibly the major one—for the view that tradition about the earthly Jesus did not constitute the gospel of the first apostles either.[87] In spite of the shift of audience and various modifications, Wellhausen did not find that the substance of the gospel of Paul differed from the gospel of Peter.[88]

Wellhausen was less interested in diversity and conflicts within early Christianity than in the main lines of development. The Gospel of Mark, the Q tradition, and Matthew represent successive stages in the growth of the tradition in Jerusalem and vicinity, with the Gospel of Luke a side branch of the same tradition, transplanted to a non-Palestinian soil.[89] The Fourth Gospel had a character and prehistory of its own, but nevertheless it represented the last stage of the development that led from Jewish origins to alienation and separation from Judaism. In spite of a late date of the last redaction, the main content of the Fourth Gospel is still assigned to the first period of Christian history and literature. By contrast, the present form of the Book of Revelation marks the beginning of a second period, characterized by the conflict between the church and the empire.[90] The first period was one of gradual emancipation of Christianity from Judaism. Within this period the most important turning point was the persecution under Herod Agrippa (44 C.E.), at which, according to Wellhausen, both James and John, the sons of Zebedee, suffered martyrdom. Peter left Jerusalem, where James, the brother of the Lord, became the leader, while Paul started out on his great missionary journeys.[91]

To the extent that it is permissible to make any generalization on the basis of Wellhausen's remarks about early Christian history, he seems to have understood history as a continuous process in which major events, in this case the crucifixion of Jesus, the persecution under Herod Agrippa, and the beginning of Roman persecutions, marked the beginning and end of discrete periods. Within this continuum great personalities might well make more impact upon posterity than upon their own generation. I find no traces of a Hegelian pattern of dialectical evolution.

RELATIONSHIP TO NEW TESTAMENT SCHOLARS

In the history of New Testament scholarship, Wellhausen's studies belong to the last phase of a period that came to an end with World War I. They were as controversial as his *Prolegomena* but never gained the same importance. The impact made by Wellhausen was conflated with that of other scholars, with the result that the specific value of his contribution has too often been overlooked.

In retrospect we tend to see Wellhausen as one among several radical German scholars who in the decades before 1914 found that the historical criticism, as practiced by persons such as H. J. Holtzmann and Harnack, had resulted in an unhistorical and uncritical modernization of Jesus and early Christianity. A closer look makes it clear that these scholars differed a great deal among themselves and were often highly critical of each other.

Already before Wellhausen, William Wrede had placed Mark at the side of Paul and John as a witness to a "dogmatic" faith in Jesus as the crucified and risen Christ. The two most outstanding representatives of radical gospel criticism reached similar results along different paths. Wellhausen could express partial agreement,[92] but he could also brand Wrede's theory a failure that rendered the gospel of the resurrection and thereby the origin of Christianity incomprehensible: "The rabbi from Nazareth could never have become the Messiah by virtue of his death"—unless he had already on earth been considered to be the Messiah and been crucified for that reason.[93]

Albert Schweitzer's thoroughgoing eschatology ran contrary to the views of Wellhausen, and their scholarly approach, method, and style differed greatly. Wellhausen's disparaging remarks about "most progressive theologians" and "ignorants" likely reflect the way in which the German academic aristocracy looked upon the impertinent young genius.[94] After the publication of the latter's major work, whose title ought to have been *From Reimarus to Schweitzer*, Wellhausen exchanged his irony for a sharp but fair criticism.[95] In fact, the two of them fought at the same frontiers, against traditional conservatism, against nineteenth-century "life of Jesus" theology, and against the history-of-religion school. The affinity between Schweitzer's "ethical mysticism" and Wellhausen's "practical monotheism" may have been greater than either of them sensed.

At least in some respects, the "Jewish Jesus" discovered by Wellhausen "closely resembles the one portrayed by the history-of-religions school."[96] The reasons for the similarity may have been that both he and the members of the school were rooted in the tradition of liberal theology and that their source criticism widened the gap between Jesus and Christianity, to the extent that Jesus appears as a lonely figure, distanced from the Judaism of his time and separated from Christianity. In contrast to H. Gunkel and other members of the school, however, Wellhausen found genetic questions about the ultimate origin to be a matter of no consequence for the meaning of the materials used by an author of apocalyptic or other writings.[97] He did not think that influence from the syncretistic environment was a factor of major importance during the first period of Christian history. Christianity attracted Gentile converts for the simple reason that it was a monotheistic religion that did not require circumcision and observation of purity laws.[98] As Wellhausen found that the historical events of the crucifixion and the resurrection appearances explained the origin of Christianity, the prehistory of christological concepts was a matter of secondary importance to him. He was himself a historian of religion—but one whose interest was focused on the origin and history of the three great monotheistic religions—Judaism, Christianity, and Islam. One might say that in Wellhausen's presentation Christianity appears as a mutation of biblical monotheism. Even the Johannine variety is characterized by monotheism, which is the motivation of moral life and the source of knowledge.[99]

Wellhausen, the historian, drew the conclusion that it is impossible to elevate Jesus to a religious principle and to play him off against Christianity. The concluding paragraph of his *Einleitung* as a classical text would have deserved to be quoted in extenso. Some excerpts must suffice: "Whence is the belief that Jesus is the religious ideal derived in fact, if not from Christianity?" One can neither comprehend Jesus nor do justice to his significance if one does not also consider the historical outcome: "Even a Jesus without the gospel and without Paul cannot be detached from the Judaism to which he adhered, although he had outgrown it. We cannot go back to him even if we would like to." The necessary consequence of making the historical Jesus a religious dogma is to eliminate "time-conditioned" features and, finally, to exchange history for a rationality about which one can hold highly divergent concepts. "As a foundation of religion, the historical Jesus is a dubious and unsatisfactory substitute for what is lost with the [Christian] gospel. Without his death he would not have become historical at all."[100]

As these excerpts indicate, Wellhausen's New Testament studies led him to the conclusion that the type of theological liberalism for which Harnack was the leading representative was built on shaky foundations. The ensuing controversy between Harnack and Wellhausen centered on the collection of sayings of Jesus preserved by Matthew and Luke, its relation to the Gospel of Mark, and its historical reliability, but both participants realized that more was at stake.[101] The two great masters had still much in common, not merely a distance from the history-of-religions school. Both emphasized the difference between the preaching (Wellhausen would have said the teachings) of Jesus and the apostles' proclamation of Jesus as the Christ, and neither of them accepted the slogan "back from Paul to Jesus." Wellhausen was even willing to concede that the religious value of the later Gospels might be greater than that of Mark.[102] Nevertheless, the two masters went separate ways.

To Harnack, the essence of Christianity was contained in the gospel that Jesus preached, with the fatherhood of God and the infinite value of the human soul at its center. The apostolic preaching about Jesus was a secondary form of the gospel, historically necessary as the means of communication and preservation of the primary gospel. For Wellhausen there was but one gospel, the gospel about Jesus as the crucified and risen Christ. Without this gospel, which had also been retrojected into the history of Jesus, there was no Christianity. Harnack, the leading liberal theologian, grew increasingly conservative in matters of historical source criticism. Wellhausen, the Semitist, historian, and radical critic, maintained that historical, genuine Christianity was faith in the crucified Jesus Christ, the faith attested by the Gospels as well as by Paul.

Having resigned from the theological faculty at Greifswald in 1882, Wellhausen stood at some distance from the theological controversies in Germany at the turn of the century. He found an appreciative and sympathetic critic in Adolf Jülicher, but even Jülicher found Wellhausen's criticism of the sayings tradition to be excessive.[103] At the time of his New Testament studies, however, Wellhausen was engaged in a mutually stimulating exchange with Eduard Schwartz, the outstanding classicist and historian of antiquity, including the ancient church, professor at Göttingen from 1902–9.[104] Like Schwartz, Wellhausen stood in the tradition of the great nineteenth-century historians. He did not see it as his task to discuss theological or philosophical issues and was reticent to expose his own religious belief in public writings. He did not share Harnack's interest in mediating between religion and culture and thought that only a religiously motivated morality could remain independent of "the variable idol culture."[105]

IMPACT AND RELEVANCE

It is not possible to add more than some scattered remarks about the more permanent effects and the lasting value of Wellhausen's work in the New Testament field. Some of Wellhausen's observations and conjectures were picked up, accepted, or at least discussed by other scholars and have passed into the learned tradition, reproduced in commentaries and other works.

Wellhausen's critical analysis of the Gospels, especially Mark, and his assumption that sayings of Jesus, as much as stories about him, were products of the creative community called for a closer, less impressionistic study of the history of tradition and redaction. Thus, Wellhausen paved the way for the fresh approach to the study of the Gospels that was inaugurated immediately after World War I. The pioneering works of K. L. Schmidt and R. Bultmann built upon the foundations laid by Wellhausen to a higher degree than did Dibelius's version of form criticism. To some extent, however, Wellhausen anticipated the type of critical analysis of Acts that was later carried out by Dibelius and Haenchen.

It had to cause some upheaval that a person with Wellhausen's authority turned against the attempt to make the Jesus of historians a foundation of Christian faith. Wellhausen had in fact done little to prevent conservative theologians from trying "to gather apologetic figs from skeptical thistles." Inadvertently, Wellhausen's studies became one factor among many that contributed to the change of theological climate in Germany after World War I. In spite of opposite points of departure, Wellhausen's conclusions had some genuine similarity to the thesis of Martin Kähler, that the impact upon posterity makes an outstanding person truly "historic" (*geschichtlich*) and that the object of Christian faith is the "biblical historic Christ" and not a reconstructed historical Jesus.[106] A confluence of impulses from Wellhausen and Kähler favored a "kerygmatic" approach to New Testament theology, an approach for which Rudolf Bultmann was not only the most outstanding representative but also the one whose critical attitude was akin to Wellhausen's. Bultmann had a remarkable ability to assimilate observations and insights of highly diverse scholars into a synthesis of his own and was little more indebted to Wellhausen than to others, for example, the members of the history-of-religions school, Wrede, Schweitzer, A. Schlatter, and even Karl Barth. One can detect in Bultmann's works, however, many passages that are reminiscent of Wellhausen's formulations, even where there is no direct quotation.

To the younger generation, Wellhausen's New Testament studies are probably known, if at all, as a presupposition for the work of Bultmann and other scholars of his time. Especially in the United States, the work of other German pioneers at the turn of the century (e.g., Wrede, Bousset, and even Kähler) has been rediscovered and translated into English in the last couple of decades. To my knowledge, there has been no comparable new interest in Wellhausen's work on the New Testament. This may, at least to some extent, be due to the lack of any major historical work and the often unsystematic, sometimes aphoristic form of presentation as well as to the extravagance of Wellhausen's radical criticism, in comparison with which even Bultmann may appear to be moderate (e.g., with respect to the parables and the sayings of Jesus about the kingdom of God). Much of what Wellhausen wrote took the form of critical comments, not to say marginal notes, upon the state of New Testament scholarship at his time, and it is therefore dated. Nevertheless, there are elements in Wellhausen's studies that are as important today as ever, especially if historical questions, rather than biblical theology and existential interpretation, will once more come into the focus of scholarly interest.

What seems most important to me is Wellhausen's insistence that the crucifixion of Jesus as King of the Jews is a historical fact that provides a major clue to the origin of Christianity as well as to the history of Jesus (see the section "Fragments of the History of Jesus" above). Wrede thought that the dogmatic theory of the messianic secret explained the contrast between the nonmessianic life of Jesus and the evangelists' conviction that Jesus was the Messiah, while Schweitzer found the nature of the Jewish messianic conception to provide the explanation. Later scholars have continued to discuss these theories, with manifold variations. Few realized that Wellhausen had pointed to the possibility of a third explanation, more solidly based upon the historical facts and therefore more plausible. One does not find a reference to this central aspect of Wellhausen's studies even where one might expect it.[107] I myself wrote an article entitled "The Crucified Messiah" without being fully aware of the degree to which Wellhausen had anticipated much of what I had to say.[108]

Few scholars will today sit down and read Wellhausen's New Testament studies in their entirety unless they have to write an article about them or have a special interest either in Wellhausen or in German biblical scholarship at the turn of the century. The works are in many respects outdated. New Testament scholarship has, after all, made progress during the last seventy years. Yet Wellhausen's works remain mines of observations, suggestions, and critical asides that have not lost their relevance. As a historian, he raised basic questions that still deserve serious reflection and further research, whether one is inclined to agree with his results or not. Depending upon one's mood, one may be irritated or amused at his terse style and dry wit, but one is not bored. Young scholars should not try to imitate him, but they might learn to concentrate on saying what they have to say. In the life of an old professor there are moments in which one is tired of reading books and articles that, if they do not rehearse old stuff, may make fresh proposals about approaches, methods, models, structures, philosophical, sociological or linguistic terminology and much else, while they have little to say about precise exegetical details and important historical events. In such moments it is a refreshing relief to sit down and read Julius Wellhausen.

Notes

[1]Some published items I did not have at hand, including the first and some of the other editions of Wellhausen's *Israelitische und jüdische Geschichte* (3d ed.; Berlin: Reimer, 1897; 1st ed., 1894; 8th ed., 1958), hereafter *Geschichte*; the second edition of *Das Evangelium Marci übersetzt und erklärt* (Berlin: Reimer, 1903; 2d ed.; 1909); and a short article entitled "Strauss' Leben Jesus," no. 234 in A. Rahlfs, "Verzeichnis der Schriften Julius Wellhausens," in *Studien zur semitischen Philologie und Religionsgeschichte: Julius Wellhausen zum siebzigsten Geburtstag* (BZAW 27; ed. K. Marti; Giessen: Töpelmann, 1914). Wellhausen reviewed several editions of Christian Syriac texts and other works of indirect interest for New Testament studies (in Rahlfs, "Verzeichnis," see nos. 180, 196, 219, 220, 223, and, e.g., 85, 96, 173).

[2]J. Wellhausen, *Prolegomena to the History of Israel* (New York: Meridian Books, 1957).

[3]J. Wellhausen, *Marci, Das Evangelium Matthaei übersetzt und erklärt* (Berlin: Reimer, 1904), *Das Evangelium Lucae übersetzt und erklärt* (Berlin: Reimer, 1904), and *Einleitung in die drei ersten Evangelien* (Berlin: Reimer, 1905; 2d ed., 1911), hereafter *Marci, Matthaei, Lucae,* and *Einleitung* (1st ed.) and (2d ed.).

[4]J. Wellhausen, *Erweiterungen und Änderungen im vierten Evangelium* (Berlin: Reimer, 1907); *Analyse der Offenbarung Johannis* (AGWG 9/4; Berlin: Weidmann, 1907); "Noten zur Apostelgeschichte," *NGWG* (1907) 1–21; and *Das Evangelium Johannis* (Berlin: Reimer, 1908), hereafter *Johannis*.

[5]J. Wellhausen, *Kritische Analyse der Apostelgeschichte* (AGWG 15/2; Berlin: Weidmann, 1914) 35 n. 1, hereafter *Apostelgeschichte*.

[6]J. Wellhausen, "Heinrich Ewald," in *Festschrift zur Feier des 150jährigen Bestehens der Kgl. Gesellschaft der Wissenschaften zu Göttingen* (Berlin: Weidmann, 1901).

[7]J. Wellhausen, *Die Pharisäer und die Sadducäer* (Greifswald: Bamberg, 1874).

[8]*Geschichte*.

[9]J. Wellhausen, "Der syrische Evangelienpalimpset von Sinai," *NGWG* (1895) 1–12; review of *Die Muttersprache Jesu*, by A. Meyer, *GGA* (1896) 265–68; *Skizzen und Vorarbeiten* VI (Berlin: Reimer, 1899).

[10]*Einleitung* (2d ed.) 162.

[11]See, e.g., ibid. 170–76, on Kirsopp Lake. Only in the years between the first and second editions of his *Einleitung* (1905 and 1911) did Wellhausen read the works of D. F. Strauss and F. C. Baur with some care.

[12]Cf. A. Jülicher, review of *Das Evangelium Marci*, by J. Wellhausen, *TLZ* 29 (1904) 256–61.

Jesus the Christ

[13]Wellhausen, "Syrische Evangelienpalimpset" and review of *Muttersprache*. Cf. *Einleitung* (1st ed.) 35–38, 57, 68 with (2d ed.) 26f., 48, 60.

[14]*Einleitung* (2d ed.) 25–28.

[15]Ibid. 11–25; see also M. Black, *An Aramaic Approach to the Gospels and Acts* (Oxford: Clarendon, 1946) 1f. and throughout.

[16]See G. Dalman, *Die Worte Jesu* (Leipzig: Hinrichs, 1898), and *Einleitung* (2d ed.) 28–32.

[17]*Einleitung* (2d ed.) 1–7 and *Johannis* 127–32.

[18]*Einleitung* (1st ed.) 53–57 = (2d ed.) 45–48.

[19]*Einleitung* (2d ed.) 59f.

[20]See Wellhausen, *Erweiterungen*.

[21]*Johannis* 119–25.

[22]Wellhausen, *Offenbarung Johannis* 4, 34.

[23]Wellhausen, "Apostelgeschichte" 16, 21.

[24]E. Schwartz, "Zur Chronologie des Paulus," *NGWG* (1907) 262–99; also in *Gesammelte Schriften* V (2d ed.; Berlin: de Gruyter, 1963) 124–69.

[25]Wellhausen, "Apostelgeschichte" 22f.

[26]E.g., *Matthaei* 75, on Herod and Jesus.

[27]*Einleitung* (1st ed.) 86, (2d ed.) 77.

[28]*Einleitung* (2d ed.) 82, 99f., 102.

[29]Ibid. 81f.

[30]Ibid. 44.

[31]*Marci* 9.

[32]*Einleitung* (2d ed.) 43.

[33]Ibid. 75.

[34]Ibid. 61f., 73f.

[35]Ibid. 54f.

[36]Ibid., 60f., 63f.

[37]*Johannis* 121.

[38]*Einleitung* (2d ed.) 76.

[39]Ibid. 60f.

[40]Cf., e.g., A. Jülicher, *Neue Linien in der Kritik der evangelischen Überlieferung* (Giessen: Töpelmann, 1906); A. Harnack, *Sprüche und Reden Jesu* (Beiträge zur Einleitung in das Neue Testament 2; Leipzig: Hinrichs, 1907).

[41]*Einleitung* (1st ed.) 74–78, (2d ed.) 65–70.

[42]*Einleitung* (2d ed.) 160.

[43]Ibid. 75–77, 160–62.

[44]Ibid. 72–75, 163–67.

[45]Ibid. 45, (1st ed.) 53 n.1.

[46]E.g., *Marci* 100; *Matthaei* 69, 133; *Lucae* 86f., 98.

[47]*Einleitung* (2d ed.) 77; see also 158f.

[48]See, e.g., *Marci* 37, 77; *Matthaei* 77.

[49]*Einleitung* (2d ed.) 103.

[50]Ibid. 104.

[51]Ibid. 77; cf. 168–70.

[52]Ibid. 79.

[53]W. G. Kümmel, *The New Testament: The History of the Investigation of Its Problems* (trans. S. M. Gilmour and H. C. Kee; Nashville: Abingdon, 1972) 282.

[54]*Marci* 136, 139.

[55]*Einleitung* (2d ed.) 82; *Apostelgeschichte* 6 n. 1.

[56]*Marci* 132f., 136, also 106; see *Einleitung* (2d ed.) 98.

[57]*Geschichte* 380.

[58]*Einleitung* (2d ed.) 94f., 98–102.

[59]Ibid. 97.

[60]Ibid. 102 and 95, where the term "evident truths," used in (1st ed.) 106, was dropped.

[61]*Einleitung* (2d ed.) 102f.; *Marci* 103f.

[62]*Einleitung* (2d ed.) 97f., 103.

[63]Ibid. 83, 123–30; and already in *Skizzen*.

[64]*Einleitung* (1st ed.) 94, slightly modified in (2d ed.) 84.

[65]*Geschichte* 382.

[66]*Marci* 94–97.

[67]*Einleitung* (1st ed.) 92 = (2d ed.) 82.

[68]*Einleitung* (2d ed.) 80f.; see also 40f. and *Matthaei* 75.

[69]*Einleitung* (1st ed.) 93; cf. *Marci* 71, 104.

[70]*Einleitung* (2d ed.) 83.

[71]*Marci* 119–26; see also *Einleitung* (2d ed.) 134.

[72]*Marci* 126; *Einleitung* (2d ed.) 96.

[73]*Geschichte* 377–84, *Marci* 103, *Einleitung* (2d ed.) 102f.

[74]*Geschichte* 388 (the last page).

[75]See, e.g., *Einleitung* (2d ed.) 71f., 77f., 102f.

[76]Ibid. 103f., 168f.

[77]*Geschichte* 384. See also the quotation from Goethe, in *Einleitung* (2d ed.) 168 n. 1.

[78]*Einleitung* (2d ed.) 84f., *Marci* 145f.

[79]*Einleitung* (2d ed.) 85 and especially 149f.; *Apostelgeschichte* 6f.

[80]*Einleitung* (2d ed.) 149.

[81]*Einleitung* (1st ed.) 96.

[82]*Einleitung* (2d ed.) 85f., 151f., 170–76.

[83]Ibid. 128–30, in contrast to *Marci* 66–69 and *Einleitung* (1st ed.) 96f.

[84]*Einleitung* (2d ed.) 147, *Apostelgeschichte* 29, *Johannis* 121.

[85]*Einleitung* (2d ed.) 155.

[86]Ibid. 148f., 168f.

[87]Ibid. 147f.; cf. 99–101.

[88]*Johannis* 121, *Einleitung* (2d ed.) 169.

[89]*Einleitung* (2d ed.) 79f.

[90]*Johannis* 126f.

[91]Ibid. 119f.; *Einleitung* (2d ed.) 142, 145f.; *Apostelgeschichte* 22ff.; cf. section "Source Analysis" above.

[92]*Marci* 70f.

[93]*Apostelgeschichte* 6 n. 1.

[94]*Einleitung* (1st ed.) 98, 107.

[95]*Einleitung* (2d ed.) 151 n. 1.

[96]Kümmel, *New Testament* 282.

[97]Wellhausen, *Skizzen* 233f.

[98]*Apostelgeschichte* 26.

[99]*Johannis* 123.

[100]*Einleitung* (1st ed.) 114f. = (2d ed.) 104.

[101]Harnack, *Sprüche und Reden Jesu; Einleitung* (2d ed.) 157–70.

[102]*Einleitung* (2d ed.) 168f.

[103]Jülicher, *Neue Linien* and *Einleitung in das Neue Testament* (7th ed., with E. Fascher; Tübingen: Mohr, 1931) 274, 346f., 366–69.

[104]See E. Schwartz, *Julius Wellhausen* (Berlin: Weidmann, 1919); also in *Gesammelte Schriften* I (2d ed.; Berlin: de Gruyter, 1963) 326–61.
[105]*Einleitung* (2d ed.) 102.
[106]M. Kähler, *Der sogenannte historische Jesus und der geschichtliche, biblische Christus* (rev. ed., ed. E. Wolff; Munich: Kaiser, 1953; orig. ed., 1892).
[107]See, e.g., A. Schweitzer, *Geschichte der Leben-Jesu-Forschung* (Tübingen: Mohr, 1913) 247 n. 2, 375, 590f.; Kümmel, *New Testament* 280–84; C. K. Barrett, *Jesus and the Gospel Tradition* (Philadelphia: Fortress, 1968) 36–39.
[108]N. A. Dahl, "The Crucified Messiah," chap. 2 in this volume.

Bibliography

Barrett, Charles Kingsley. *Jesus and the Gospel Tradition*. Philadelphia: Fortress, 1968.
Black, Matthew. *An Aramaic Approach to the Gospels and Acts*. Oxford: Clarendon, 1946.
Bultmann, Rudolf. *Geschichte der synoptischen Tradition*. Göttingen: Vandenhoeck & Ruprecht, 1921. 2d ed., 1931.
Dahl, Nils Alstrup. *The Crucified Messiah and Other Essays*. Minneapolis: Augsburg, 1974 (Now *Jesus the Christ*).
Dalman, Gustaf. *Die Worte Jesu*. Leipzig: Hinrichs, 1898.
Eissfeldt, Otto. "Julius Wellhausen." *RGG*, 3d ed., 6 (1962) cols. 1594–95.
Harnack, Adolf. *Sprüche und Reden Jesu*. Beiträge zur Einleitung in das Neue Testament 2. Leipzig: Hinrichs, 1907.
Jülicher, Adolf. *Einleitung in das Neue Testament*. 7th ed., with Erich Fascher. Tübingen: Mohr, 1931.
———. *Neue Linien in der Kritik der evangelischen Überlieferung*. Giessen: Töpelmann, 1906.
———. Review of *Das Evangelium Marci*, by J. Wellhausen. *TLZ* 29 (1904) 256–61.
Kähler, Martin. *Der sogenannte historische Jesus und der geschichtliche, biblische Christus*. Rev. ed. Ed. E. Wolff. Munich: Kaiser, 1953. Orig. ed., 1892.
Kümmel, Werner Georg. *The New Testament: The History of the Investigation of Its Problems*. Trans. S. M. Gilmour and H. C. Kee. Nashville: Abingdon, 1972.
Rahlfs, Alfred. "Verzeichnis der Schriften Julius Wellhausens." In *Studien zur semitischen Philologie und Religionsgeschichte: Julius Wellhausen zum siebzigsten Geburtstag*, ed. K. Marti, 351–68. BZAW 27. Giessen: Töpelmann, 1914.
Schmidt, Karl Ludwig. *Der Rahmen der Geschichte Jesu*. Berlin: Trowitzsch, 1919.
Schwartz, Eduard. *Julius Wellhausen*. Berlin: Weidmann, 1919. Also in *Gesammelte Schriften* I, 326–61. 2d ed. Berlin: de Gruyter, 1963.
———. "Zur Chronologie des Paulus." *NGWG* (1907) 262–99. Also in *Gesammelte Schriften* V, 124–69. 2d ed. Berlin: de Gruyter, 1963.
Schweitzer, Albert. *Geschichte der Leben-Jesu-Forschung*. Tübingen: Mohr, 1913. (2d ed. of *Von Reimarus zu Wrede*, 1907.)
Wellhausen, Julius. *Analyse der Offenbarung Johannis*. AGWG 9/4. Berlin: Weidmann, 1907.
———. *Einleitung in die drei ersten Evangelien*. Berlin: Reimer, 1905. 2d ed., 1911.
———. *Erweiterungen und Änderungen im vierten Evangelium*. Berlin: Reimer, 1907.

_____. *Das Evangelium Johannis*. Berlin: Reimer, 1908.

_____. *Das Evangelium Lucae übersetzt und erklärt*. Berlin: Reimer, 1904.

_____. *Das Evangelium Marci übersetzt und erklärt*. Berlin: Reimer, 1903. 2d ed., 1909.

_____. *Das Evangelium Matthaei übersetzt und erklärt*. Berlin: Reimer, 1904.

_____. "Heinrich Ewald." In *Festschrift zur Feier des 150jährigen Bestehens der Kgl. Gesellschaft der Wissenschaften zu Göttingen*, 61–88. Berlin: Weidmann, 1901.

_____. *Israelitische und jüdische Geschichte*. 3d ed. Berlin: Reimer, 1897. 1st ed., 1894; 8th ed., 1958.

_____. *Kritische Analyse der Apostelgeschichte*. AGWG 15/2. Berlin: Weidmann, 1914.

_____. "Noten zur Apostelgeschichte." *NGWG* (1907) 1–21.

_____. *Die Pharisäer und die Sadducäer*. Greifswald: Bamberg, 1874.

_____. Review of *Die Muttersprache Jesu*, by A. Meyer. *GGA* (1896) 265–68.

_____. *Skizzen und Vorarbeiten VI*. Berlin: Reimer, 1899. (pp. 187–215, "Des Menschen Sohn"; pp. 215–49, "Zur apokalyptischen Literatur").

_____. "Der syrische Evangelienpalimpset von Sinai." *NGWG* (1895) 1–12.

Index of Biblical and Other Ancient Literature